# copywriting

J. Jonathan Gabay

TEACH YOURSELF BOOKS

Long-renowned as the authoritative source for self-guided learning – with more than 30 million copies sold worldwide – the *Teach Yourself* series includes over 200 titles in the fields of languages, crafts, hobbies, sports, and other leisure activities.

*British Library Cataloguing in Publication Data*

A catalogue record for this title is available from the British Library

*Library of Congress Catalog Card Number on file.*

First published in UK 1996 by Hodder Headline Plc, 338 Euston Road, London NW1 3BH

First published in US 1996 by NTC Publishing Group, 4255 West Touhy Avenue, Lincolnwood (Chicago), Illinois 60646 – 1975 U.S.A.

Copyright © 1996 J. Jonathan Gabay

Typeset by Transet Ltd, Coventry, England
Printed in Great Britain by Cox & Wyman Ltd, Reading, Berkshire.

Impression number    10 9 8 7 6 5 4 3 2 1
Year               2000 1999 1998 1997 1996

# CONTENTS

**Introduction**                                                   1

**1  What is a Copywriter?**                                       8
Who makes a good copywriter?                                       8
The art of copywriting                                             9
First steps up the ladder                                        12

**2  The Big Idea**                                               19
The basic steps towards a new idea                               20
Creative thinking                                                21
Turn a blank page into a powerful sales message                  34

**3  How to Structure Your Copy**                                48
The creative brief                                               48
Creative copy approaches                                         54

**4  Getting to Grips with Your Copy**                           61
Grammar                                                          61
Creative structure                                               70

**5  Body Building**                                             92
Understanding bodycopy                                           92
Taking the right direction                                       94
Straplines, slogans and other payoffs                           103
Flesch out the copy                                             107
Copy fitting                                                    109

**6  Media and Understanding its Creative Language**            113
Choosing your medium                                            114

**7  The Press Up Close**                                       125
Recruitment advertising                                         125
Business-to-business press advertising                          131

**8  Off-the-page Advertising**                                 151
Completing the off-the-page sales cycle                         152

**9 Selling Through the Letterbox**      **166**
Open the envelope, pull out a benefit      168
Is there anybody out there?      169
Direct mail contents      170
Twenty-six creative mailing ideas      190
A word about catalogues      203

**10 Direct Mail and Charity**      **206**
Donors      207
Types of creative message      208

**11 Moving Pictures**      **212**
Attracting viewers' attention      214
Practical creative approaches      217
Direct response television      236
Now here's the bill      239
The future of television      241

**12 Listen to This!**      **244**
Creative advantages of radio      244
Turn up the creative volume      249
Radio production      256

**13 Posters**      **259**
Three signs to watch for      260
Targeting your message with posters      262

**14 Trade and 'Yellow Page' Directories**      **266**
Other directories      268

**15 The INTERNET**      **270**
Origins      270
Marketing on the web      272

**16 Press Release Copy**      **279**
General news release      280
Other types of press release      282
'Bad news' releases      287

**Glossary**      **292**

**Appendix A** Typical all-embracing creative brief form      **313**

**Appendix B** Sample production time plans      **317**

**Useful Addresses**      **320**

**Index**      **327**

# About the author

Jonathan Gabay has been a full-time professional copywriter, journalist and author for over a decade. His work has won awards and has been featured in the international press. He has written many creative advertising campaigns for internationally famous brands. Currently he divides his time between running his own creative consultancy, being an author and enjoying family life.

*My thanks to those who have taught me.*
*My appreciation for the knowledge I've yet to learn.*

# INTRODUCTION

## *I am a copywriter. Care to join me?*

Thank you for buying this book. Over the next 330 pages or so, I hope
to reveal and review the key aspects of copywriting.

*Hmmm. How does that opening paragraph sound to you? Well, it
starts off with a positive statement – 'Thank you'. Next, it is relevant to
this product, and finally, it is enticing. Do you think you could do a
better job? Perhaps you could redirect the approach? Instead of thank-
ing the reader up front for buying this book (which, I suppose, may
sound a little insincere) you could proceed directly to the benefits
derived from reading it. Then, of course, you have to consider the type
of person who might buy this book.*

We haven't met face-to-face but, based on research, I can make a few
assumptions about you. First, the obvious – copywriting interests
you. Next you are the sort of person who believes that, given the right
guidance, you could pursue a career in advertising or creative marketing. Or maybe you want to publicise your own business or local
theatre group. Perhaps you want to promote a fundraising campaign
for a charity. If you already work in the advertising industry, you
may be interested in picking up some helpful tips that would help to
make your job more involved, rewarding and (let's face it) 'fun'.

For the sake of logic and order, I will take you through all the main
aspects of practical copywriting, starting from who makes an ideal
copywriter, to the technicalities of awareness advertising, direct mail,
sales promotion, and so on.

Why do companies and organisations spend so much time and energy
getting the right mix of words and pictures to convey a message? The
obvious answer is simply to *sell*. This is indisputable. Advertising is

big business. Figures produced by the Advertising Association show that, on average, over £8 billion is spent each year in the United Kingdom on advertising. Of this, according to Register–MEAL (Media Expenditure Analysis) in 1992 alone, the top three advertisers including all their subsidiaries invested an incredible amount into promoting their products and services:

| Parent Company | Subsidiaries' Expenditure £000 | Total expenditure TV, press and radio £000 |
| --- | --- | --- |
| Unilever | Lever Brothers 74 737 | 181 905 |
| | Elida Gibbs 30 905 | |
| | Birds Eye Walls 26 304 | |
| | Brooke Bond Food 22 516 | |
| | Van den Berghs and Jurgens 18 830 | |
| | Rimmel International 2670 | |
| | Mattesons Wall's 2534 | |
| | Elizabeth Arden 1697 | |
| | John West Foods 1165 | |
| | Unipath 548 | |
| Proctor & Gamble | Proctor & Gamble 94 537 | 130 096 |
| | Proctor & Gamble – Health and Beauty 35 730 | |
| | Hair Care 8 | |
| Nestlé Holdings (UK) | Nestlé Rowntree 30 001 | 81 028 |
| | Nestlé (Grocery) 23 016 | |
| | Nestlé (Food) 15 250 | |
| | Cereal Partners (UK) 11 353 | |
| | Nestlé Ice Cream 1399 | |
| | Nestlé Food Services 10 | |

Annual specific expenditure varies. In 1994 Unilever's TV, radio and press expenditure was £212 320. However, the one thing which remains constant is the indubitable commitment that big business has to advertising. Why does advertising need clever words? With so many brand names being promoted you could argue that there is too much choice! That is where thoroughly planned copywriting comes into the picture.

This book will show that copywriting places a huge amount of importance on directing a targeted message to a specific group of consumers. Copywriting – supported by evocative images – explains the benefits of a product or service to an individual and then allows that person to make a considered decision based on facts, aspiration and association.

But, before you write a single word you have to consider your general approach to copywriting. If your attitude is wrong, then as sure as William Shakespeare could write a good plot, so your readers will know that you are not 100 per cent committed to communicating an effective message. Like a wooden stool, there are three supports to provide creative stability to your copy. Remove one support and your creative argument and integrity topples over.

*Involvement* between the consumer and seller. (Usually through creating an empathy in a desired lifestyle.)

*Reward* in terms of personal gain, to a consumer for purchasing a product.

*Fun* – the third vital element which concerns you the writer more than the consumer. I am referring to 'fun' in terms of 'enjoying the job' of writing. Without it, no matter how serious or frivolous a product may be, the conviction behind your words will never become apparent to the consumer.

As a first step, it's a good idea to look at the basic ingredients of copywriting. These are 50 per cent information, 15 per cent inspiration, 25 per cent personalisation and 10 per cent perspiration! The more you can balance the first three ingredients, the less you need to mop your brow!

An important aspect of this balancing act is to understand your audience. You have to adapt your style and tone of voice to establish a rapport and hence credibility with your intended reader, viewer, listener, and so forth. This is equally important whether you address a buyer of soap suds or the Chairperson of the Board.

It's getting to know what makes people listen,

... read ...                                        ... continue to watch ...

...what you have to say ...

        ... that you can write effective copy.

## *Introducing Scotdale Northside and Penpod*

At this point I think it is a good time to introduce two fictitious companies. They are representative of typical organisations of their size and type. Throughout this book, we'll be looking at how these different companies make use of copywriting techniques to enhance their ongoing development plans.

**SCOTDALE**

**NORTHSIDE**

This is a large multinational food company. It supplies a vast range of Fast Moving Consumer Goods (FMCG). This refers to goods that usually move off the supermarket shelves quite quickly. Examples of FMCG items include tinned foodstuffs, toothpaste, ready made meals and soft drinks. FMCGs require stores to keep fresh stocks of the products to replace those that have been sold.

Scotdale Northside has been established for 100 years. Because this year is their centenary year, they are planning an extensive publicity and advertising drive. During the year, among other things, they intend to launch several new products, reinforce their corporate awareness advertising and open a nationwide restaurant chain.

This is a small business. As yet, it hasn't even been formally launched in the market. PenPod has two key company directors. One invented the 'PenPod'. The other is the Managing Director who is in charge of sales.

The so-called 'PenPod' is an ink pen encased in steel. It is guaranteed to write underwater as well as at any angle. The real ingenuity of the 'PenPod' is that its nib can be changed easily from a fountain pen to ball-point style, and even to broad marker pen.

As with Scotdale Northside, this is going to be a very important year for PenPod and much of the company's success will depend on effective advertising.

## *How to use this book*

Whatever your copywriting needs, this book can help. Whether you are looking for some creative ideas for a small business or a local theatre group or whether you are working in advertising and want to dip in for extra hints and tips, this book is for you.

At the end of each section you'll find a summary and example exercises. If you want to brush up on all aspects of copywriting, then you should find something of interest in each section. If, on the other hand, you prefer to concentrate on one particular subject, simply look it up in the table of contents or by subject name in the index. At the end of the book, you'll find a practical glossary of terms along with useful addresses. If you are looking only for the basics on copywriting, I suggest you follow the flowchart on pages 6–7. Whichever route you take, I hope that you'll find this book informative and enjoyable.

With this introduction in mind, please join me as we embark on our journey to the world of copywriting through a method that helps **you** to become come your own best teacher.

## COPYWRITING ESSENTIALS FLOWCHART

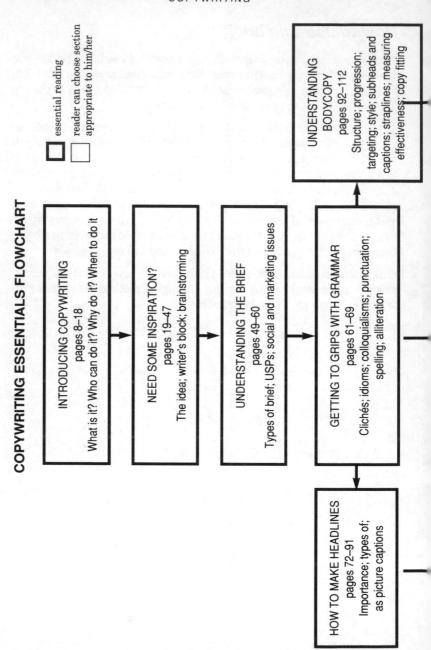

- essential reading
- reader can choose section appropriate to him/her

**INTRODUCING COPYWRITING**
pages 8–18
What is it? Who can do it? Why do it? When to do it

**NEED SOME INSPIRATION?**
pages 19–47
The idea; writer's block; brainstorming

**UNDERSTANDING THE BRIEF**
pages 49–60
Types of brief; USPs; social and marketing issues

**GETTING TO GRIPS WITH GRAMMAR**
pages 61–69
Clichés; idioms; colloquialisms; punctuation; spelling; alliteration

**UNDERSTANDING BODYCOPY**
pages 92–112
Structure; progression; targeting; style; subheads and captions; straplines; measuring effectiveness; copy fitting

**HOW TO MAKE HEADLINES**
pages 72–91
Importance; types of; as picture captions

**HOW TO WRITE
GREAT RECRUITMENT ADVERTISING**

pages 125–130

Line ads; classified ads; display ads

**HOW TO WRITE GREAT
BUSINESS-TO-BUSINESS ADVERTISING**

pages 131–150

Research; gaining attention; targeting;
corporate press ads; response; trade magazines

**HOW TO WRITE
GREAT OFF-THE-PAGE ADVERTISING**

pages 151–165

Style; incentives; coupons;
telephone hotlines; premium rate lines

**HOW TO WRITE GREAT
TRADE DIRECTORY ADVERTISING**

pages 266–269

Layout; approach

**TARGETING DIRECT MARKETING**

pages 166–205

One-to-one; direct mail; reply devices;
creative ideas; questionnaires; catalogues

**HOW TO MAKE CHARITY
MORE APPEALING**

pages 206–211

Targeting donors; direct mail;
action lines; begging; emergency appeals

**WRITING RADIO COMMERCIALS**

pages 244–258

Script writing; targeting;
production techniques

**THE INTERNET ESSENTIALS**

pages 270–278

The web; forums; IP address; HTML;
marketing

**HOW TO WRITE
GREAT PRESS RELEASES**

pages 279–291

Style and content; targeting;
dealing with 'bad' news

# 1
# WHAT IS A COPYWRITER?

According to the *Oxford English Business Dictionary*, a copywriter is 'a person who writes the text for advertisements or other promotional material. Copywriters are usually employed by an advertising agency, although for highly technical matters they are often employed directly by the company manufacturing or distributing the product.'

Here's my own definition: a copywriter is a salesperson who manipulates words within the communication media. A particularly effective copywriter is someone able to balance and integrate the marketing and sales principles of a specific industry sector with provocative writing that explains the benefits of a product or service. That literary style may be informative, persuasive, subliminal, or a combination of all three.

## — Who makes a good copywriter? —

*It could be you.*
(Headline produced by Saatchi and Saatchi for the multi-million pound launch campaign for the UK National Lottery.)

I have met scores of copywriters and even more would-be copywriters. They do not all automatically have a particular outstanding academic background. However, they all share one remarkable ability – to pinpoint, in words and pictures, the key benefits of a particular product or service. They interpret those benefits convincingly, concisely and with originality, through text, pictures, sounds or images.

A good copywriter needs to possess or develop certain qualities.

Are you the kind of person who:

- Has an insatiable curiosity about how and why things work?
- Looks at a word or situation and conjures up images to match?
- Is worldly wise?
- Sees both sides of an argument?
- Is often asked for your opinion?
- Part teacher, part confidant, totally interested in what makes people tick?
- Has a good imagination?
- Can take a logical, lateral approach to technical matters?
- Has a good sense of humour?

If you want a job in copywriting, a first-class degree in English certainly will not do you any harm. Also a respectable grade in business studies and marketing is useful, as is a fair knowledge of history and social psychology. However, if you do not possess any of these academic skills, do not lose heart; they are desirable, but not essential.

---

The Thomas Smith agency in London was the first (in 1889) to employ full-time 'ad writers'. The first international agency was Gordon & Gotch which opened for business in Melbourne, Australia, in 1855. Its first overseas branch opened in London in 1867.

---

—————— **The art of copywriting** ——————

## How is copywriting related to the sales process?

Copywriting is not just the art of eloquent writing. In fact in grammatical terms, it is often an English professor's nightmare. So rather than narrow your view to looking at copywriting as a branch of creative writing (see *Teach Yourself Creative Writing*), you should consider copywriting as primarily a selling skill.

All successful salespeople need to be able to think laterally. Likewise, they need to possess an above average degree of original thinking. This enables them to assimilate various pieces of information into a finely tuned message.

Frankly, it boils down to this: you need to make your product or service

**A**ttractive      **I**nteresting      **D**esirable      **A**ctionable      (AIDA)

Each attribute will be examined in greater detail as we progress through this book.

## Copywriting and subjectivity

'Great!' I hear you saying. 'I write really interesting copy.' Well, just because *you* like a piece of creative writing, it doesn't necessarily follow that your target audience will agree with you. (Remember, it is they who ultimately have to buy a product or service). Even when you think that you have correctly adjusted the balance of inspiration, imagination and personalisation, you have to consider the 'tricky' area of subjectivity. What one person finds interesting another finds irrelevant.

As you can see, getting the message 'right' is not as straightforward as you might at first think – but hang on, your very early creative writing and learning experiences may have already prepared you for a copywriting career. From a very early age, creative writing plays an important role in your life. By understanding its influences, you can see how it can be harnessed. Words, accompanied by provocative images, conjure powerful feelings and attitudes towards outselves as well as towards the outside world. For example nursery rhymes have a tremendously strong influence on young children and encourage group play. Holding hands with each other and then falling down to the ground on a key phrase – as in 'Ring a Ring of Roses' may be a dynamic concept to a toddler. Such concepts encourage us to further explore the world through words.

What may appear as everyday sentences to you or me are potentially, for the pre-school child, great adventures of discovery. Consider this sentence: *'The child's funny green hat made everyone laugh'*. To the child, the hat belongs to him or her. He or she *is* the child and more importantly has the ability to make everyone laugh. It makes the child feel good, by being accepted by the peer group.

## Directions through words

The influence of the creative word through media such as books, newspapers and magazines, videos, CD-ROM, and so on, has a trickle-feed effect on our subconscious. Take, as an example, tales from the Koran or Bible. They are retold time and time again. Through listening to them, we are supposed to gain some sort of moral direction.

By studying history we discover how throughout time, people handled key decisions – whether to fight, to try to negotiate, to explore – the very same judgements which we may be called upon to make.

It is, perhaps, not surprising that the written word concerning historical, religious or fictional characters – or more significantly, what they represent socially and psychologically – impresses us deeply.

## Role playing and leading

When we enter adolescence, words become an even greater influence in our lives. Some of us turn to reading or writing poetry, others keep a diary. Words in popular songs become relevant. Love songs, for instance, can help us recover from a first romance at school. Other songs may even help us to express feelings of rebellion against all the history that has preceded us and declare our intentions to change the world.

For some, the allure of songs and song writing is so strong that we form our own bands. This creative lyric writing process can turn into a voyage of self awareness. For others, just listening to the songs or maybe reading teenage magazines about the singers, can provoke powerful images of empathy with the singer whose words and performance so reflect an adolescent's needs. This empathy with the singer often develops into a fascination with the singer and all that he or she does. So begins a form of hero worshipping where trends and ideals are set and followed.

All these forms of creative writing are ideal training for the future copywriter. However, this style of writing about yourself, and the world in relation to yourself, needs to gradually shift emphasis from what is personally motivating to what touches an audience. Curiously, more often that not – as in the case of the singer who is followed by adoring fans – this can be the same thing.

# ——— First steps up the ladder ———

As you explore the copywriting avenue further, you can delve deeper into areas which do not specifically have much to do with your own life. It is time to put yourself in someone else's shoes. You will need to prioritise the pros and cons of a proposition that is being put before you.

The following example provides the first thinking steps to becoming a copywriter. Don't worry if you feel that the situation is a little far fetched. At this stage, the thought process behind the advert is more important than the actual circumstance. Ready to explore? Let's go!

Imagine yourself in the shoes of teenage leader of a band. You need to get hold of a 150-watt set of speakers for a rock gig performance. You don't know where to find this piece of equipment and you are restricted to a limited budget. You decide to pin up a notice on a local information board. What should you write?

**WANTED**
A PAIR OF **150-WATT SPEAKERS** WITH 'C' CONTROL AND AMPS.
MUST BE CHEAP AND IN GOOD CONDITION.
CALL SAM ON 01234 56789

Well, that certainly gets the message across. However, does it cover *everything* you need? For instance, you are pretty desperate for this pair of speakers because the gig is on Friday night. So, ideally, you will need to have everything in place at least by Wednesday. Next, what about that limited budget of your? You have only £100 to spend and so you cannot be too choosy.

On the other hand, who would want to 'give away' a perfectly good pair of speakers for below the 'going' price? And let's consider your request that the speakers should be in 'good condition'. Can you be a little more precise? Finally, the 'call to action' (how people can get in touch with you) – is it strong enough?

At this point you may be forgiven for thinking that if you were to include every requirement detail, you would need a lot more space than an A4 sheet stuck on a notice board! First, consider the main restrictions of your advertising space. It cannot cover more than an A4 sheet. You don't want to use too many words as your advertisement will become too cluttered and so difficult to read. Could you pep it up a bit with some colour in the headline? Next, think about the type of people who are going to read this advertisement. It will be pinned up on the local community notice board – so people may know you or at least assume that you live nearby. (This is important if they are going to deliver the speakers to you.) Naturally, those intended would want to get as high a price as possible for their speakers. Part of that bargaining ploy would be the condition of the equipment. Next, think about how these people will perceive you? To begin with, you probably don't have much money because, if you did, you would surely be advertising in a trade magazine.

Let's sort all this information into sections:

| Your needs | The ad space | Your prospects' needs |
| --- | --- | --- |
| 150-watt speakers | A4 size | Sell speaker(s) |
| Dolby 'C' control | Colour available | Good price |
| Good condition | Not too many | Not too many |
| Cheap | words | delivery hassles |
| Immediate | | |
| availability | | |

Now consider the possible motives behind this sale.

| You | Your prospect |
| --- | --- |
| Want your band to be heard! | No need for extra set of |
| Can be more creative with | speakers |
| sound output | Needs to raise cash – quickly |
| Can get more gigs ... | Given up on music |
| ...and experience | Wants new, higher spec. |
| Have more fun playing as part | speakers |
| of a band | Needs the space that is taken |
| Band can practise and perfect | up by the speakers |
| the 'act' | |
| Don't want your band to | |
| become disbanded! | |

Finally, imagine the speakers as a catalyst for emotions. In terms of feelings how do they affect each interested party?

| You | Your prospect |
|---|---|
| *Happiness* – as you can team up with your friends | *Nostalgia* – for when you played in a band |
| *Confidence* – as you can express your feelings creatively | *Happiness* – when you recollect adventures that you had with the band |
| *Pride* – when you consider what you and the band have already achieved | *Sadness* – when you either a) had to give up playing with the band b) recollect more sobre times with the band |
| *Sadness* – when you worry about what will happen to the band without the speakers | *Confidence* – when you consider how playing with the band helped you develop your own character |
| *Optimism* – that your band will be successful | *Remorse* – when you think about what the band was supposed to achieve and never did |
| | *Pride* – when you recollect the achievements you enjoyed with the band |

Now that you have identified all your elements, you can consider revising the advert. A good copywriter gets to the heart of a proposition. In doing so, he or she 'brings out' a convincing set of motives for a prospect to find out more about a product or service. In this case, among the creative solutions, you could try:

- Pampering to your prospect's nostalgia values;
- Addressing the practicalities of disposing of cumbersome and bulky pieces of equipment;
- Combining both the approaches.

Your tone of voice could be:

- serious
- humorous

- begging
- challenging
- irreverent
- formal
- casual

What do you think your prospect would want to hear?

## Targeting your message

One way of 'targeting' your message is to match mutual key motives.

| You | Your prospect |
|---|---|
| *confidence* | confidence |
| *happiness* | happiness |
| *pride* | pride |
| *sadness* | sadness |

I wouldn't think that this particular advert calls for an all-out negative approach. Creative propositions rarely do, except in notable areas such as charity and some aspects of general public information. For example:

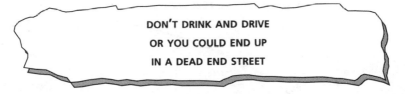

DON'T DRINK AND DRIVE

OR YOU COULD END UP

IN A DEAD END STREET

Let's get rid of the negatives. What's left?

| You | Your prospect |
|---|---|
| *happiness* | *happiness* |
| *confidence* | *confidence* |
| *pride* | *pride* |

Imagine standing on a graph line which shows where your musical ambitions could take you. Now do the same for your prospect. This time, however, just summarise the emotions behind his or her experiences (see Figure 1.1).

**Figure 1.1** Advertiser and prospect's ambitions

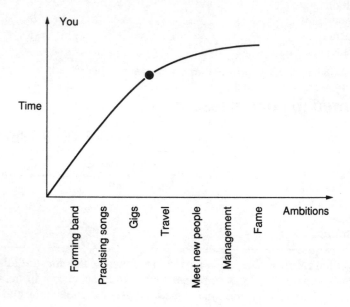

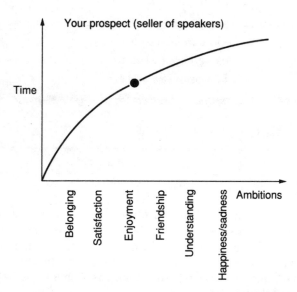

Now, return to your original catalyst list. There is one word for your prospect which connects all of these experiences – *nostalgia*.

The word 'nostalgia' derives from the Greek word *nostor* meaning 'return home'. Copywriting which directs itself at a subject's 'home truths' is copywriting at its best. So, if you rewrote the advert using nostalgia as a direction to take, you could incorporate all the powerful nostalgic feelings associated with an up-and-coming band.

- *Challenging* – like the motives behind the lyrics;
- *Casual / easy going* – like the key band members;
- *Ambitious* – like you, and perhaps your prospect when he originally purchased the speakers;
- *Witty* – like the band;
- *Direct* – like all youth;
- *Intimate* – like your songs.

Using the limited space available, let's give the advert another shot. My suggestion would be to 'connect' your practical *and* emotive needs with those of your prospect:

## CAN YOU HEAR US AT THE BACK?

*They could with your help!*

*We need a pair of 150-watt speakers (inc. dolby 'c' and amps).*

*We offer £100 ono + the chance to see our band playing live.*

*Please don't turn a deaf ear on us.*

*Call Sam on 01234 56789 ASAP we play on Friday!*

## *Over to you*

1 Based upon the 'speakers' advert, write a similar advert adopting the following approaches:
  *a)* serious
  *b)* practical
2 Write another advert, this time from a person wishing to sell, rather than buy the speakers.

**3** Think about the nursery rhyme 'Humpty Dumpty'.

> *Humpty Dumpty sat on a wall*
> *Humpty Dumpty had a great fall*
> *All the King's horses,*
> *And all the King's men,*
> *Couldn't put Humpty together again.*

*a)* List six practical reasons why Humpty Dumpty needs to be put together again.

*b)* List three practical problems that the King's men face in putting Humpty Dumpty together again.

*c)* Assuming Humpty Dumpty is the heir apparent to the throne and a father of two children, what would be his three prime motives to be put together again?

*d)* What would be the King's men's three prime motives?

*e)* Discuss three main shared motives for Humpty Dumpty and the King's men to put him together again?

# 2

# THE BIG IDEA

How many times have you watched television and admired the clever combination of words and images in a commercial? I've done just that many times. Often I ask myself, 'How and from where did they get such a good idea?'

The philosopher Plato (427–347 B.C.E) believed that the mind and body were made up of different things. Each followed separate sets of rules. He taught that the mind was the most important of the two and the general 'body', (things you could see, touch, and so on) formed the foundations for reality. 'Platonic ideas' came about through a process of reasoning, by drawing a general conclusion about something mainly based on experience or through experimenting with the available facts. Plato also maintained that ideas represented the genuine basis for reality. Why? You see Plato believed that once you had an idea about something, to you that idea was real. For example, you walk by a coliseum. You think, 'Wouldn't it be great if the coliseum had a roof to protect everyone from the sun?' As far as your perception of the world is concerned, simply by having the ability to visualise the coliseum with a roof, the roof may as well be there.

Some centuries after Plato left this earth for the Great Coliseum in the Sky, another mathematician and philosopher called René Descartes entered the philosophical world. He extended Plato's theory by concluding that the processes that controlled the mind and soul were indivisible. On the other hand, the basic controls that governed the body could be divisible and understood through mathematics and physical study. So, according to Descartes, ideas were directly perceived in the mind without any influence of the 'body'.

Today, many generally believe that an idea is a mental episode created in the mind and based on real experiences or known facts.

## The basic steps towards a new idea

1 Specific experience;
2 Thought about that experience;
3 Other experiences – material 'facts' (perhaps not directly related);
4 Consolidation of all the experiences;
5 Fresh opinion or insight relating to the original experience;
6 The formulation of a plan to implement a completely new experience;
7 The materialisation of that plan and so a completely new experience or material fact.

Example – a Greek philosopher has an idea about the local coliseum

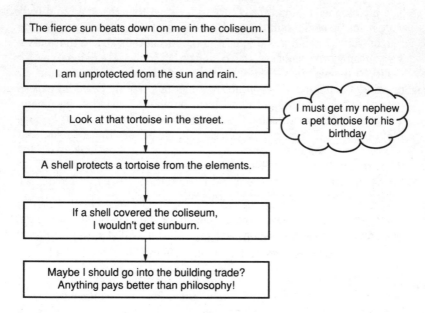

Hence, without prior knowledge and experience of a) the fierce sun, and b) the tortoise's shell protection, the Greek could not have concluded that it would be a good idea for the coliseum to have a roof.

───────── # Creative thinking ─────────

## *Writer's block*

Most people have heard of the expression 'writer's block'. It refers to that frustrating point in a creative writing project when no great ideas come to mind; at least nothing directly connected with the writing assignment itself. Every experienced writer faces this. There you sit, staring at the blank piece of paper and there it rests, lifeless.

So, you make a token effort and start to concentrate on the project. Then you become distracted by thoughts such as 'Should I eat chips or baked potatoes with my dinner?', or 'How long would it take to type out every number from one to a million?' (Incidentally, the answer is 5 years and 2473 sheets of US letter size paper, with normal line spacing.)

Whatever the cause of your writer's block, study this book and many excuses will become redundant.

To begin, let's address the problem of the roving mind. At the start of this chapter, I spoke about the basic principles behind arriving at ideas. If you understand the logical process behind thought association you will be able to redirect your thoughts towards the specific task at hand.

If your mind is still roving along, rather than worrying about your writer's block, indulge in it. Take a break, have a quick nap. Writer's blocks can sometimes be your subconscious saying, 'This is tiring. Let's have 40 winks and see if we can think of something else'. So relax, allow yourself to daydream for a while. Often it leads to a thought that is so different from your original line of thinking that it spurs the innovative idea that you were looking for in the first place.

Don't always reach for the obvious approach to a copy assignment. Just the act of thinking laterally about a project is often enough to push out all the superfluous 'stuff' in your head that's standing between you and your VDU or piece of paper.

A few years ago, I attended a course in problem solving. The tutor drew a box containing nine crosses like this:

| X | X | X |
|---|---|---|
| X | X | X |
| X | X | X |

The tutor asked the class to connect each of the crosses by drawing no more than four straight lines through them, without taking a pen off the paper or retracing any line in any direction.

The class started to scribble various lines. Most either retraced a line or went beyond the four permitted lines.

The solution was to *think outside the box*. Human nature being what it is, most people assumed that the box conatining the crosses also held the parameters within which they had to work. However, the

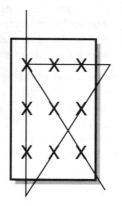
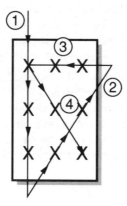

tutor never actually said that the class should be restrained by such confines. The tutor wanted the class to think laterally – go beyond what would, otherwise, be predictable ways of looking and use creative initiative.

## Should you follow the crowd?

Whatever your commercial walk of life, it seems that just about every industry sector likes to produce its pet formulae for instant and guaranteed success. The information technology industry uses mnemonics like GIGO (Garbage In, Garbage Out). 'Green' companies like to refer to the levels of threat to the environment in terms of ALATA (As Low As Technically Achievable). Out-placement practices refer to QWL (Quality of Working Life) a holistic approach to careers that takes into account time spent on leisure, the family as well as career progression.

Perhaps the most famous of all creative formulae is AIDA.

### My Aunt AIDA

AIDA was created during the roaring 1920s. It is actually derived from another theory that advocated that all advertising must be:

**S**een
**R**ead
**B**elieved
**R**emembered
**A**cted upon

The trouble with this theory is that it is not that well defined. For instance, when it says 'remembered', how detailed should your memory be? When it says 'read', does that mean you should read every single word and think about it at length? Besides, (perhaps a little frivolously) how do you pronounce SRBRA (answers on a postcard, please).

And so SRBRA begot AIDA and an entire nation of copywriting theories was born.

AIDA stands for:

**A**ttention
**I**nterest
**D**esire
**A**ction

AIDA's logic has stood the test of time

**Attention** leads to   **Interest** in the product or service

**Interest** leads to   **Desire** to get hold of the offer

**Desire** leads to     **Action** to either make a purchase or follow an instruction to take the next step. For example, call a freephone telephone number.

A near cousin of AIDA is AIDCA. Here, once your target audience desires what you are offering, you need to **Convince** them of your facts before they **Act**.

Once the word about formulae got around, just about everyone was producing them.

## Some classic formulae

*Bob Stone's mail formula*
(Author of *Successful Direct Marketing Methods* – Crain Books, Chicago, 1979.)

1 Promise your most important benefit;
2 Enlarge on it;
3 Specify the order in full;
4 Provide proof and endorsements;
5 Say what you might 'lose';
6 Rephrase benefits.
7 Incite action now.

*Reed's three Bs*
(Quoted in *Direct Mail and Mail Order Handbook* by Dick Hodgson, Dartnell Press, Chicago, 1980.)

**B**enefits
**B**elievability
**B**ounce

*Hoke's four Ps*
(Quoted in *Elements of Direct Marketing* by Martin Baier, McGraw Hill, New York, 1983.)

**P**icture  Get attention early in the copy to create desire;
**P**romise  Tell what the product or sevice will do; describe its benefits to the reader;
**P**rove  Show value, backed up with personal testimonials or endorsements;
**P**ush  Ask for the order.

## Sumner's ten commandments
(Quoted in *Direct Mail and Mail Order Handbook*.)

1 Know your proposition fully;
2 Organise your material (buyer's priority, not yours);
3 Decide to whom you are writing;
4 Keep it simple;
5 Use meaningful words;
6 Avoid humour;
7 Be specific, especially about names and places;
8 Inspire confidence;
9 Make copy long enough to tell a story;
10 Ask for action – make it easy.

I agree with most of these points except six and seven. On the whole, humour should be avoided, especially when you try to use it in place of a convincing sales message. However, there are times, such as when writing radio or television commercials, when humour can play an effective role in copywriting (see Chapters 11 and 12).

The idea of always detailing names and places is perhaps only relevant when: the names and places have a direct relevance to your sales proposition; you have enough space to include such minutae without spoiling your copy flow.

Any of these formulae can be followed in part or as a whole. Generally speaking, they are certainly worth your consideration.

## DAGMAR
Another variation on advertising effectiveness theory is DAGMAR. This was first discussed in a book by Russell Colley called *Defining Advertising Goals for Measured Advertising Results* (hence, DAGMAR).

Mr Colley suggested that the person to whom the advertisement is directed must have four levels of understanding:

1 Awareness of a brand or company;
2 Comprehension of what the product is and what it can achieve for him or herself;
3 Conviction to buy it;
4 Motivation to act.

The trouble with DAGMAR is that it assumes that every advertisement will automatically lead a prospect through the four levels of understanding. This doesn't take into account the fact that consumers do not buy something just because it is practical or 'sensible'. Sometimes, people are in two minds about decision making ....

## Copywriting and its influence on the mind

Some people believe that each side of the human brain specialises in certain regions of consciousness. The left side deals with practical issues and controls the right-hand side of the body. The right side deals with creative and emotional issues and controls the left-hand side of the body.

Advertising researchers developed this into an area called 'Braintyping'. A typical 'left-brain' thinking person is very good at organising things and appreciates order and structure. A typical 'right-brain' thinking person is very creative and emotionally led. Most people have a bias towards one side or the other.

As advertising relies heavily on images and emotive issues, a great deal of it is processed within the right brain' ....

| Left brain | Right brain |
|------------|-------------|
| alert | intuitive |
| unprejudiced | subjective |
| lucid | hypothetical |
| deliberate | lateral |
| focused | contrary |

Once you undertstand this dual thinking, you can appreciate why copywriting must do more than inform: it must address basic human traits. That is why it should be one or more of the following:

intriguing
involving
charming
surprising
understanding
caring and, above all,
rewarding.

## Satisfying your consumer's needs

Arguably, one of the twentieth century's greatest psychologists was a gentleman called Abraham Maslow (d. 1970). He devised a model of human motivation which many creative marketing experts refer to when assessing the motivation factors that influence a typical buyer.

Maslow's pyramid is constructed from five 'need' levels (see Figure 2.1). Like every construction, the overall strength relies on the integrity of the foundation. Once your creative message satisfies one 'need' level it should lead on to address the next.

**Figure 2.1** Maslow's pyramid

So, for example, in the case of promoting PenPod, you could adapt the model in the following way:

1 Physiological needs
  Is it portable?
2 Safety needs
  Will it leak?
3 Social needs
  Does it match my business or leisure requirements?
4 Esteem needs
  Will people admire my writing instrument and will it help me to produce well-presented work?

**5** Fulfilment needs
Can I rely on it to adapt to any future requirements? Will it enable me to write down essential pieces of information at any given time?

In the case of a charity, the Maslow's model may work like this:

**1** Physiological needs
Will donating make me feel better about myself?
**2** Safety needs
Will the donation help save lives?
**3** Social needs
By making a donation, will I feel that I have gone some way towards contributing towards a better society?
**4** Esteem needs
Will people admire my generosity? Will I gain satisfaction from knowing that I have been able to help a good cause?
**5** Fulfilment needs
Does this charity make me feel good?

## Brainstorming

Now you are beginning to get the idea. It's wonderfully indulgent to bask in the warmth and glory of a creative idea that you thought of for yourself. Unfortunately, coming up with great ideas isn't as mechanical as producing, for example, computer screens on an endless production line in China. (Mind you, just imagine it: a world full of people having non-stop creative ideas. Even the rational would be irrational.) In the real world of copywriting it often takes team work to really understand a product or service and come up with some original ideas to communicate its benefits.

One way of achieving this is to organise a 'brainstorming' meeting of the minds.

Brainstorming is so called because it involves a downpour of spontaneous ideas – however practical or impractical they may be. The ideas can be generated by anyone, irrespective of the person's position within a company. If you are running a very small business, you can even consider asking friends to come over for a brainstorming afternoon. (Serve drinks and you could even call it a brainstorm in a coffee cup meeting!) Whoever is present and wherever you attend a brainstorm meeting, the main ingredient for success is to remove all forms of creative inhibitions.

This can be more difficult than it first appears. At virtually every brainstorming group that I have attended, at least one of two types of people has been present. The first is the extrovert who refuses to believe that a personal idea is unviable. The other is the introvert who at best refuses to believe that he or she is capable of having any good ideas in the first place; at worst that he or she is simply too shy to co-operate in the meeting.

To get around this, wherever possible, try to appoint a 'facilitator' – an independent person who controls the meeting and ensures that everyone gets a fair chance to speak and so express ideas, originally or otherwise.

The first mistake often made by most facilitators is to immediately introduce people to the creative problem at hand. Bear in mind that this is supposed to be a meeting where freedom of thought gives rise to coherent and effective expression. So throwing people in at the deep end without giving them the chance to limber up creatively won't enable the facilitator to get the most out of people.

## Take the mind out for a brisk walk – brainstorming techniques

Any professional dietician will tell you that the worst way to slim is to stop eating. This deprives the body of essential nutrients which burn to produce energy which, in turn, burns the calories. Similarly, it is important to encourage participants (brainstormers) at a brainstorming meeting to exercise their minds and indulge in a creatively controlled feast of ideas. The 'pooling' of information and sharing of ideas stokes up the furnace of imagination. This, in turn, generates ideas. So let's get the fires burning.

All fire needs air to breathe. Take your brainstormer's minds out for a brisk walk in the pressure-free environment of random expression. Discuss issues that are not immediately connected with the project at hand. For example, your brainstormers could be called to come up with a new name for a chocolate bar. It is well known that eating chocolate makes people happy. You might, therefore, kick off by talking about what makes people happy. Reading a good book? Having a meal in a restaurant? Playing golf? Going to the movies? Sex...

WHAT, SEX!!!!! *Hold on a minute you can't suddenly talk about sex! It's unprofessionally personal and has nothing whatsoever to do with chocolate bars...*

Well, that's where you are wrong. A colleague of mine – Jamie Dow, one of the UK's leading independent consumer psychologists – invariably throws in the subject of sex at the beginning of a new product-naming brainstorming session. He finds this annoys, amuses, intrigues, offends or pleases people. All of which, of course, sets the creative idea process in motion.

By now your brainstormers should be feeling less inhibited and more susceptible to lateral thinking. The time is right to speed up from a brisk walk to a faster jog around a routed course.

The facilitator must never forget to encourage each brainstormer individually. Therefore, a set of rules is needed to prevent each person from stumbling on to the creative path of another.

## The nine rules of effective brainstorming

1 Every brainstormer is equal;
2 No brainstormer is permitted to evaluate another brainstormer's ideas;
3 The more off-the wall – an idea is, the better;
4 All ideas can be coupled and encouraged;
5 Never mind about the quality, feel the width. Brainstorm sessions should generate a long list of ideas, however good or bad those ideas may be;
6 Include every idea in the final list. To censor ideas is to judge them;
7 Brainstormers cannot ask leading or intimidating questions. For example, 'Don't you agree that when it comes to experience of this kind of thing, my idea must surely be the best?'
8 Whether an idea sounds good or odd, let curiosity encourage it to be developed;
9 Once you have all agreed on the most accurate and informed creative options, let the final analysis take pure 'gut feeling' or intuition into account.

## Fifty practical brainstorming ideas for any occasion

The following is a list of 50 typically used ideas to help stimulate creativity. I chose 50 as an arbitrary figure. In practical terms, each idea may lead to many more. So you can add to the list to make it as long and as  in-depth as your imagination will allow.

1 Enlarge it
2 Reduce it
3 Lengthen it
4 Shorten it
5 Set it to music
6 Illustrate it
7 Program it
8 Incorporate music and words
9 Incorporate pictures and words
10 Incorporate words, pictures and music
11 Cut out the words
12 Cut out the music
13 Cut out the pictures
14 Repeat the message
15 Add an extra dimension
16 Reshape it
17 Sell it by mail order
18 Sell it to everyone
19 Make it exclusive
20 Add texture
21 Make it serious
22 Make a joke out of it
23 Strengthen it
24 Dilute it
25 Change the style
26 Change the typeface
27 Change the pictures
28 Make it contemporary
29 Make it classical
30 Heat it
31 Cool it
32 Sniff it
33 Make a fashion statement
34 Aim it at women
35 Aim it at men
36 Aim it at children ⎫
37 Aim it at the elderly ⎭ (within the advertising codes of practice)
38 Revolve it
39 Put it on the INTERNET
40 Use new materials

**41** Make it mobile
**42** Personalise it
**42** Understate it
**44** Exaggerate it
**45** Rename it
**46** Suspend it
**47** Immerse it
**48** Concentrate it
**49** Give it away
**50** Endorse it

## Fifty excuses to avoid in a creative brainstorm

Wherever possible, you should try to avoid any means of 'killing' an idea before it even has a chance to breathe. The following are 50 common excuses that you should be wary of before and during a creative brainstorming session. If any should crop up, be prepared to address them individually. However, remain cautious that you don't waste a brainstorming session by fighting negativity with quick-fix solutions.

Above all, remember that each of the following excuses can, if left unchecked, fester into a creative epidemic where an entire group can feel embarrassed or restricted to express ideas based on lateral thinking.

**1** That's impossible;
**2** It's been tried before;
**3** We do things differently here;
**4** It's too expensive;
**5** It's not my responsibility;
**6** We don't have the time for that;
**7** We're too busy;
**8** We don't have the support;
**9** We've never done it before, so why should we start now?
**10** That's too radical for us;
**11** It's not corporate policy;
**12** The management would never go for it;
**13** The workers would never go for it;
**14** Come on. Let's be realistic about this;
**15** That will ruin our planned cash-flow;
**16** (No comment – just a sarcastic smile or snigger);
**17** Call that an idea?

**18** I agree, but...
**19** We're not at that stage as yet;
**20** Please don't try to 'teach grandma to suck eggs';
**21** You can't teach an old dog new tricks;
**22** People are happy with the way things are;
**23** The budget won't stretch that far;
**24** Nice idea but totally impractical;
**25** Oh, not that old chestnut again;
**26** We can't just jump into something;
**27** We'll be the laughing stock of the profession;
**28** We have to put profits before people;
**29** Well, we've got along quite nicely without it, thank you very much;
**30** I like your enthusiasm, but please, respect my seniority;
**31** Okay, let's put that idea on the back burner for a while;
**32** If we still like the idea in a couple of months, we'll look at it again;
**33** Is it just me or does everyone think it's ridiculous?
**34** We have set systems in place that have cost fortunes to set up;
**35** The Chairman will never approve;
**36** I don't know about you, but I for one would never have the gaul to present that idea to the board;
**37** Let's sleep on it;
**38** It will take too long to realise a return;
**39** The shareholders would never go for it;
**40** I once knew someone who tried it and failed;
**41** We haven't got time for new ideas;
**42** Don't rock the boat;
**43** A secure job is better than a crazy idea;
**44** The staff can only do so much, you know;
**45** It's not part of the training programme;
**46** It's never been tried before, why we should be the guinea pigs?
**47** Please, stop dreaming;
**48** It sounds like too much hard work;
**49** If I wanted a wild idea, I'd go to San Francisco;
**50** (The ultimate creative brainstorm killer excuse...) *Let's form a committee.*

## Synectics sessions

There is a branch of highly structured brainstorms, originally developed at Harvard University in the United States, called synectics sessions. These feature a research director who heads-up the thinking and a senior member of the team who suggests possible directions to pursue. Another key feature of a synectics session is that people who are unconnected to the product, service or even company are invited to 'pitch in' ideas. All ideas are jotted down on a flip chart and made available for everyone to review. Invariably, fresh ideas from a mass of off-the-wall thinking emerge at the end of the session.

## Give your chair a rest

It can be difficult to be 'creative' when you are constantly being interrupted by everyday office duites. If the creative project is substantial enough, you may consider holding your brainstorm session away from the office. For example, an 'away day' frees you and your colleagues from possible interruptions and allows you to relax in a different atmosphere such as an hotel. For this reason, on the whole, synectics sessions are held away from a client's or creative person's usual premises.

# Turn a blank page into a powerful sales message

Let's return to the idea process itself. Ideas can't develop without facts. Inspiration can't become fact without ideas.

As I have discussed, if you accept Plato's theories, innovative ideas come about through either direct or indirect connection of one set of facts with another. ('Mind' and 'body' in unison.) It's a bit like a detective looking at all the available clues, examining the facts, drawing conclusions and piecing together a picture of the truth.

You could argue that a great deal of the business of creative copywriting requires pure detective work. After all, like a detective, you need to identify all the material facts. Then consider how you can pair these pieces of information in an original and apt way.

Later in this book I am going to show how to ensure that your copy flows logically and effortlessly towards a strong selling conclusion. However, before you can even start to think about copy structure, you have to return to the job of assimilating all your facts. That way, you can go on to the next step when you create an innovative style of presenting your case.

Imagine that the individual facts form a kind of indetikit general description of a product or service. Consider each fact to be a 'suspect'. Any 'suspect', either individually or working as part of a team, could be the main culprit(s) who wants to *make the buyer an offer they simply cannot refuse*. This 'offer' is known as the Unique Sales Proposition or USP. Your job is to narrow down the guilty 'suspect(s)' from an identification parade.

As with all identity parades, you shouldn't enter into the exercise with preconceived prejudices about any of your 'suspects'. For example, let's say you are asked to write about nuts and bolts. It doesn't necessarily mean that these particular nuts and bolts have nothing new to offer the people who use them, or that they could be as unreliable as those which you recently used to fix a cupboard at home.

Your initial subjective views about the benefits of a product or service may have nothing to do with the specific facts relating to the product at hand. Besides, your target audience may not share your assumptions. It is they who have a greater appreciation of how a specific product or service can be directly applied. It is you who has to introduce them to the product that will do the job.

If you are the supplier of a product or service, you have to be prepared to accept that the consumer may base a purchasing decision on reasons other than those first assumed by you. In many cases, these reasons can actually enhance your sales pitch.

As a copywriter you have to balance each party's indisputable facts with their subjective views – including your own. That is why you must always enter into a copywriting project with an open mind and an attentive attitude. Somewhere in the middle of what you assume, what the product claims and the target audience needs is the creative Holy Grail (see Figure 2.2).

Go find that Big Idea.

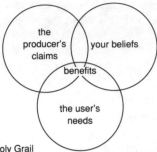

**Figure 2.2** The creative Holy Grail

## *The nine-point cross-examination*

Okay. So you are a copywriting detective. Take a good, long, hard look at your apparent facts or 'suspects'. *Ugly mugs ain't they?* Now it's time to flick on the spotlight and uncover the truth. Pull up a chair and get ready to interrogate. You are going to need to work with a set of prepared questions:

### 1 What are we doing here?

It may sound obvious or even the sort of question put to a philosopher, but why exactly does the client want to advertise in the first place? To make money? Perhaps. Is that all? Maybe there is a hidden agenda? It may be to inform, educate, compete, launch, announce... Once you know what is really trying to be achieved you can approach the business of fact interrogation accordingly.

### 2 Face the facts

What do the facts genuinely inform you about the product or service?

### 3 Who or what is the missing link?

Consider what the facts have told you. Are there any missing bits of information that would help you complete the picture?

### 4 Where will you uncover the clues?

You need to get to the bottom of this issue. That calls for diving into a lot of carefully planned questions. From where and how will you get your answers?

## 5 Do you believe the facts?

Do the 'factual' claims make sense to you? Put yourself in the target audience's shoes. Would the product or service instil confidence?

## 6 Clamp down on any unsubstantiated claims

A fact is not a fact until it is proven. Address this by arguing a good case why it could be suspicious.

## 7 Listen to factual strengths

Try to understand completely the factual strengths for what they are and how your target audience could benefit from them.

## 8 Coax the facts

Encourage the facts to speak out. Offer suggestions for the facts to stand on a platform – however broad, narrow or otherwise structured such a platform may be. Allow the facts the space to sell themselves.

## 9 Get it all down on paper

You have ascertained the facts. It's time to review all the information and strengthen the benefits by researching your creative plan.

If at any stage you are unsure of the basic facts, return to the start of your nine-point interrogation plan. Remember, the facts are in your custody. You won't release them until, and unless, you have an idea that can totally convince the outside world of their value and relevance. Once you have narrowed down your USPs, you can use this nine-point interrogation technique at any level of the brainstorming process.

# Research

There are virtually hundreds of ways to find further details about people, places, companies, systems, products and services. All forms of research should be undertaken with one clearly defined aim – to understand a) why and how a client wants to sell 'it', and b) why the buyer wants to buy 'it'.

Specific ways that research can help identify a target audience are discussed in Chapter 9.

You can use research to reinforce facts and give you a basis for a sound strategy, this enabling you to define clearly a creative and coherent message that stimulates fresh ideas.

So-called 'desk research' makes use of a wide variety of sources. These include available published work such as company reports, clippings from trade magazines, information on the INTERNET and specialist on-line (available via a computer link) subscription-based services.

Of course, your project may be so innovative that there isn't any directly relevant and useful available information. In this case, you need to look at the service or product closest to the one that you intend to promote.

Find out if there would be a demand for your product or service and, if so, why and potentially how great is that demand? In such an event, the services of a market research specialist may be just what you need. Market research companies can provide an entire portfolio of research techniques ranging from group discussions to regional surveys and questionnaires by post or telephone.

The field of advertising research is wide enough for an entire book of its own. For the present, you need to bear in mind that, particularly in the case of a small business carrying out its own copywriting, the other important reason for research is to 'check out the competition'. It is commonly misunderstood that companies primarily carry out research on competitors to find out inside trade information. The true main objective for studying competitors is to know at least as much as your customers do about what is available, where and at what cost.

Once you have uncovered these facts, you can begin to compare your (or your client's) products in terms of price, quality and distribution against those of your competitors. Most important of all you can understand what I call the 'Elvis factor'.

## *The Elvis factor and the 'G' spot*

There have been many contenders to the throne left open by the late King of Rock and Roll – Elvis Aaron Presley. Even during his reign the likes of Cliff Richard, Bill Haley and Jerry Lee Lewis hotly contested the crown. However, although many talented contenders had personality and star quality, none could ever quite match Elvis in his universal appeal.

Ultimately, you or your client's company have to demonstrate at least one aspect (the Unique Sales Proposition – USP) about a product or service that no other company can either match or beat. I like to refer to that certain something (or if you are really fortunate, list of aspects), as the Elvis factor.

As technology spreads from helping one person do his or her job better, to helping one person do two people's jobs equally well, successful distinction between one company and another relies on a variation of the 80–20 rule, sometimes called the Pareto principle. (The greatest proportion of a company's sales and profits may derive from a relatively small proportion of its customers and products.) In this case, 20 per cent of the workforce can produce 80 per cent of the product or serivce. Given that more and more companies take on dual roles (e.g. a building society that's also a bank), you have to ask yourself to define the 20 per cent Elvis factor. Scotdale Northside's Elvis factor could be that they are the country's favourite food and grocery retailer. PenPod's Elvis factor could be that they are the first company in the world to incorporate space technology into an interchangeable pen. Everyone else can only imitate, never lead.

Get to know other companies' Elvis factors. They could be heritage, size, cost, age appeal, fashion, quantity, quality, range, taste, scent, or whatever. Then you can identify the most important market segment of them all – what I like to call the 'G' spot.

'G' is short for Ginza – one of the world's most sought-after pieces of commercial land. Ginza is situated at the heart of Tokyo in Japan. It is surrounded by other tremendously sought-after areas such as the financial district. Ginza land values can be as much as one hundred times more expensive than, for example, Mayfair or Knightsbridge in London.

The 'G' spot is the commercially sensitive region that lies in between two 'Elvis factor' areas that already capture loyal customers. Initially, these customers would take far too much of your time, effort and cash to woo away. However, once you have established a 'G' spot of your own, you can concentrate on enhancing your position. This is far easier than simultaneously defending it against a bigger competitor, as well as finding creative ideas to sell a product or service.

## Make your 'G' spot into a 'G' force

Be specific about your 'G' spot. For example, if your company or client produces a vast range of products, that's fine. However, if range is one of your main strengths never put all your product 'eggs' into one basket by featuring them all in advertisements. Instead, concentrate on each product at a time. Then, you can always build individual brands.

A good portfolio of brands is like a well-trained army of troops. Use the 'G' spot methodology to creatively address and so add value to every product or service in your range, however great or small each may be. The result is an invincible force ready to withstand any competitor.

## Give your troops brand names

Each brand ('division' or 'regiment') has a core value. In creative marketing terms, brand structures can be depicted as in Figure 2.3.

Middlemen or dealers such as major retailers can also put their name to a brand. For example, Scotdale Northside Baked Beans. (These are also known as 'own-label' brands.)

Brand loyalty is when consumers return to a specific brand time and time again. Brand loyalty relies on a core set of values that never change. These can include quality, service and care. Creatively, you have to be cautious of brand loyalty. British Medical Association research in 1995 suggested that heavily advertised cigarettes may create more child smokers than loyal adult smokers. Over time, competitors will try to 'fight' loyalty. The classic reaction to this is to produce advertising known as sales promotions. This is often price or styling led. (Buy two for the price of one. Buy a limited edition box set...)

Sales promotions helps to fight off hostile armies of would-be 'G' spot owners. However, in the long term consumers tend to return to those brands whose core values remain sound. For example, cola brands may compete on price to such an extent that a 'price war' overtakes the original reason for buying a cola – taste. At the end of the day, one cola may be cheaper than another or both may be equally priced. You can be certain that eventually the consumer will return to his or her favourite brand – one that has endured the test of time, money-off promotions and contenders to its Elvis factor. Ultimately, consumers pay for quality and reassurance of a well-known brand.

**Figure 2.3**   Brand structures

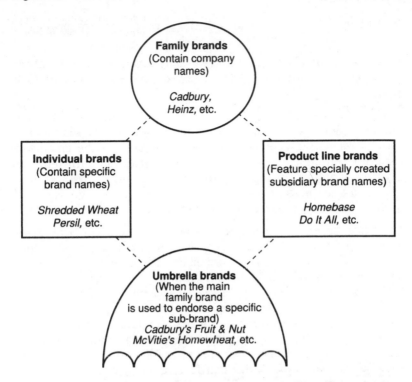

Interestingly enough, in recent years, unrelenting fierce sales promotions challenging major brand names have forced core value brands to become mass market commodity-led ('cheap and cheerful' clones) products. Typical examples of this include executive pens, sportswear, wrist watches, personal organisers, personal stereos and radios.

On the other hand, such competition has also made some major brand names enhance their product by constantly adapting to change through restyling, repricing, reinforcing service and recreating a healthy and fresh image.

The first gift coupon appeared in 1865. New Yorker Benjamin Talbert Babbit overprinted soap wrappers with the word 'coupon'. Ten coupons entitled the customer to claim a 'beautiful' lithograph picture'.

## Circle of life

Another way to help you plan each stage of your creative message is to consider the typical life of a new product.

The *introduction* phase of the cycle usually features low sales. (After all no-one has heard of the product as yet.) Marketing costs are high and advertising is directed towards the key distributors such as retailers. In this phase, profit margins are low if not non-existent.

The next phase is *growth*. By now sales slowly start to build. The price of converting enquiries into sales improves. If the product is good, competitors start to move towards your 'G' spot. In terms of advertising and marketing, it is time to look at price, product variations and guarantees. Creatively, the message usually directs itself towards the broader market by building awareness and so interest.

The next phase is *maturity*. Sales reach their pinnacle level. From here on, they either maintain their position, rise or fall as casualties of competition. Your costs are low and profits are high (assuming you have firm control of your 'G' spot). Your initial, more adventurous customers would have gone on to try other products. However, your mainstream customers will be prime targets for loyalty type creative messages. Competitors will either operate in parallel against you or drop out of the game. New product ranges are introduced, pricing is aimed against competitors, and sales promotion campaigns are introduced to combat brand switching. (Incidentally, consumers who frequently practise brand switching are sometimes called spinners or rate-surfers.) All of these aspects require strong creative messages.

The final phase is *decline*. Profits fall, sales fall. Even the mainstream consumers begin to move on to fresher ideas. Brand lines are rationalised, distribution is revisited. The bulk of your creative message is directed towards keeping the loyal customer. Usually a company will make six times greater annual profit from a customer who has remained loyal over seven years than from a brand new customer, as shown in Figure 2.4.

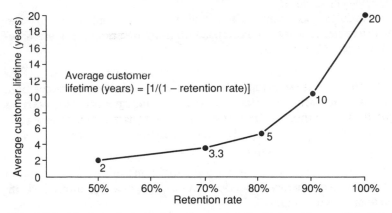

**Figure 2.4** The impact of retention rate on customer lifetime (Source: Bain & Co)

Let's look at an example to show how the circle of life could affect PenPod.

*Introduction*
PenPod launches on to the market – big spend on marketing in order to announce its launch.

*Growth*
People hear about PenPod. They try it out at demonstrations. They like it. They tell their friends. Their friends see the advertising and so the sales grow. Unfortunately, all this good news about the exciting product also reaches the ears of competitors who launch their variations of PenPod.

*Price variations and guarantees*
With others encroaching into PenPod's 'G' spot, it's time to consider strategic tactics to prevent sales from declining. The company tries marketing 'special offer' pens and even brings out new accessories.

*Maturity*
It was a long hard fight, but PenPod made it through – at least for now. The consumers know that PenPod is first in the market not just historically speaking, but in terms of quality, innovation and reputation. Now all PenPod has to do is maintain their pole position – which requires a new kind of advertising strategy.

*Position enforcement*
A hard-hitting campaign is launched to reinforce PenPod's values and at the same time keep the competition from matching price and product range.

*Decline*
PenPod falls into the trap of becoming complacent about its position. It slows down the advertising and marketing process. This opens a gap for the competition. People get bored with PenPod. Spinners start to influence buying habits. The competition is much more fierce and products are more useful. Farewell PenPod.

The product life cycle phases vary in length and duration according to the individual product or service. An example of a typical product life cycle is shown in Figure 2.5

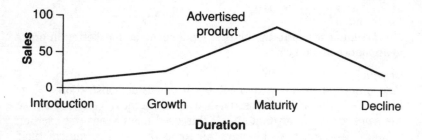

**Figure 2.5**  Product life cycle

In terms of creative message, you can see how it is possible to configure the strength and exposure of your creativity over a given period. Figure 2.6 is an example of just this. By extending the graph beyond the decline stage, it shows how the creative message may help restimulate product interest.

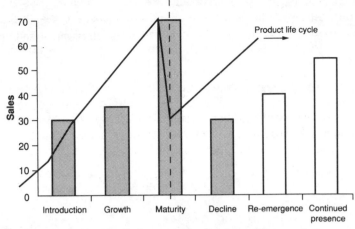

**Figure 2.6**   How advertising helps to re-stimulate interest in a product

## Who's trying to move on to your patch?

The business of research and competitors now takes on a different angle. You can be even more selective about competitive research:

- Who is trying to 'move into' *your* territory with similar services or products?
- How are they attempting to achieve their goal?
- To whom is their advertising directed?
- Which advertising media do they use?
- How often do they advertise?
- What kind of creative messages do they use?
- Is their creative tone of voice friendly, professional, casual…?
- If you are trying to compete, what would your creative message say?

## Make the right impression – first steps in media selection

I will discuss specific media later in this book (see Chapter 6). However, as part of your plan of action it is important to start to consider which media to use. (e.g. newspapers, TV, radio, and so.) Read the relevant papers for style and content. What kind of advertiser advertises in it? Does it have a recruitment section – if so what kind of jobs do the readers hold or aspire to have? How will an ad reproduce on paper? Get hold of what is called a 'Media Pack' – a fact kit that tells you about, for example, a newspaper's readership (the total number of people reached by a specific publication and circulation; the officially audited number of subscribers to a publication).

## Swot up on your findings

A useful method to summarise your findings is the SWOT analysis technique. SWOT helps you consider:

**S**trengths
**W**eaknesses
**O**pportunities
**T**hreats
**S W O T**

*Strengths* can relate to either your company's or your competitors' enhanced value to a customer. For instance, a supermarket may offer shorter queues at their checkouts. Or a manufacturer may have a particularly good distribution system, so you can purchase a particular product virtually anywhere in the country.

*Weaknesses* could refer to a small advertising budget or an inefficient customer service department.

*Opportunities* could relate to changing consumer habits. Or to competitors who have become 'uncreative' in their approach and offer.

*Threats* may arise from a competitor moving on to your 'G' spot.

The SWOT analysis is also useful for assessing media (see page 116).

Now you have an idea of what to write about, pick up a pen or sit down in front of a computer and start to type!

## *The Big Idea quick tips*

- Follow the seven steps towards a new idea.
- Turn a daydream into an idea generation opportunity.
- Never settle for an obvious answer.
- Follow the AIDA or DAGMAR formula.
- Appeal to both sides of the brain.
- If you are stuck for inspiration, try brainstorming.
- Remember the nine rules of effective brainstorming.

- Never instantly dismiss an idea.
- Balance your views with those of your client and its customers.
- Interrogate your client's product.
- Research a brief as fully as possible.
- Know your USPs and those of your competitors.
- Fight for and then defend your 'G' spot.
- Consider the different areas of branding and where your product or service sits in the branding hierarchy.
- Adapt your creative message to suit the life cycle of the product or service
- Use a SWOT analysis on your company and its competitors.

## *Over to you*

1 Imagine you are the inventor of PenPod. Refer to the seven basic steps towards a new idea. In seven steps, explain how you might have arrived at the idea to invent a pen that has an interchangeable nib?

2 You are the Marketing Director of Scotdale Northside. Using the AIDA formula, which of the following statements best applies to an effective advertising message?

   *a)* We sell an extensive range of goods.

   *b)* We sell an extensive range of goods that are reduced in price until the end of the month.

   *c)* We sell an extensive range of goods that are competitively priced and available from a shop near you.

   *d)* We sell an extensive range of competitively priced goods.

3 List the AIDA points in the statement you selected in question 2.

4 You are once more in the hot-seat at PenPod. This time, you are the Managing Director. You are planning a meeting with a particularly demanding client. She's expecting a dull introduction to PenPod's product benefits.

   *a)* In two minutes, list six 'one-line' ways that you could praise PenPod's tremendous benefits.

   *b)* Jot down the most attractive idea of the possible six.

   *c)* In two minutes, list every secondary idea that your chosen benefits suggest.

5 Think about promises that politicians make, in one minute, write down the first 20 things that come to mind.

6 Take a break – have a quick nap.

7 List other ideas (if any) that come to mind thanks to your 'quick nap'.

8 Now list the top three ways to praise PenPod that come to mind.

# 3

# HOW TO STRUCTURE YOUR COPY

## The creative brief

The creative brief is one of the most important documents for a copywriter and the client who instructs a creative team. A proper creative brief is a necessity for both advertiser and copywriter alike. Without it, the facts are vague. This may result in misinformation, misinterpretation and missing the point of why something is being produced in the first place.

All too often you may find that clients may not want to take the time to commit an instruction to paper. The easy way to overcome this is to design a briefing form that is as easy to complete as it is to understand. A sample form is included in Appendix A.

### Three stages of briefing

Ideally, there are three stages to effective briefing. The first is the client brief. This is a management tool that often doesn't directly affect the creative team, but helps the client to define who will be responsible for what.

Next there is the informal pre-brief. This is usually no more than a casual meeting that prepares for a forthcoming full creative brief. This may entail considering research (see page 37) or ensuring you have enough available time get the job done.

The third stage is the creative brief. The quicker an advertiser produces a creative brief, the more time there will be for you, the creative person, to do a good job. Creative briefs should be submitted before any work gets underway. If that means leaving out some facts, it doesn't matter as long as those gaps can be filled at a later stage. After all, having something to think about is better than having nothing.

Indisputably, a creative brief should contain everything a person needs to produce effective creative work. However, you should bear in mind that your job as a writer is to communicate with an audience. Therefore don't be afraid to communicate with the person who wrote the brief. Clarify your own understanding of what is required. You may even disagree with something. Now is your chance to question the brief before committing anything to paper.

## *The brief itself*

There are two kinds of typical creative brief. The first, the all-embracing brief, assumes you know nothing or very little about a product or service. The second, an *aide-mémoire* brief, assumes you know something or a lot about a product or service. The first is meant to educate and inspire. The second is meant to clarify and inspire.

### The all-embracing brief and its components

This brief document is self-contained and provides all the information a writer needs.

*1 Who's advertising?*
Company name only. If you feel it is important to include a company report, attach this separately under the heading of 'Background'.

*2 What does the company do?*
A general heading, like 'Publishing', or perhaps 'Medical book publishing'. *You don't need to talk about the plots of their last five hospital dramas.*

*3 What is required?*
A one-line description, such as 'TV commercial' or 'Poster'. Don't worry about specific media details at this stage.

## 4 What is the format?
For example, if you have to write a brochure, how long will it be? Is it in colour? Will there be any illustrations (essential if you want to take advantage of captioning). If it is a direct mail letter, is there a specific length required... and so forth).

## 5 What do you specifically expect the creative work to achieve?
Again, something precise. For example, you might want 75 people to call and ask for more details.

## 6 What are your marketing objectives and your corporate objectives?
Try to summarise each in one line. For example, 'to increase market share by 15 per cent, and to be recognised as the leader in our field.

## 7 What's the story so far?
This is relevant background detail. You could include where the company stands in its market-place; where it would like to be; where the creative work will appear; what will support the work – for example, other ads ...? (See page 38).

## 8 Describe the product
Include any previous leaflets, advertisements, etc. What is it? How is it used? How does it work?

## 9 Why should someone want it?
List the USPs. Why buy this one rather than those offered by a competitor? A classic misunderstanding is that the copywriter is responsible for creating the USPs. This is, in fact, the role of the marketing department or in smaller companies, the salesperson or managing director. It is up to the writer to communicate those benefits.

## 10 Who wants it?
Who would want to buy this product/service? Where do they live? How old are they? Discuss their social economic groupings. What kind of jobs do they have? If the audience is a type of business, what sort of business is it? How big is it? Describe its business sector. Who makes the buying decisions? How does the buying process work? For example, a secretary sees a new kind of pen. She informs her boss, asks the stationery buyer to include it on the next stationery order. How do they perceive themselves in the market? (See page 15.)

## 11 Are there any special offers?
For example, do you need to write about a special discount or free gift? If so, what is it? What is its value? What do you have to do to get it and why would anyone want it?

### 12  How do you see yourself?
Based on your company's image, what style should the copy adopt? Serious? Casual? Caring...?

### 13  Tests
This is often used in direct marketing briefs (see Chapter 9). However, it could also refer to tests of advertisements by size, frequency, colour and media.

### 14  What media will you use?
For example, national newspapers, trade press. In all cases, try to include a sample.

### 15  Why did you choose this media?
A probing question, this one! However, a very useful one if you are to 'get a firm grip' on your target audience and the advertiser's marketing rationale.

### 16  What is your budget?
No-one likes to discuss money. If, for instance, you intend to feature photography, it's less shocking for an advertiser if you announce *from the start* your intention to shoot your pics in Mauritius, 'Because the sun has a certain hue in that part of the world'. Wherever possible, it is shrewd to agree available budgets with everyone, including, if you work in an agency, the production department. You can always base costs on previous projects.

### 17  What is taboo?
Advertisers are invariably keen to list every USP under the sun. Just as important are the 'unmentionables'. Advertisers may also have to refer to corporate restrictions and trade legislation within copy. This may include financial services' rules, as regulated by bodies such as the Personal Investment Authority which reports to the Securities Investment Board (SIB), the Investment Management Regulatory Organisation (IMRO) which deals with issues such as Unit Trusts, or the Securities and Futures Authority (SFA) which deals with stockbrokers, also controlled by SIB. (Membership to any of these regulatorswill require acknowledgement within the copy.

For example:

*Financial Touch Marketing Ltd*
*Registered in the United Kingdom No. 12345.*
*Registered Office: 107 Empire Road London EC21 6BW.*

*Representative of the Financial Touch Marketing Group, members of which are regulated by the Personal Investment Authority and/or IMRO, for the purposes only of advising on and selling life assurance pension and unit trust contracts and investment services bearing Financial Touch's name.*

If applicable, credit examples may also have to be shown. Other restrictions could be dictated by database protection laws and, of course, limitations as described by specific advertising codes of practice.

### 18 How will you keep a tab of things?

All advertisers should monitor the effectiveness of their advertising. If this includes coupons, you will need to know if you should include any special details. Likewise, if a premium rate telephone response number is to be featured, you will also need technical information such as costs to the caller.

### 19 Who can tell me more?

However detailed the brief may be, you may still have further questions. Who can answer those questions and where can you find that person – phone numbers, e-mail numbers, fax numbers.

### 20 What do you expect to see?

Does the advertiser expect to see a finished creative job, all the way to artwork? Perhaps a rough visual will do? How about the copy without any visuals or even just some headlines?

### 21 When do you expect to see it?

When does the advertiser want to see your presentation and when does he expect to see the finished work? Again, try to involve everyone connected to the production side of things. This way you can account for printing times, filming schedules, publication dates, etc.

Whenever possible, get the advertiser to 'sign off' the creative brief. Other details that may be included are internal project or 'job' numbers.

## The *aide-mémoire* brief components

This kind of creative brief is designed for the copywriter who is already quite familiar with a particular product or service. It lists the main questions that always need to be addressed:

The Magnificent 13.5

| 1 | What's the big message? |
|---|---|
| 2 | What's needed? |
| 3 | What's on sale? |
| 4 | What's the USP? |
| 5 | Who wants it? |
| 6 | What do you want the folks to do? |
| 7 | What do they get out of it? |
| 8 | When and where is the communication going to appear? |
| 9 | What's the budget? |
| 10 | What's taboo? |
| 11 | What's the format? |
| 12 | What's the background? |
| 13 | What's next and when do you want it? |

Once you have constructed the *aide-mémoire* brief, you may go on to develop the ultimate creative copy brief called 'the copy platform'. Here, in just a few sentences you describe the product or service. Next, you provide a clear statement outlining your objectives. This is followed by a short note about your target audience, and no more than six leading benefits. Finally, you can include two other statements. One that describes your product positioning in the market and a second relating to the tone of voice that the advertising should take.

# —— Creative copy approaches ——

Ask any Wall Street financier or newspaper journalist to list the key attributes of a successful business or compelling news story and the chances are high that 'have a good angle' is in a leading position.

The 'angle' in question is the approach that you adopt to a message. By now, thanks to your thorough research and comprehensive creative brief, you should have enough knowledge about the product or service to work out your angle.

The most valuable information that helps you decide the best angle is your understanding of the target audience. This is point number nine of the all-embracing creative brief (see page 50).

## *USPs are more than skin deep*

Throughout this book, I discuss the various merits of the Unique Sales Proposition. I tell you to concentrate on a product's or service's main USP as a firm foundation for constructing an advertisement. Yet even when you believe you have found the ideal USP, how can you be certain that it is the appropriate one for the project in hand?

The solution is to think of the USP as sort of seductive Arabian exotic dancer.

### The USP's dance of the seven veils

Let's imagine that Scotdale Northside wants to promote its range of baby food. You have managed to target the USP as one of several possibilities.

- convenient, innovative packaging
- fresh ingredients (never more than 24 hours old before being canned)
- tasty – recipes from award-winning chefs
- cost effective – usually 10 per cent cheaper than the leading brand
- healthy – winner of several healthy eating awards

Now, start peeling off each seductive veil of promise.

**Convenient**
- for mum
- for baby
- for storage
- no cooking
- self-contained in the package
- no mess
- long shelf life

Next, go through the same process with each of your other USPs. In this example, this will provide you with up to 35 possible USPs. (If you really cannot find seven distinct USPs in each heading, do not spend all your time looking for one just to make up the numbers – USPs should leap out at you.)

You can perform the same exercise in reverse, casting away each USP that is weak or too similar to another. Try to get down to one or two USPs per heading. Consider, in terms of benefits, which USPs 'cross over' and then discard them.

Your final list can be shown to a person or group who is not directly involved with the project. Alternatively, if it's down to you to decide which USP wins, think about who or what ultimately benefits from the USP. For example, you may cut your baby food USP down to: fresh; tasty; healthy. Of these, which is probably the most beneficial to the baby? My suggestion would be 'healthy'.

(See 'Targeting your message' on page 15).

## Conceptions and perceptions

There are four key factors that influence a person's positive or negative attitude towards a group or individuals, namely:

1 cultural issues
2 situational (or interpersonal issues)
3 historic and economic concerns
4 individual experience

## Cultural issues

Where people live and how people work influences the type of approach to everything from purchasing washing-up liquid to investing in the stock market. For instance, local area overcrowding affects how people relate to each other. On the negative side, it may lead to increased crime. On the positive side, it may lead to a greater integration of cultural backgrounds and so to a broader understanding or different cultural values. This, in turn, affects the street language and interpersonal relationships of the 'locals'. It may lead to great competition in the job market. It may also result in a wider acceptance of new technology such as computers. This means a heightened need for products such as CD-ROMs, hardware and software.

## Situational (or interpersonal issues)

Following the crowd is a basic human instinct. Peer pressure is tremendously powerful throughout our lives. People like to conform. Even non-conformists conform with non-conformists. The reward for conforming is peer-group acceptance. For example, in the US 'Deep South', restaurant owners used to display signs that read: 'I'm not prejudiced, but my customers wouldn't like it.' This was meant to justify their refusal for blacks to eat at their premises.

Many house-cleansing material commercials are typical examples of how the advertisers try to be sympathetic towards a particular social peer group (often a housewife or, to a lesser extent, house husband). They discuss the possible repercussions to a family unit if the spouse and kids discover that their clothes are not as clean as they should be. Worse still, the possible scandal if poor domestic management by the housekeeper was discovered. The subtle thing to bear in mind is, if you do use this as a concept don't overplay the scenario or it could end up as a farce – unless, of course, you want to appear to be one of the social group making fun of itself. A concept should, therefore, be 'angled' to cater for the cliques without appearing to come across as a cliché.

## Historical concerns

Often people's aptitudes are social inheritances from a bygone age: 'We don't trust doctors because our parents didn't'; 'We drink it because we've always done so.' Socially, entire national prejudices may be based on historic concerns. For instance, British Asians were originally imported to the United Kingdom as slaves. A slave has no rights. Several centuries later, sadly there are still pockets of people who feel that Asians can never be 100 per cent British, or that blacks are less intelligent that 'real Brits'.

Historic influences are relatively easy to manipulate because, more often than not, people are unlikely to question why or exactly for how long their 'tradition' has been practised. If they did, they could upset their own social peers and so be rejected. For example, a local sign for Hindustani-speaking building contractors read: 'You've tried the cowboys now try the Indians'. Is this racist or is it harmless humour?

## Individual experience

As much as people like to feel that they 'fit' in society, they also like to retain their individuality. Doing so may, to a greater or lesser extent, result in some harsh lessons about life. For example, early in 1995 the British banking community suffered one of its greatest investment losses in its entire history, some £600 million, through apparent mismanagement.

While many financial institutions threw up their arms in horror, others used the disaster to highlight the fact that investments were safer with their banks. Advertisers liked to remind people that thanks to their product or service, the consumer need never be put in an uncomfortable or compromising position.

These four concepts typify the many complex types of character traits. The headings themselves contain many subheadings with refinements of each character trait. These can also be cross-referred against other traits. Ultimately you arrive at a unique DNA-type of advertising targeting. Ideally, this can be properly addressed only through traditional one-to-one selling techniques. Alternatively, it requires direct marketing (see Chapter 9). For now, it is important to remember not to misinterpret the categories by stereotyping. If you did, all your copy would be one-dimensional. It would have no substance and sound insincere.

# Square pegs, round holes and other categorisation

'Socio-economic groups' or 'social grading' was first developed for the Institute of Practitioners in Advertising. It is a system for classifying social status according to interests, social backgrounds and occupations. Each piece of data reflects the job of the head of the household. In the past, however, socio-economic classification tended to grade people by their income.

| Social grade | Social status | Occupation of head of household |
|---|---|---|
| A | Upper middle class | Higher managerial, professional |
| B | Middle class | Intermediate managerial |
| C1 | Lower middle class | Clerical |
| C2 | Skilled working class | Skilled manual worker |
| D | Working class | Unskilled manual worker |
| E | Lowest level | State pensioner, widow, casual worker, people dependent on social security |

(Source: JICNARS national readership survey)

Armed with this level of information, you can home-in on your target audience's lifestyle with greater accuracy. (Interestingly enough, in the United States, there is no such universal system for social grading. Instead, copywriters have to rely on lifestyle data and neighbourhood data such as those used in UK direct marketing (see Chapter 9).

## Psychographic targeting

Psychographic or psychometric classification of target customers by attitudes and other intellectual characteristics has led to various acronyms and classifications. One way of 'name-tagging' groups of people into types is the Values and Lifestyles approach (VALS). This tracks people as they progress from being totally unmotivated to having outstandingly balanced perceptions of society and their role in it.

| | |
|---|---|
| **Survivors** | Extremely poor and despondent |
| **Sustainers** | Poor but slightly optimistic about the future |
| **Belongers** | Conventional, middle of the road type who likes to fit in |
| **Emulators** | Aspiring, upwardly mobile and status-conscious |
| **Achievers** | Successful leaders |
| **I-am-me's** | Young, self-aware and self-driven; usually acting on the spur of the moment |
| **Experimentals** | Sybarites ready to try out a new experience; very inner-directed |
| **Society conscious** | Strives to wipe out examples of all social injustice |
| **Mature integrated** | Socially balanced, inwardly confident |

In order to segment lifestyles, many marketing companies develop acronyms even further. Here are a few popular psychographic terms including acronyms, that may help you define your target audience.

| Very young | Youthful and dynamic | Married | Established | Retired |
|---|---|---|---|---|
| *Baby boomer* The original term referred to people who grew up after the baby boom of the 1960s. The term has been also used to refer to people born at various key historical periods of population increase. | *Skotey* Spoiled kid of the Eighties. *Buppies* Black upwardly mobile professionals. *Road warriors* Professionals who spend over 100 days per year on business travel. | *Dinkies* Double income, no kids married couple. *Empty nesters* Married couple without children. *Managing mums* Guilt-ridden women dedicated to their families. | *Woopies* Well-off older people (over 55). Pre-retirement. *Glams* Greying, leisured, affluent middle-aged. *Markas* Middle-aged re-nester, kids away. | *Wrinklies* Elderly people who were in their twenties during the Second World War. *Crinklies* (Same as 'Wrinklies') *Silver market* People aged 60+. |

| Baby busters | Yuppies | Minks | Jolies | Grey panthers |
|---|---|---|---|---|
| People who were born just after the original baby boomers' generation and so, in the 1990s, had less need for housing and goods. | Young upwardly mobile professionals. | Multiple income, no kids. | Jet-setting oldies aged 49–59, free of financial worries. | Financially astute people aged 80+. |
| | *Puppies* Previously upwardly mobile professionals. | *Ticks* Two incomes with kids. | *Whannies* We have a nanny. | |
| | *Yuca* An American term for a young upwardly mobile Cuban-American. | *Muppie* Middle-aged urban professional. | *Holiday junkies* People 'hooked' on taking lots of holidays. | |
| | *Y-people* (Y-person) Another term for Yuppie. | *Droppies* Disillusioned relatively ordinary professionals preferring independent employment situations. | *Methuselah market* Rich people within five years of retirement. | |
| | *Grumpies* Grim ruthless upwardly mobile professionals. | | | |
| | *Guppies* People who have special interests and hobbies (such as people who breed guppie fish). | | | |
| | *Lombard* Lots of money but a real dickhead | | | |

# 4
# GETTING TO GRIPS
# WITH YOUR COPY

## Grammar

Hopefully, my English teacher will be happy that I 'ended-up' as a copywriter. However, knowing how much of a 'stickler' he was for precise grammar, I think that he would give up on my sentence construction.

Often, copywritten sentences are a complete grammatical nightmare. For example, this advertisement headline for a computer desktop recorder:

**Drive. A Hard bargain.**

This is not even a complete sentence because the verb doesn't agree with the subject. However, the advertisement's text (commonly referred to as bodycopy) may explain that the company is offering a desktop recorder (Hard Drive) at a competitive price. In this context, the headline seems appropriate. Even as it stands, the headline is intriguing enough to make you take a second glance at the advertisment and so, hopefully, lead you into the bodycopy. (I discuss bodycopy at greater length in Chapter 5.)

Copywriting is very different from formal business writing, journalism or novel writing. For example, the responsibility of most national tabloid journalists is confined to the details of the story. The job of writing an eye-catching headline or caption rests with the sub-editor. The picture editor deals with photographs. The page layout is managed by the page make-up person. Typography may be the job of a typographer (although with the advent of desktop publishing this is much less likely to be the case).

The copywriter, on the other hand, often has to consider the advertisement from every creative angle:

| | |
|---|---|
| headlines | sub-headlines |
| bodycopy | design |
| illustration | size |

frequency of appearance

You can, therefore, liken a copywriter to a musical composer and a conductor. The advertising message (copy) is the musical score. It is up to the copywriter to ensure that every note is harmonious and keeps tempo.

## Copywriting works in mysterious ways – using clichés

Unlike other forms of writing, copywriting tends to rely on one of the all-time big 'no, nos' of correct grammar – the heavy use of clichés. Clichés help to make advertisements immediate. They provide impact and can stimulate action. Copywriters like them because they help to convey a message quickly.

Flick through most mainstream magazines and newspapers. Before long, you should come across one of the following advertising clichés:

| | |
|---|---|
| Buy now | Act now |
| Exclusive offer | Yours free |
| Limited offer | Open now |
| Order now | At last |

## Take my word for it – introducing idioms

Copywriting also uses a lot of idioms, especially in slogans. They help a copywriter to achieve the ultimate goal – capture within a single sentence a product's key consumer benefit. Often an idiom is used completely out of context. This helps to add intrigue.

Idioms can be used in a corporate context. For example, imagine you are asked to produce an advertisement for Scotdale Northside. Your idiom could be used as a strapline (a sign-off line that appears at the foot of an advertisement). You could choose something like:

> SCOTDALE NORTHSIDE –
> FOR GOODNESS SAKE.

Why not combine two idioms:

> YOU'RE WELCOME,
> ANY DAY OF THE WEEK.

(Assuming the stores are open all week.)

Perhaps you want to advertise the Scotdale Northside horticultural division:

> EVERYTHING IN THE GARDEN
> IS LOVELY.

Alternatively, you could extend the idiom:

> EVERYTHING IN THE GARDEN IS ROSY, POSY, DAISY...
> AN ENTIRE BOUQUET OF DELIGHTS AT
> SCOTDALE NORTHSIDE.

(I will tell you more about the specific use of straplines, later in this chapter, so, *wait for it* and in the meantime, *just mark my words*.)

## *Colloquialisms*

Another needle in the side of grammarians is the use of colloqui-alisms. Generally, mass-media advertising that directs itself towards the 'ordinary person in the street' tends to adopt a lot of colloquial language. It enables the copywriter to communicate to people at an informal 'one-to-one' level. Colloquial use of language subtly 'tones down' the advertising sales pressure. See for yourself:

THE COMPANY WOULD LIKE TO
INVITE YOU TO PARTICIPATE
IN A VERY VALUABLE PRIZE DRAW PROMOTION.

*Versus*

JOIN OUR BIGGEST
EVER PRIZE DRAW.

Or

OUR OFFICE IS LOCATED ON THE CORNER OF BRITON AVENUE,
OPPOSITE THE REAR ENTRANCE OF
SCOTDALE NORTHSIDE'S SUPERSTORE.

*Versus*

YOU'LL FIND US BEHIND
SCOTDALE NORTHSIDE.

A word of warning about the use of colloquialisms: a specific colloqui-al vocabulary should reflect that of your target audience. For exam-ple, 'catch this crucial message' probably wouldn't be that effective if you were addressing a company chairperson. Likewise, usually there is little to gain from poor sentence construction 'just coz you reckon your audience is downmarket'!

(I remember once being briefed by someone to construct an advertisement that would appear in *The Sun* newspaper. The person said, 'Make it really simple and 'downmarket', don't use clever words or long sentences. After all, the audience are *Sun* readers.' My response was to 'dip into' my briefcase, remove a copy of a novel by Tolstoy and then produce a copy of my morning's paper – *The Sun*).

Just remember when it comes to colloquial English, as T S Eliot so aptly put it, 'If we spoke as we write, we should find no-one to read'.

Proverbs should be used only if relevant to a product or service. They are one of your tools to create word pictures. The best way to use them is to add a different angle to their meaning. So, if Scotdale Northside wanted to advertise 'two for the price of one' chickens, they could adapt a proverb like this:

> **A BIRD IN THE SHOPPING BASKET**
> **IS WORTH TWO AT THE CHECKOUT.**

## *Creative persuasion*

Copywriters can be sneaky. They walk a very fine line between overtly 'pushing' a product or service and gently persuading a person to buy it. The art of persuasion is far more covert that the job of 'ram-raiding' the sales message. On occasion, you have to think of various indirect ways of making sure a product name is seen, or a message is heard, time and time again.

Use direct or indirect repetition in the headline.
Repeat your point in the picture caption.
Repeat it in the bodycopy.
Repeat it in the coupon.
Repeat it in the strapline.
Repeat it in a jingle.
Let them hear what you have to say, first time.
Leading to a buying conclusion every time.

A classic way to 'slip in' repetition is to turn a product name into a noun. For example:

> **ADD STYLE TO LETTERS.**
> **PENPOD THEM.**

## *Punchier punctuation*

### The Victorian Rules of Punctuation

*Sentences start with a Capital letter,*
*So as to make your writing better.*
*Use a full stop to mark the end.*
*It closes every sentence penned.*
*Insert a comma for short pauses and breaks,*
*And also for lists the writer makes.*
*Dashes – like these – are for thoughts.*
*They provide additional information (so do brackets, of course).*
*These two dots are colons: they pause to compare.*
*They also do this: list, explain and prepare.*
*The semicolon makes a break; followed by a pause.*
*It does the job of words that link; it's also a short pause.*
*An apostrophe shows the owner of anyone's things,*
*It's quite useful for shortenings.*
*I'm glad! He's mad! Don't walk on the grass!*
*To show strong feelings use an exclamation mark!*
*A question mark follows Where? When? Why? What? and How?*
*Can I? Do you? Shall We? Tell us now!*
*"Quotation marks" enclose what is said.*
*Which is why they are often called 'speech marks' instead.*

(Based on *a Victorian Schoolmistress's Rules of Punctuation*)

Advertising copy needs to be as arresting as possible. The heart of copy construction is punctuation. Long sentences are rare. Yet in certain circumstances, their size can contribute to a sales proposition, especially when it is important to squeeze in every relevant detail which enhances the product sale, so leaving the prospect gasping for a breath.

Often, sentences are short.

Taken out of context.

Like building blocks.

Individually intriguing.

Collectively inspiring.

Ellipses such as,

> **NOW... FOREVER...**
>
> **FLOWERS SAY IT ALL.**

reinforce the tempo.

Short, sharp headlines with an emphatic full stop can make a proposition particularly arresting. For example:

> **CHEAT ON YOUR WIFE.**

(Don't let her known that the meal came out of a packet).

> **GET AHEAD. CHANGE YOUR HEAD.**

(Could be for tape-head reader or perhaps the PenPod product.)

> **GET STUFFED.**

(Scotdale Northside's range of chicken stuffing?)

These particular headlines could work as complete advertisements without supporting bodycopy. (See also 'Heads you win', page 88.)

Punctuation is like an artist's brush. Depending on its usage, at a stroke, you can create a picture that is highly complex or simple. You can surprise people. sentences may start with lower-case letters.

They could incorporate a dropped initial capital letter. (This particular technique is at least as old as the Magna Carta.)

Apart from arresting a reader's attention, the second most important use of punctuation in copywriting is to condense copy. Highlight key points. Drive the fundamental message home.

## Check you're spelling – the nineties' role four correct spelling

Always check your spelling manually. Don't just rely on your word processor's internal spell-checking program. This is highlighted by a verse that reputedly circulated around a large company in Houston, USA. It perfectly demonstrates the folly of copy checked by computer alone.

I have a spelling checker.
It came with my PC.
It plainly marks for my revue
Mistake I cannot see
I've run this poem threw it.
I'm sure your plees too no.
It's letter perfect in it's weigh,
My checker tolled me sew.

## Creative alliteration

The tills are alive with the sound of copy. Browse around your local High Street. Read the slogans on the posters or the leaflets, even the product packaging and you can hear musical advertising alliteration:

Finger lickin' good
Beans Meanz Heinz
You can't fit better than a Quick Fit fitter
Don't just book it, Thomas Cook it
Anytime, anyplace, anywhere

A theatre group could use the technique like this:

CENTRE STAGE, CENTRE ATTRACTION.

LIFE. WHATEVER YOUR STAGE, WE STAGE IT ON OURS.

LOCAL THEATRE. ONCE YOU'VE BOOKED, YOU'LL BE HOOKED.

A charity could use the technique like this:

HELPING THE HANDICAPPED TO HELP THEMSELVES.

EVERY PENNY MEANS EVER SO MUCH.

SHOW YOU CARE ABOUT THE AIR. (Environmental charity)

MAKING IT BETTER BY GETTING TOGETHER.

(Charity to find parents for children)

Alliteration through the repetition of letters, words or syllables has the same kind of effect as one of those tunes you can't seem to get off your mind. (Notable classics that pop into my head include: 'Ooh Waka Doo Wacka Day' and 'I've Got a Little Something For Ya...') Eventually the message becomes deeply embedded within a prospect's mind. Every time he or she thinks of a particular type of product or service, the slogan comes to mind and the prospect selects that brand. This technique is even more effective if the slogan is written as a musical jingle.

## Grammar quick tips

- Never use two words if one is enough.
- Never opt for a long word if a short word will do.
- Be specific – *talk*, not *communicate*.
- Check your words; *Computer program*, not *computer programme*.
- Don't use bureaucratic banality. Not *in due course, the Management board will inform you of its decision*. Instead *we'll let you know*.
- Always veer towards the positive thought rather than the negative. *You've won second prize in our contest*, not *you have not come first in our contest*.
- Link word couples. *Scotdale Northside's new shopping centre is always busy; customers love to shop there*, not *Customers that shop at Scotdale Northside's new shopping centre make it very busy because they love to shop there*.
- Heu, modo itera omnia quae mihi nunc narravisti, sed nunc, Anglice. (Oy! Repeat everything you just told me, but this time in English). In other words, we speak English, not Latin – in case you haven't heard, Caesar et Mort. So use *Every* not *per*. *Year* not *annum*...
- Above all, don't get too obsessed with grammatical correctness. The most important thing is to make your message interesting, easy to read and straightforward. If that means offending grammar puritans to achieve a winning creative response, go forth young person and offend!

# Creative structure

Before you write a word, always bear in mind that your priority is to carry a message to the *attention* of your audience, stimulate *interest*, solicit *desire* and then get your audience to take some kind of *action*. AIDA. Let's get down to the nitty-gritty.

## *The design*

The first thing that a person sees when looking at your creative advertisement is its shape. Your message has to compete against the many other messages that the consumer will see during the course of an average day. These messages are not just on posters, television, mail or in the press. They're also on pieces of sales promotion like drink coasters in pubs, or on T-shirts. Messages are heard on the radio, transmitted via the INTERNET, passed on by word of mouth… (Recent UK surveys suggest around 3000 visual communications are seen each day.)

So you have to think of an original way to present your piece of communication visually. Often this is the job of an art director. An art director is responsible for the visual appearance and concept of a piece of advertising. As a copywriter you will either be working independently or as part of a copywriter/art director team. Whether or not that team is a permanent feature, it is important to bear certain *musts* in mind when considering the look of a piece of communication.

*1 People look at pictures before they read words*
As children we grow up to recognise pictures before words. Pictures are worth a thousand words, but the 1001st word – your final word – completes the story.

*2 Never clutter the look, or 'layout'*
However trendy you wish to make your piece of communication look, always make it flow logically.

*3 Don't use two pictures when one will do*

*4 Don't use one general picture when one relevant detailed picture will do*

## 5 The logo is sacred
Never mess with a company's logo and always include it in the piece of communication. It acts as corporate seal of approval.

## 6 Develop a certain 'look' for all your pieces of communication
This, too, acts as a subtle corporate seal of approval. Each time your creative work is seen, even if people don't read it, they know from its style that you are active in the market place. A 'look' includes consistent use of typeface, consistent use of borders and, wherever possible, consistent shape of each layout.

## 7 Balance your copy with pictures
Depending on the power of the image, adjust your copy to compliment the image rather than undermine it. Likewise, never allow the images to undermine your copy.

## 8 Adapt the look
Adapt your creative work to blend into the media in which it will appear. (See Chapter 6.)

## 9 Always stick to one theme
Too many ideas in one piece of creative work dilutes your key message (USP).

## 10 Make room for impact
Include a sensible amount of 'white' or empty space that tones down the overtly 'hard sell' in the layout.

## 11 Make a citizen's arrest in $3/4$ of a second
It is thought that, on average, a person spends about 1½ seconds looking at a printed advertisement. So your picture has only half of that time to make a suitable impact.

---

The world's first photographically illustrated advertisement was placed by the Harrison Patent Knitting Machine Company of Portland Street, Manchester in the UK. It appeared on 11 November, 1887, and showed the company's attendent staff near a display stand.

---

## Making the headlines

If your prospective buyer reads only one thing, it's going to be your headline. So it's not surprising that copywriters spend so much time in getting 'it right'. If your headline is dull, your bodycopy will never see the light of day.

As I listed in point seven (overleaf), it is important to balance your copy with your visual elements. Curiously, you may be able to write an advertisement without the support of a graphic, such as a photograph. However, you rarely create an advertisement without a headline. (Unless you are trying to 'tease' your audience.)

That is not to suggest that all pictures need a headline to explain their relevance. In fact, none do. Headlines and pictures are equal partners in the communications business. One (either one) brings one of the following elements to the venture and the other brings the other element!

*Intrigue*

*Impact*

One further thought on photography and headlines: during a political advertising campaign for the UK Conservative Party in the late 1950s, it was planned to run a series of advertisements featuring a photograph of bright-eyed, ready-for-anything, person waking up. The headline read: *Get up and go with the Conservatives*. Everyone thought it was a good advertisement. However, just as it was about to run in the press someone noticed the bedside alarm clock in the photograph – it read the time of 09:45. (Not exactly very 'get up and go'!) The entire advertisement had to be scrapped. Moral: It's true, photography may offer details that can never be matched by illustration – however, unless you pay attention to everything during the shoot, those details could be your downfall.

### Headlines as picture captions

Although headlines should never be literal translations of pictures, they can enhance a message by referring to the picture, and hence explaining certain of its elements. This could include:

Who's in the picture?
Why is the person doing something?

What is the product?
In a word or two, what makes all of this relevant to a reader?

Returning to point 11 (overleaf), you have a total of 1½ seconds to make a citizen's arrest, so it is vital that you use the time effectively. In tests, virtually everyone reads the first two or three words in a headline. In terms of percentages, only 70 per cent of people will read six or seven words. Thereafter attention begins to go astray. The only exception to this rule is sometimes found in direct marketing copy (see Chapter 9). Response advertising often requires time and space to convey an evolving story. You can find lots of examples of long copy headlines in direct response advertising. Long headlines offer two advantages over the shorter piffy lines:

1  There are millions of short pithy headlines, so a longer one helps to make an advertisment outstanding;
2  A longer headline can be viewed as an expanded lead-in to the bodycopy, thus luring the reader deeper into the text.

For example, I once wrote the following headline:

> **720,459 PEOPLE AGED OVER 50**
> **DIDN'T PLAN TO DIE LAST YEAR,**
> **BUT THEN AGAIN,**
> **SOMETIMES LIFE DOESN'T ALWAYS GO TO PLAN ...**

This approach enabled me to complete the story in the text (bodycopy) and, at the same time, stir sufficient curiosity to stimulate the reader's interest.

Even if you manage to refine your message to only two or three words, there's no point in writing an arresting headline if it isn't relevant to your message. Worse still, if it doesn't make the reader want to find out more by reading the bodycopy. So, your main priority must always be to create a headline which delivers an immediate and relevant benefit to the consumer; anything else is just icing on the cake.

# Grabbing attention

There are eleven basic headline themes:

1 question
2 'Jump to it!' – command
3 comparison
4 challenge
5 invitation
6 promise
7 anticipation
8 location
9 representation
10 demonstration
11 news making

## Question headlines

*Who?*
There are two ways to consider the who? approach to headlines. The first is quite simply to include 'who' in the headline.

> **WHO KNOWS WHAT CHIPS**
> **KIDS LOVE BEST?**

(A Scotdale Northside advertisement for frozen chips.)

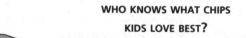

> **WHO CAN YOU TURN TO**
> **FOR IMPARTIAL ADVICE?**

(A financial services advertisement.)

The other route to consider is the testimonial type of advertisement. Testimonials add credence to a benefit through including a celebrity of character (fictional or historic) or person who is typical of the audience that you are trying to attract. Testimonial headlines must be believable, otherwise they fall flat. If you are going to quote a person or have permission to construct a quote for a person, always ensure that it is written in the style in which that person would say it.

> **"PenPòd is the only pen I ever need."**

As opposed to:

> **"Of all the pens I use, more often than not I find myself using this most excellent instrument called PenPod."**

*Can I quote you on that?*
In a word, 'No'. Copywriters often use quotations as an emergency exit out of a difficult project when they cannot find anything original to say.

Sometimes Who? headlines refer to historic or fictional characters. Again, try to use this technique only if it is relevant. There wouldn't be much point in a headline for an advertisement for baked beans that incorporated a picture of Winston Churchill and read:

> **"Give us the tools and we will finish the job."**

(Mind you, as an advertisement for PenPod...)

Finally, when it comes to quotations in headlines, try to remember to let the product take the sales lead – not the models or personalities.

*Why? Which? and How?*
Questions always provoke a response – or do they? They pose puzzles that people instinctively have to either answer or wait to be answered. More importantly they act as a kind of mental tickling stick to tease your audience.

Consider this headline:

> **Would you like to get £5,000 a week for nothing?**

The headline achieves three things:

1 It poses a question;
2 Considering human instinct, you, the copywriter, can take an intuitive 'stab' at the likely response – 'Yes, but what's the catch?'
3 Based on all these things, you can proceed with the bodycopy.

One of the danger signs to watch for when writing question-led headlines is never to allow the question to answer itself. If you do, nobody will bother to read any further.

For example:

**'WOULD YOU LIKE SOME LIFE INSURANCE'?**

**'ARE YOU OVERWEIGHT'?**

Either 'yes' or 'no' answers choke the interest factor at birth. One way to avoid this is to answer the question in a subhead.

**'ARE YOU OVERWEIGHT?'**
CALL US ON **0800 123 124**.
WE'LL SAVE YOU POUNDS THE MOMENT YOU DIAL.

Clever manipulation of words can help you avoid the definite 'yes' or 'no' answer to a question, without having to include a subhead solution:

HOW DO YOU THINK PENPOD
SAVES YOU MONEY?

*When questions make answers*
One final use of questions in a headline is when you turn a bland statement into a powerful sales message, just by adding a simple 'why' or 'where' or 'how'.

For example:

> **WE SELL THE GREATEST RANGE OF BABY NAPPIES.**

This is a strong statement. However, add the word 'why' and it lifts off the page.

> **WHY WE SELL THE GREATEST RANGE**
> **OF BABY NAPPIES.**

Another copywriting 'trick' is to use a leading questions as an explanation to demonstrate a product's simplicity.

Consider this:

> **BUILD A 150 MILE PER HOUR SPORTS CAR IN YOUR GARAGE.**

The same could be applied to:

> **THIS INSURANCE POLICY WILL COVER**
> **ALL YOUR COMPANY'S BAD DEBTS.**

Both examples can be made more rewarding to the reader:

> **HOW CAN YOU BUILD A 150 MILE PER HOUR**
> **SPORTS CAR IN YOUR GARAGE?**
> **HERE'S HOW...**

> **HERE'S HOW THIS INSURANCE POLICY**
> **WILL COVER ALL YOUR COMPANY'S BAD DEBTS.**

## Jump-to-it headlines

Don't walk on the grass!
Eat your greens!
Clean your teeth!
Stop biting your nails!

Headlines are stuffed from capital letter to full stop with orders. With so many commands being seen and heard through the media, it's a small wonder that anyone has time to get on with their lives! Likewise, with such a plethora of messages, the net impact of the instructions faces a danger of being completely diluted to a mish-mash of disorder. It is thought that the average person 'takes-in' around 200 'jump-to-it' messages a day, but will recall fewer than 10 per cent.

So what makes people listen to one instruction and ignore another? Simply, it's the way you phrase your instruction. It's the attitude your advertisement takes. If you aggressively order people about simply to bully them into doing something, often all you achieve is their doing the opposite – just to spite you. Likewise, if a creative approach is too shocking, verging on the tasteless, people turn away (see page 208). That doesn't mean that you shouldn't use verbs in headlines. Instead, you need to plan how best to use verbs as a persuasive tool. Wherever possible, it is worthwhile considering the use of verbs in a headline. Not every headline features a verb. You may prefer to imply it.

For example a headline referring to PenPod's durability and reliability. The text could appear as though it had been written on a piece of paper that stretches for miles:

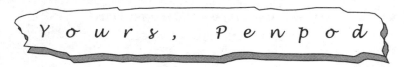

Verbs add impact to a headline. Without them you can still conjure up provocative images. With them you drive your message home. For example, Scotdale Northside wish to announce a new phase as part of their anniversary celebrations. The press release is headed:

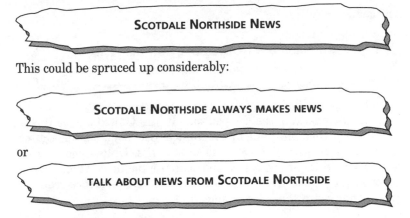

**SCOTDALE NORTHSIDE NEWS**

This could be spruced up considerably:

**SCOTDALE NORTHSIDE ALWAYS MAKES NEWS**

or

**TALK ABOUT NEWS FROM SCOTDALE NORTHSIDE**

## Comparison headlines

Comparison headlines prove highly effective ways to stimulate reader participation. They usually incorporate a striking visual that shows the clear difference between one thing and another. Historically, comparison headlines work particularly well for health and diet plans, when the advertiser wishes to show clearly the results of a diet after participating in the plan. One trick is to highlight how the 'after' result has had a dramatic effect for the user of the diet plan by showing the 'before' appearance in its worst possible light. So, the person in the 'before' shot would be wearing something dowdy and plain. Whereas in the 'after' shot, the same person wears something quite fetching and stylish.

Comparison ads work equally well with inanimate objects. For example, Scotdale Northside wants to show how they include more biscuits in their packets than those offered by their competitors. The Scotdale Northside ad would feature a stylishly photographed mound of biscuits on a plate, whereas the competitor's plate would be only half full.

As another example, a video-tape manufacturer wishes to demonstrate the durability and quality of 'its product compared to the other manufacturers'.

Visualise two pictures ('a' and 'b'):

a) shows a clear television picture clip of *Gone with the Wind*;
b) has a fuzzy television picture of *Gone with the Wind*.

The headline reads:

> **WHY SHOULD WATCHING *GONE WITH THE WIND***
> **LEAVE YOU HUFFING AND PUFFING?**

The only drawback of comparison-type headlines is that they can be construed as 'knocking the competition'. In the United States this is often more acceptable than in the United Kingdom. In the United Kingdom, such aggression can lead to lawsuits. Unless you wish to create a stir in the marketplace and so invite public relations' coverage, the best way to avoid this is to have all the evidence ready to support your claim. (See also Chapter 16.)

## Challenge headlines

> **I BET YOU THAT AFTER TWO WEEKS**
> **OF SWITCHING TO BRAND X**
> **YOU WILL PERMANENTLY USE IT IN**
> **PREFERENCE TO YOUR USUAL BRAND.**

> **I BET YOU WON'T BE ABLE TO TELL THE DIFFERENCE**
> **IN TASTE BETWEEN BRAND X AND BRAND Y.**

The beauty of challenge headlines is that the only way a customer can dispute your claim is to pick up the gauntlet and accept your challenge.

There are several methods to help enliven challenge headlines. One is the blindfold test approach, where the identities of your product and those of your competitors are concealed until the results are presented. Often, blindfold testing produces surprising results.

|  | Open | Blind |
|---|---|---|
| Prefer Pepsi | 23% | 51% |
| Prefer Coke | 65% | 44% |
| No preference | 12% | 5% |

Source: *Relationship Marketing* by Martin Christopher, Adrian Payne and David Ballantyne

Apart from highlighting people's perceptions about the drinks, this table also demonstrates the power of brand loyalty. (See 'Give your troops brand names; page 40).

Another option is to offer to refund the cost of your product. It works like this: if the prospect believes that, after an acceptable period of time 'testing out', your product is still better than your competitor's, you refund the money. Of course, refunds are made only upon proof of purchase. After, say, a two-week challenge period for a relatively low-priced item, how many people will really be bothered to claim back their money – would you?

## Invitation headlines

Everyone likes to receive an invitation to participate in something. Even if you don't accept the invitation, it's nice to know that you were asked in the first place. Invitation headlines work particularly well for launches or in conjunction with demonstration headlines.

> COME AND VISIT THE NEW SCOTDALE NORTHSIDE STORE.

> TEST DRIVE OUR LATEST CAR.

> BE ONE OF THE FIRST TO VISIT OUR NEW RESTAURANT.

Invitation headlines work well when they incorporate a reward for accepting the invitation.

> BE ONE OF THE FIRST TO VISIT THE NEW
> SCOTDALE NORTHSIDE STORE
> AND WE'LL GIVE YOU A £10 GIFT VOUCHER.

> TEST DRIVE OUR LATEST CAR AND YOU COULD WIN IT IN A PRIZE DRAW.

> **BE ONE OF THE FIRST TO VISIT OUR NEW RESTAURANT.**
>
> **NEXT TIME, YOUR MEAL IS ON US.**

In order to clarify these examples, I have made the offers quite implicit. However, in practice, you should try to allow your headline to withhold an element of your offer, either for further explanation within the bodycopy or to be completely realised when the invitation is accepted.

> **BE ONE OF THE FIRST TO VISIT OUR NEW STORE AND OUR**
>
> **CHECKOUT ASSISTANTS WILL PAY *YOU*.**

> **TAKE OUR LATEST CAR FOR A SPIN AROUND THE BLOCK**
>
> **AND KEEP THE KEYS.**

> **A PERFECT MEAL, COMPLIMENTS OF THE CHEF.**

## Promise headlines

Promise headlines are reserved for advertisers who are prepared to put their money where their sales pitch is. A promise headline obliges the advertiser to offer guarantees on the product or service. A guarantee is a legal commitment that needs to be honoured. So, if you decide to make a guarantee, you have to be specific about its duration, value and restrictions. You also have to ensure that any promise doesn't affect statutory consumer rights. (You may need to take legal advice on this, or consult your local Citizen's Advice Bureau.)

Some may say, cynically, that guarantees create more loopholes than sales. The answer is, it depends on how you phrase your guarantee. You don't want to end up with a headline that is two pages long with clauses. Nor do you want to design an advertisement with more small print than bodycopy. Therefore, keep your guarantees simple and, as is invariably found in direct mail advertising, your guaranteed confidence should enhance the message. (And you can take my word on that – or your money back!)

## Anticipation headlines

An old Vaudeville magician once said, 'To grab an audience, keep them waiting and they'll come back for more.'

You can imagine the scenario. The magician would claim that he could escape from a locked tea chest immersed underwater. He climbed in. Someone sealed the chest with heavy chains and complicated locking devices. The chest was lowered into a huge glass container. Water split out everywhere. After about 30 seconds, the audience began to grow concerned for the poor performer locked in the chest. Sixty seconds passed. No sign of the chains being removed. Two minutes elapsed. A distraught woman appeared from backstage and screamed for the stage hands to help her retrieve the chest. By then, five minutes had passed. The bandmaster stopped playing. He tried to console a member of the orchestra who had broken down in tears. The chest was finally winched out and dropped, dripping wet, on to the stage. Someone approached with a huge chain-cutting device. The case was thrown open. Out spilt gallons of water, but the magician had vanished. At that precise moment, he appeared in perfect shape at the back of the auditorium. The audience applauded.

Keeping your advertising audience waiting almost contradicts the 'get the message quick' approach of headlines. However, you can still 'keep them waiting' by featuring several well-tried techniques.

The first is to place your product in an impossible situation. For example, you want to demonstrate PenPod's amazing strength? So why not drive over it with a Jumbo jet? Similarly, you want to demonstrate the creamy thickness of one of Scotdale Northside's yoghurts. Why not 'load' it with lots of fruit that defy gravity by nestling on the yoghurt's surface? If you want to demonstrate the strength of a piece of string, why not suspend a fork lift truck from it?

The second technique is to feature a headline that can be fully understood only if the person purchases the product. These headlines are great if you have a product that you wish to position as being so refined that it can be appreciated only by the very few – nobody else will understand the proposition. Usually, these types of headlines produce what I call the 'niggling itch' effect. This is when the consumer sees the advertisement and, not wishing to appear stupid, makes every possible effort to show his or her peers that he or she understands the message, so nervously 'scratches' away at the obscure message.

Drink brands often produce advertising that evokes a sense of belonging to a group of people who share a special outlook and appreciation of life. It works along the same lines as adolescent gangs. One gang has its own mode of travel or dress, even perhaps special language, while another group promotes a different view. Once you belong to either gang you can enjoy the status that such membership brings. This is made even more valuable if that gang forces you to keep secrets that can never be revealed to anyone outside the group. That's why you may get a beer advertisment wrapped up in riddles. Then, when you go to the pub to order a beer you find a certain group of people adopting the beer not just as a refreshing drink, but as a statement that reflects their social attitudes (see 'rebel advertising' in 'Glossary' page 312).

A third anticipation headline technique is the 'taste of the things to come' approach. The chocolate bar that looks so good you could eat it off the page. The holiday that looks so relaxing you can't wait to get on to the beach, and so on.

Finally, you could try the leading...
        ... teaser headline. However I have found that this seems to work only if you reserve it for mailing pieces where the headline may start on the outer envelope ...

... And conclude as you open the envelope. I sometimes refer to this technique as the greetings card device because so many greetings rely on such leading headlines.

> **FOR YOUR BIRTHDAY I WANTED TO BUY YOU**
> **SOMETHING THAT COUNTS...**

(Open the card)

> **... HERE'S AN ABACUS.**

## Location headlines

A short cut to direct a consumer towards your brand is the creation of unique locations where your brand has the freedom to really excel. Location headline approaches can be useful when you want individual brands to be perceived as being part of a bigger family of products and services. As you learnt in 'The Elvis factor and the 'G' spot', (page 38) brands should be able to stand alone as well as part of a whole.

The ultimate brand location must surely be Disneyworld. Here, individual brand items such as specific film titles with unique characters, club together with carnival rides and attractions to produce a transglobal parent brand with a cultural following all of its own. Indeed, it is so successful that even the location has become a brand with several sister sites around the world.

You may not have the odd couple of billion pounds to build such a themed location – in advertising terms, that is not important. Many of the world's leading brands have used advertising to create artificial locations that are just as evocative as the real thing. Alcoholic beverage brands often conjure up a paradise island where their drinks are served all day. Artificial locations can also work for specific one-off brands. The most famous example of this is Marlboro Country. A place where the air is clean, a man is free and the environment is natural. (Where better to escape for a quick ciggie?)

## Representation headlines

Now you have invented your magical 'Oz' you will need a guide to show your prospective buyer around. You can either invent a character to complement your imaginary location, or you can feature yourself or your client in the advertising.

As you know, good advertising leads a prospect to associate a product or service with something that can be personally relevant. Often advertising promises, or at least hints towards the promise, that a product or service will help the prospect reach a sort of utopia. (Just in case you didn't already know, there is no such place as Utopia. However, everyone wants to find it, and if people were to give up the search, many aspects of life would collapse – and you as a copywriter would be out of a job!)

## Imaginary characters

Just as an imaginary land paints a vivid picture of a type of utopia so it makes sense to invent an imaginary escort to guide you through it. Catering companies often use this approach by inventing everything from a character made of dough to one built from liquorice. Erotic magazines publishers build entire Xanadus on the basis of the ideal lover.

Animated characters can be manipulated to show precise facial characteristics. The combined detachment from reality and precision of facial expressions may actually enhance the impression that you want your brand to leave on a prospect. Highly successful animated characters have included giants, walking milk bottles, dancing credit cards, singing raisins, marching toothbrushes, flying sprays of polish, and a variety of others.

Imaginary characters need not be animated, however. Some of the world's longest-running advertising campaigns have been built around fictitious characters played by actors. These include advertisements featuring the 'ideal' mum who always serves a particular gravy brand, and one of the most famous of all classic advertising characters – the 'man in the Hathaway shirt' (an eye-patched man whose sophisticated lifestyle always meant that he had to be suitable attired – in a Hathaway-branded shirt).

## Appearing in your own advertising

Should you or your client appear in an advertisement? Few people are great media communicators. It doesn't matter how good a salesperson you or your client may be, the chances are strong that once you appear in your ad, your charming personality, however wonderful it may be, could come across as one-dimensional and insincere. Effective advertising pre-empts risks. Unless you are prepared to ask an unbiased panel for their honest views of you or your client's appearance in an advertisement, don't risk it.

Yet… like everything, there are exceptions to the rule. A notable one is when the company representative is featured as part of a mailing piece. For example, a fashion buyer may write to explain why a certain line of suits caught his or her eye.

Occasionally, you come across someone who really does have what it takes to appear sincere in every medium. If you do happen to find such a company representative, and he or she is senior enough within the organisation, an endorsement ad from 'the top cat' will help sales. However, I remain sceptical.

## Demonstration headlines

Demonstration headlines can be startlingly effective. Ask any vacuum cleaner salespeople how to impress a prospective buyer and they'll throw a bin-full of rubbish on your lounge carpet. The real shock is that the vacuum cleaner tidies up the mess in minutes, leaving not even a speck of dust behind. Demonstration headlines are closely related to anticipation headlines in that they feature the product in an unusual setting, such as a man stuck to a flying plane by nothing more than a brand of glue.

One of the best mediums for demonstration headlines is television. Here you can play out an entire scenario in front of an audience (see Chapter 11).

## News making headlines

When you read the heading above, did you interpret it as reading that advertising headlines makes news? If you did, you read it correctly. If you did not, your interpretation is still correct.

A lot of people still believe that advertising sets trends. For 99.9 per cent of the time, this is nonsense. Advertising pampers to society's needs by understanding how people see their roles in society. To do this, it has to listen and watch trends, then follow those trends alongside the consumer. Topical headlines can either be directly or indirectly connected to the company. Directly topical headlines could refer to specific use of the product in a news-making context. For example, you produce the oil in a Grand Prix winning vehicle, so you write a headline that refers to the great race.

Alternatively, a topical headline could be indirectly associated with the topical news. For example, a national football team wins the World Cup. Scotdale Northside could refer to it with the following headline:

> **CONGRATULATIONS ENGLAND**
> **FROM ONE LEAGUE LEADER TO ANOTHER.**

Topical headlines help to make a company appear to be part of a living community. They can provide scope for humour, compassion or responsibility.

What about the 0.1 per cent chance that advertising sets trends? Sometimes advertisers create risky advertising that is bound to be banned and so makes headlines. Other times advertisers use themes that suddenly become fashionable such as the use of an evocative piece of music. However, you invariably find that the advertisement is based on a variation of a published theme. An example was a 1995 jeans commercial which featured the song *Boombastic* by Shaggy.

Advertising doesn't invent. It innovates.

## *Heads you win – painting pictures with copy*

I can't leave the world of headlines without discussing one of its most fascinating aspects. Word pictures. Once you have decided which of the 11 headline themes you wish to take – or even which combination best suits your needs, you must consider the appropriateness of word pictures.

Word pictures draw the reader to a product's personality. In addition to highlighting a benefit, they set the agenda for the advertisement's tone of voice.

Here are examples of word pictures:

BANANAS SO CHEAP,
YOU WON'T WANT THEM TO SLIP BY.

THE WALLS HAVE EARS.

Word pictures match elements of a product's name, or use, with the given situation or location that you place it within. So, for example, you wish to talk about a relaxing ferry journey.

Headline:

**THE NOT SO CROSS FERRY.**

(Picture of contented passenger *versus* frustrated passenger)

Another variation of a word picture is when you combine and illustrate two separate words into one message.

Possible examples

**SMOKE RING**

(Give up smoking, dial this number)

**ACTION REPLAY**

(Action-packed computer game that you'll want to play time after time)

**AIR LIFT**

(New kind of hydraulic elevator system)

**IRONING BOARD**

(Company's own management tests a new iron)

**VAMPIRE BAT**

(High-impact cricket bat)

**BOTTOM LINE**

(A successful dieter's figure)

... and so on.

Never confuse word pictures with puns. Puns are over-used and poor substitutes for clear messages. Copywriters have the tendency to play with sentences for no other purpose than to make something sound funny when it is not relevant to do so. (See also 'Punchier punctuation', page 66, and 'Colloquialisms', page 64.) One of the crudest puns I have ever seen was for a scaffolding company whose trade advertisement headline read: 'Satisfaction guaranteed with every erection'. Unlike puns, word pictures open doors to creative writing. Once you enter into a proposition, bodycopy takes over to complete the story.

## Nitty-gritty quick tips

- Design your advertisement to gain the maximum impact on the page.
- Invest the time to create a powerful headline.
- People read or reject a headline within 1½ seconds.
- There are 11 basic headline themes.
- Testimonials must 'sound' realistic.
- Quotations are an excuse to avoid writing something original that's quotable.
- Wouldn't you use a leading question to direct a prospect to a sale?
- Persuading a prospect is different to pushing a prospect.
- Consider writing 'before and after' creative copy.
- If a product is difficult to sell, consider throwing down the gauntlet by setting a challenge.
- Invite your prospect to view your product before buying it.
- Prospects are VIPs – Very Important Prospects.
- Guarantee your proposition.
- Make your product or service something that's worth waiting for.
- Position your product or service in a special unique location.
- Add product personality by inventing a unique character.
- Demonstrate your product or service.
- Advertising doesn't invent, it innovates.
- Link words to create pictures.

## *Over to you*

1 Using six headline themes, write headlines to advertise three of your favourite films, and for three current news stories.
2 Write 50 words to persuade a person not to jump off a mountain.
3 Apart from slimming products, list six other products or services which could use a 'before and after' technique.
4 Write ten word pictures.
5 Write a headline which captures the spirit of:
   *a)* The Mona Lisa
   *b)* A traffic light
   *c)* The gum on the back of a stamp
   *d)* Witticism

# 5

# BODY BUILDING

## Understanding bodycopy

Without bodycopy a firm sales proposition hasn't any substance. One of the most common questions asked about bodycopy is, 'How long should it be?' There are three replies:

1 As long as it takes to convey all the information;
2 The greater the commitment that you are asking the consumer to make, the longer the copy;
3 As long as it takes until you lose enthusiasm for the project.

Your headline, accompanied by a suitable visual, provides the carrot that entices the reader into your message. If your copy is not at least equally provocative, the entire exercise is redundant. Bodycopy provides the detailed reasons a buyer needs to make a purchase or take appropriate action.

Depending on the type of advertisement, you need to *identify* either a product or service or provide *information* about the product or service. Your bodycopy should adapt accordingly. In the case of identifying products or services, strong headlines and visuals usually suffice. Examples of this are on posters for impulse purchases such as sweets or household detergents. (This can also include in-store posters.)

In the case of providing information about a product or service, bodycopy takes the lead from headlines. Informative advertising needs time to convey the benefits of a product or service. Good examples of this are technical or financial products. Often business-to-business advertising also relies on longer copy.

## *Copy with conviction*

Bodycopy has to be convincing. To achieve this, you have to have confidence in your proposition. Believe me, your mood is always 'read' in the copy. Too often copywriters let themselves and the advertisement down by either being forced to write over-long copy, just to fill in space, or write copy that's too short, just to accommodate a certain style. If you are sincere, the copy will sound sincere. If you are blasé, the copy will appear crass.

Another cause of unbelievable bodycopy is the unbelievable claim. Very few people will believe that a particular item will change their lives for the better: especially if your bodycopy oversells. The only exception to this rule is when you adopt the technique to overtly oversell in order to draw attention to your style of selling. This is often used by American-style car salespeople who may make claims such as 'Our deals are so good that if you don't buy, we'll eat the car'! Likewise, claims direct from a product supplier or manufacturer can also sound feeble when compared to endorsements from users of the product or service. (See also 'Testimonials', page 74.)

An extreme example of a manufacturer overselling a product is:

> ONE SPOONFUL OF OUR YOGHURT WILL
> MAKE YOU FEEL LIKE A MILLIONAIRE.
> ONE SPOONFUL OF OUR COMPETITOR'S YOGHURT WILL
> MAKE YOU FEEL SICK.

Sure, someone somewhere will buy the yoghurt. However, it will be a one-off purchase. Once they try your competitor's yoghurt, the chances are pretty strong that won't be sick so, you have deceived them. (By the way, if you make such a direct competitor-knocking claim, it could infringe the rules of the Advertising Code of Practice.)

The best course of action is to remember that you want to keep a customer for good, not for just a moment. Therefore, keep your claims believable and people will come back again and again.

# ⎯⎯ Taking the right direction ⎯⎯

By the time you start to write your bodycopy, you should be very familiar with all aspects of the brief. Generally, your headline sets the tone of voice for the copy. Light-hearted headlines lead into light-hearted copy. Technical headlines demand technical explanations.

The first sentence of your bodycopy (also known as the lead-in sentence) is the second most important part of your main text. (The most important is the call to action.) The lead-in sentence links your headline with the rest of your piece. It's as if your headline is a shop window and the bodycopy is the showroom with all the gadgets ready to be discussed by a salesperson. (If you want to go into any further detail, you'll need a brochure.)

As the lead-in sentence links two complimentary lines of thought, you should never use it to repeat the headline or try to fill in gaps that your headline and/or visual failed to achieve. That is a waste of words and doesn't make the link secure enough to keep a prospect 'hooked' to your message. Get to the point, lead your prospect to all your USPs.

For example, Scotdale Northside are opening a new chain of restaurants.

Headline:

> **WILD WEST GRUB?**
> **FAR EASTERN CHOW?**
> **SOUTHERN FRIED CHICKEN?**
> **NORTHERN HOSPITALITY?**

Subhead:

> **BETTER HEAD IN OUR DIRECTION.**

Lead-in sentence:

> WHEN YOU'RE PECKISH AND JUST CAN'T DECIDE WHICH FOOD MATCHES
> YOUR MOOD, HEAD TO THE ONE PLACE THAT HAS IT ALL – DIRECTIONS...

*Not*

> FRESH FOOD THAT'S IDEAL FOR ALL YOUR FAMILY CAN BE
> FOUND IN OUR NEW RESTAURANT CALLED DIRECTIONS.

## *Are you following all of this?*

Now that you have set a copy agenda, allow your creative ideas to flow effortlessly. So-called 'copy tracking' provides a catalyst for ideas to flow in a logical sequence. The test of good copy tracking is to remove one of the sentences from a paragraph. If the rest of the sentences still add up to a reasonably plausible message, your copy tracking hasn't gone off the rails.

Next, you need to prioritise product benefits in the order you want them read. For example, here are some of the USPs for Scotdale Northside's 'Directions' chain of restaurants:

● Locations throughout the country;
● Delicious food from all corners of the world;
● Reasonably priced;
● Special pre-measured portions;
● Excellent service;
● Tempting dishes for young and 'not so young';
● Different speciality menu every day;
● Homely decor.

Depending on where your advertisement appears, your bodycopy should concentrate on a suitable benefit. So, if your advertisement appears in a family-style publication, 'Tempting dishes for young and "not so young" ' should take priority.

## *Address the arguments before the questions start*

Once you have prioritised your benefits, you have to state them as well as address arguments that may arise. To do this, as you write each sentence think of how it will affect any of the following sentences. More importantly, think how each sales proposition creates a possible argument against it. For example, you want to address families using their cars for long journeys.

Headline:

> **IF YOU'RE FEELING PECKISH PULL OFF AT JUNCTION 5 AND FILL THE WATFORD GAP.**

(Picture of a family in a car. One of the kids is acting quite wild. Another is looking glum. The front passenger is trying to placate everyone and the driver is looking desperate.)

Bodycopy:

> **WHEN YOU'RE STUCK IN A FIVE-MILE TAILBACK**
> **AND THE KIDS ARE SCREAMING FOR LUNCH,**
> **YOU NEED A NEW DIRECTION – PRONTO.**

(What are you going to do about it?)

> **LOOK OUT FOR THE SPECIAL DIRECTIONS COMPASS SIGN**
> **AND YOU'LL BE JUST A JUNCTION AWAY FROM A**
> **SATISFYING MEAL THAT ALL THE FAMILY WILL RELISH.**

(What's so satisfying about it?)

> **DIRECTIONS FEATURES SCRUMPTIOUS DISHES FROM ALL**
> **FOUR CORNERS OF THE WORLD, INCLUDING WILD WEST FEASTS,**
> **FAR EASTERN SPECIALITIES AND LOTS MORE BESIDES...**
> **IN FACT, SOMETHING TO PLEASE EVERYONE.**

(Is there anything else that's special?)

YOU CAN CHOOSE FROM THREE MENUS:
THE HEARTY FILLER — IDEAL FOR A WHOLESOME SNACK;
THE BIG DEAL — BIG ON PORTIONS, SMALL ON PRICE;
THE GIANT SLAYER — A MASSIVE PORTION THAT WILL KNOCK YOUR
EYES OUT AND FILL EVEN THE BIGGEST APPETITE.

(Sounds expensive. What does it cost?)

JUST BECAUSE WE SERVE THE BEST CHOICE OF FOOD FROM
AROUND THE WORLD, IT DOESN'T MEAN THAT OUR PRICES ARE
OUT OF THIS EARTH.
A HEARTY FILLER COSTS AS LITTLE AS £4.99,
AND EVEN OUR GIANT SLAYER STARTS FROM ONLY £9.99.

(I want some of that. What do I do next?)

THE NEXT TIME YOU'RE FEELING PECKISH,
PULL IN AND FILL UP AT DIRECTIONS.

(Where can I find it?)

Include a map or list of restaurant locations. Alternatively, you may consider featuring a special telephone number which people can ring for further details.

## Don't cramp my style

### (Writing for a specific audience)

As I mentioned at the start of this section, your headline sets the tone of voice for your bodycopy. Your copy style needs to adapt to the target audience, as well as to the company which is advertising.

All professional copywriters are also copyreaders. Whenever possible, study previous examples of corporate copy style. Use the technique discussed in 'Make the right impression' (page 46). Read the papers that target audience will read. Should your style blend into that of your competitor's or should you be bold and produce something completely different?

There are hundreds of ways in which you can blend styles of copywriting. To simplify matters, I have narrowed them down to half a dozen main types of bodycopy styling.

## Six elements of style

### 1 *Get on with it*
This method picks up where the headline and visual left off. It prioritises USPs and then explains each one at a time.

- A great panacea for all styles of bodycopy;
- Essential if you have a lot of benefits to convey;
- Maintains momentum.

### 2 *View from the top*
This method takes a corporate view of a product or service. It concentrates on the ideology behind an advertised item, rather than on its immediate specifics.

- Often used by large corporate organisations;
- Helps boost confidence in a company;
- Waves the corporate flag;
- Useful to promote umbrella brands;
- Can be used in conjunction with public relations activities;
- Commonly used to imbue confidence with shareholders or financiers;
- Facts must be word perfect;
- Exaggerations must be avoided.

### 3 *Story line*
This method tells a narrative that develops into discussions of your salient USPs.

- Ideal for lifestyle copy where feelings associated with a product or services are equal to, if not stronger than, features. For example, 'gold' credit card advertising often uses a storyline (narrative copy) to describe a rich lifestyle;
- 'Pigeon holes' readers;
- Reinforces a company's corporate image;
- Can be written from the user's viewpoint or writer's description of the user's viewpoint;

- A good story needs a long description;
- Adds human interest to products or services;
- Helps you use emotive copy when there are not many USPs to discuss.

*4 Character-led*
This method lets the character in your advertisement introduce your message. Characters may include celebrities, end-users or even comic strips.

- Covers all kinds of testimonial bodycopy. (See also 'Question headlines, page 74 and 'Representation headlines', page 85)
- Testimonials must be clear, plain and, above all, sincere;
- Use only relevant celebrity testimonials. (e.g. Don't get a magician to sell a cure for cancer.)
- If you are going to write a testimonial on behalf of a celebrity, write it as if they would say it;
- Never write a testimonial that forces the celebrity or end-user to state something that he or she would not normally know. For example,

> "I ALWAYS WRITE WITH A PENPOD.
> THE **30** PER CENT EXTRA OIL IN THE INK
> MEANS THAT IT EVEN CLINGS TO NON-POROUS PAPER.'

(*Yuk!*) It would sound more credible if you wrote:

> THIS PENPOD IS GREAT.
> IT WORKS ANYWHERE.

- Testimonials can be implied through bodycopy style rather than actually including a named person.

*5 Different strokes*
This method relies on unusual language such as poetry, humour and foreign words.

- Rarely used: however, particularly potent for bodycopy aimed at the younger side of the market or when something quirky is required;

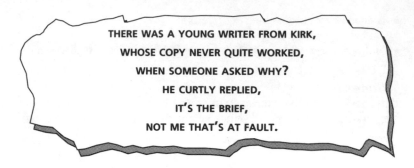

THERE WAS A YOUNG WRITER FROM KIRK,

WHOSE COPY NEVER QUITE WORKED,

WHEN SOMEONE ASKED WHY?

HE CURTLY REPLIED,

IT'S THE BRIEF,

NOT ME THAT'S AT FAULT.

**6  Caption captured**
This method uses visuals such as photographs or illustrations, together with appropriate captions.

## Subheads and captions

You may have wondered why I did not expand on subheads and captions in the previous section about headlines? The answer is that they act as direction indicators within a bodycopy context rather than conspicuous 'headline' sign posts. Subheads allow you to segment your copy into specific areas of interest. With subheads a reader can read bodycopy from anywhere within the piece of communication without disrupting the copy tracking or flow. Subheads highlight key points of interest to be explained by the bodycopy. Captions for visuals either encapsulate the spirit of what is being shown or hint towards something that is unseen (and usually brought to light through the bodycopy).

Subheads and captions should be short. First, people read less nowadays and so purely rely on subheads or captions to 'complete the picture'. Second, if subheads or captions are not kept brief, they can become chunks of bodycopy in their own right. As with lead-in copy it is important that picture captions should not repeat what the visual shows.

Too many subheads can slow down a message, especially when space is at a premium and ideas can be expressed in very simple terms. Therefore, before you decide to include subheads, think about how they will affect your flow of copy. Subheads can be compared to refreshment breaks on a motorway journey. The longer your journey, the greater the need for a refreshment break and direction check. The shorter your journey, the less the need.

Many copywriters use headlines and captions as guides to lead themselves through the process of writing bodycopy. Often, subheads are 'padded-out' with one or two lines of copy that suggest the style and content of the bodycopy for each heading.

## Keep your copy chatty

Advertising is a high-profile business. Your client pays a lot of money to be in the public spotlight. Understandably, many novice writers are over-sensitive about this to such an extent that their copy sounds stilted or distant. This is particularly apt in the case of 'view from the top', corporate-style bodycopy. Some writers believe that big corporations deserve aloof, third-person language. On the contrary, the bigger the organisation, the more intimate you should make your copy.

> **JUST BECAUSE WE'RE BIG**
> **DOESN'T MEAN THAT WE'RE NOT PERSONAL.**

Actually that line could be improved, particularly in the case of corporate-style advertising.

> **WE'RE THE BIGGEST BECAUSE**
> **YOU'RE THE MOST IMPORTANT.**

In other words, whenever possible, try to avoid using 'we'. Instead use 'you'. If you have to use 'we', complement it with a 'you'. As you will see later, this technique is particularly effective when incorporated in direct mail letters.

## And they lived happily ever after

All good things have to come to a close – or do they? Closing your bodycopy requires more than a final full stop. You need to tie up any loose ends and feel confident that your reader will know how to proceed further. If you are after a response, you can choose options such as telephone numbers or coupons (see Chapter 8). On the other hand, you may have written your advertisement purely to stimulate awareness. You may want the reader simply to have a good feeling about the company. Either way, you still have to close your proposition and leave the reader wanting to do something; invariably, buy.

One of the best techniques for closing copy is to refer to the headline and lead-in copy. Turn the proposition into a full circle, where the beginning leads to a middle, the middle leads to an end, the end refers to the beginning. By this, I do not mean that you should just keep your reader going endlessly around in circles. Instead, use a subtle reminder of where the proposition kicked off. For example, Scotdale Northside are celebrating their centenary.

Headline:

> **WE'RE REALLY GOING TO HAVE A BLOW-OUT FOR OUR 100TH BIRTHDAY**

(Picture of a 100th birthday cake of Scotdale Northside with a person about to blow out the candles.)

Lead-in copy:

> **YOU AND YOUR LOCAL SCOTDALE NORTHSIDE HAVE SOMETHING SPECIAL TO CELEBRATE**

(Then central explanation bodycopy.)

Close:

> **SO NOW YOU *REALLY* CAN HAVE YOUR CAKE AND EAT IT.**

# Straplines, slogans and other payoffs

A slogan, also known as a strapline, is the last thing people see but the first thing they remember about a company. This makes slogans a powerful form of communication. They have to be designed to leave a warm and lasting impression on your target audience.

More often than not, slogans are inherited and so you don't need to become involved with their conception. However, copywriting, like all forms of business life, is unpredictable and so you may have to devise a slogan sooner than you think. How do you do that?

First, you have to consider the purpose of slogans.

- They add continuity to a campaign;
- They instil public confidence in a company;
- They act as a surrogate logo (a company's trademark) when logos are impractical (such as on radio commercials).

Slogans should be short. If possible, a message should be conveyed in fewer than seven words, preferable three to five. Slogans need to be conversational. They need to be memory joggers so that when a consumer considers making a purchase the slogan will remind him or her of a specific supplier. Often slogans evolve from headlines or particularly succinct pieces of bodycopy. Over the years, I have noted a dozen different slogan observations.

## *The 12 slogans of constructive persuasion*

*1 Slogans are about you*
Successful slogans tend to use the word 'you' somewhere in the copy. Occasionally, they may feature 'we' but if they do, the overall benefit is still aimed at 'you', the consumer.

SCOTDALE NORTHSIDE

YOUR NAME IN THE HIGH STREET.

> **SCOTDALE NORTHSIDE**
> WE ALWAYS SELL LOWER.

*2  Slogans make promises*

> **PENPOD**
> RELIABILITY ON PAPER.

> **PENPOD**
> QUALITY YOU CAN SIGN YOUR NAME BY.

*3  Slogans call for action*

> **SCOTDALE NORTHSIDE**
> SHOP WITH US.

(Scotdale Northside)

> **DIRECTIONS**
> COME AND GET IT.

*4  Slogans create ideals*

> **PENPOD**
> THE LITTLE PEN THAT DOES IT ALL.

(Scotdale Northside ice-cream)

> DON'T YOU WISH EVERY DAY WAS A SUNDAE?

> **PENPOD**
> IF ONLY LIFE WAS THIS SIMPLE.

*5 Slogans may rhyme*

> **SCOTDALE NORTHSIDE**
> TOP FOR SHOPS.

(Scotdale Northside)

> **DIRECTIONS**
> MEALS THAT APPEAL.

*6 Slogans are 'it'*

| | | |
|---|---|---|
| GO FOR IT | IT'S TOGETHER | IT'S THE BEST |
| BUY IT | YOU CAN'T LICK IT | IT'S YOURS |
| IT'S HERE | YOU CAN'T BEAT IT | IT'S EVERYTHING |
| IT'S NOW | YOU CAN'T TOUCH IT | TRY IT, |
| IT'S MORE | IT'S HOT | YOU'LL LIKE IT |
| IT'S LESS | IT'S TASTY | BE PART OF IT |
| IT'S FOREVER | IT'S COOL | LIVE IT |

*7 Slogans are in a 'world' of their own*

> **PENPOD**
> STEP INTO A NEW WRITING DIMENSION.

> **PENPOD**
> ENTER A NEW WORLD OF WRITING.

*8 Slogans can be full of alliterations*

> **SCOTDALE NORTHSIDE**
> SUPREMELY SCOTTISH.

> **SCOTDALE NORTHSIDE**
> BUY BETTER. BUY BIGGER, BY FAR.

*9 In order to sell, slogans don't have to be clever*

> **PENPOD**
> THE BEST PEN YOU CAN BUY.

> **PENPOD**
> THE WRITER'S CHOICE.

*10 Slogans conveniently package everything in one sentence*

> **PENPOD**
> AFFORDABLE RELIABILITY IN YOUR POCKET.

> **SCOTDALE NORTHSIDE**
> A WORLD OF SHOPPING UNDER ONE ROOF.

*11 Slogans repeat key word patterns*

> **SCOTDALE NORTHSIDE**
> THE RIGHT PRICE. THE BEST QUALITY.

**PenPod**

**THE WRITING CHOICE FOR THE RIGHT OCCASION.**

*12 'The' slogan is king*

| | |
|---|---|
| THE BEST. | THE EXPERIENCE. |
| THE GREATEST. | THE GENUINE ARTICLE. |
| THE ONE. | THE ONE YOU NEED. |
| THE SHAPE. | THE INDUSTRY'S CHOICE. |
| THE ANSWER. | THE PROFESSIONAL'S CHOICE. |

Used subtly, slogans reinforce brand values. However, many advertisements still appear without slogans and are highly successful. There is an argument that applying a slogan to a one-person business may be considered a little self indulgent! If you do have to work on a slogan, remember to keep it short and keep it sweet.

## ——— Flesch out the copy ———

Bodycopy can be an uphill struggle to read. Over the years, various people have come up with methods or formulae to measure the readability of copy. Academics who have contributed to this field include C R Haas who produced two significant formulae. One to highlight the readability differences between literary texts and advertising copy: another to evaluate the effectiveness of advertising copy based on the relative number of verbs and nouns. Then there was R Gunning who devised the so-called Fog Index. This was based on the average length of sentences and percentage of words with three or more syllables. The Dale–Chall Index was a formula based on a list of 3000 words most easily understood by at least 80 per cent of pupils in the 4th Grade of US schools, after 1945. Its 'backbone' took into account the average length of sentences. As with similar tests, the Dale–Chall Index and Fog Index are sometimes used by copywriters who are particularly concerned with the readability of copy, although their use is becoming rarer today.

One of the most commonly used readability tests is the Flesch Formula devised by Rudolph Flesch (1911–86), an Austrian born in the United States.

Flesch provides a 'Reading Ease Score' based on:

**1** the average number of words per sentence
**2** the average word length (number of syllables per 100 words)
so providing
a) percentage of personal words
so providing
b) percentage of personal sentences

Mathematically, the formula works like this:

$$RE + 206.835 - 1015\frac{P}{F} - 8.46S$$

Where:

| | | |
|---|---|---|
| $RE$ | = | Reading Ease Score |
| $P$ | = | number of words |
| $F$ | = | number of sentences |
| $\frac{P}{F}$ | = | average number of words per sentence |
| $S$ | = | number of syllables per 100 words |

The Reading Ease Score (RE) index can vary between 0 and 100. The lower the score the more complicated the copy.

| Level of difficulty | RE |
|---|---|
| Very difficult | Below 30 |
| Difficult | 30–49 |
| Quite difficult | 50–59 |
| Average | 60–69 |
| Quite easy | 70–79 |
| Easy | 80–89 |
| Very easy | 90 and above |

The Flesch's Formula shows what many writers have always surmised: short sentences with short words are easy to read. Flesch never underestimated the power of personal words and sentences to keep the reader reading! By 'personal words' Flesch meant words like 'guys', 'okay' and 'cheers' as well as personal pronouns and names. 'Personal sentences' had quotation marks as well as sentences aimed directly at the reader.

There are several drawbacks to the Flesch Formula. First, it works only if your bodycopy is fairly long. Next, it assumes that every target audience wants to read colloquial copy or fits within a 'mass market' category. Just because you receive a high readability score, it doesn't necessarily follow that your copy is suitable for your target audience. Otherwise every writer would produce pithy sentences with short words. Also, the formula doesn't work in broadcast media where the spoken word reigns supreme. Finally, it fails to judge the sales effectiveness of copy. (It may read well but does it provoke the reader to buy?)

To its credit, however, you can use the formula as a fair indicator that the bodycopy is either quite readable or too stuffy for most people (see 'fuzzword' in 'Glossary' on page 300). It also warns you of impersonal writing: 'the company', rather than perhaps, 'the team'. Finally, it helps you to keep an eye on the lengths of your sentences.

# Copy fitting

Imagine that having spent time and effort producing what appears to be a fine example of work, you are told that it doesn't fit into a page or that you need more. (As if creative talent is measured by quantity rather than quality!) If this happens, set aside your Prima Donna feelings and see how copy can be made to fit.

There are several ways to ensure that your copy will fit snugly into a specified space. Most designers and typographers rely on copy-fitting tables. These are mathematical mazes. First, you have to measure character lengths. Next, you find the right pica (a unit of measurement used in typesetting) for the selected character. Finally, you multiply the number of characters per pica by the length of line to be typeset.

Believe me, if you think that sounds complicated, it is. Thankfully, there are other methods available.

You could count the average number of words per line, then multiply them by the number of lines per page to arrive at a final total. However, this system is unreliable when your sentences include long words (an extreme case would be 'pneumonoultramicroscopicsilicovol-canoconiosis' – (the longest words in the *Oxford English Dictionary* meaning a lung disease occasionally contracted by miners). Even a humble, short word like 'a' can confuse things.

## The quick-fix copy fit

There is a way round the problem of estimating copy fit. Of course, different type styles effect the space on the paper: 12 pt in one typeface will take up a different amount of space from 12 pt in another typeface. However, you can refer to the following as a good copy-fitting guide.

Here's how it works:

Firstly, decide what type size you wish to use – say 12 pt Times. This, including spaces, allows for 14 characters per 30 mm. So 135 mm will allow for 56 characters. Program your word processor to take 56 characters per line and you're off and running.

All you have to do from this stage is type until you have reached the permissible number of lines per page. If you are asked to write a specified number of characters per page, simply multiply 56 by the number of lines on the page. You can then see how close or how far off you are from a target figure.

### Examples of type sizes

Below are examples of type sizes ranging from 9-point (pt) type to 24 pt type. Newspaper copy often uses 10–11 pt type. Most business letters feature 12 pt type. All the following examples are set in single line space – justified.

9 point (Times)

Advertising has been described as the science of arresting the human intelligence long enough to get money from it. Mind you, few people at the beginning of the nineteenth century needed an adman to tell them what they wanted.

12 point (Times)

Advertising has been described as the science of arresting the human intelligence long enough to get money from it. Mind you, few people at the beginning of the nineteenth century needed an adman to tell them what they wanted.

## 18 point (Times)

Advertising has been described as the science of arresting the human intelligence long enough to get money from it. Mind you, few people at the beginning of the nineteenth century needed an adman to tell them what they wanted.

## 24 point (Times)

Advertising has been described as the science of arresting the human intelligence long enough to get money from it. Mind you, few people at the beginning of the nineteenth century needed an adman to tell them what they wanted.

# Body building quick tips

- Bodycopy should either be as long as the space that you have to write in, or as long as it takes to write a convincing and reasonable argument.
- A writer must have conviction in his or her own copy.
- Never oversell in your bodycopy.
- The first lead-in sentence of bodycopy is called just that.
- Get to the crux of your bodycopy message quickly.
- Keep your line of thought on track.
- Address arguments before they arise.
- Write for your audience – not yourself.
- Remember the six elements of style.
- Use captions as directions within the bodycopy.
- Keep your copy user-friendly.
- Close your bodycopy in a logical sequence that is relative to the rest of the text.
- Use the 12 slogans of constructive persuasion.
- One of the most common ways to measure copy readability is the Flesch Formula.

# Over to you

1 Write six slogans which describe your friend.
2 Rewrite the first two paragraphs of copy from a leaflet setting out the terms and conditions for a credit card, to make it sound chatty.
3 Rewrite a newspaper headline as if the subject was a product.
4 List 12 features of your left-hand thumb.
5 Your product is a paper clip. Write a headline, lead-in sentence and closing sentence connected by an underlying theme.
6 List the six elements of style.
7 Write an advertisement for an encyclopaedia that never actually hints towards any form of direct sale.
8 Write six captions which could be read in sequence – without the support of bodycopy.

# 6
# MEDIA AND UNDERSTANDING ITS CREATIVE LANGUAGE

The advertising industry map can be divided into three territories. The first is ruled by the advertiser. Here, the servants are the agencies and media. The second is governed by the agencies. Here, associated suppliers like TV commercial producers and printers group together with media owners to sell their wares to the advertising agencies. The third territory is dominated by the media. Here, media owners make decisions according to the needs of their audience – readers, viewers or listeners. They rely on advertiser's budgets to serve those needs and extend their territory to accommodate an even larger audience. Together, all three territories make up a thriving community and depend on each other for survival. The advertisers want to reach the maximum number of appropriate people. So a medium has to be editorially as well as commercially attractive to a specific audience. This requires investment, which calls for more advertising.

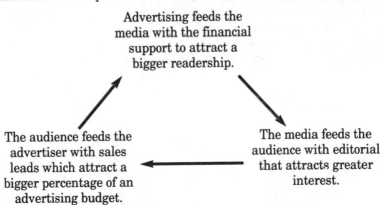

Advertising feeds the media with the financial support to attract a bigger readership.

The audience feeds the advertiser with sales leads which attract a bigger percentage of an advertising budget.

The media feeds the audience with editorial that attracts greater interest.

Media is split into two categories: above-the-line media and below-the-line media. The 'line' originally referred to the commission paid to advertising agencies for booking advertisements in mainstream media like the press, television, cinema, posters and radio. All these 'above-the-line' media paid commission directly to the agencies. 'Below-the-line' suppliers such as direct mailing companies, design agencies, incentive brokers and sales promotion specialists did not pay commission, and so the agencies invoiced a service charge to clients. Today, most suppliers are willing to pay commissions and areas such as direct marketing use 'above-the-line' media such as television and radio. So the term 'through-the-line' has been created, which covers *any* aspect of communication media (see 'Selling through the letterbox, Chapter 9).

Your choice of above-the-line media is staggering. During the mid-1990s, according to *Benn's Media Directory*, in the UK alone there were around 19 000 titles. (It listed over 50 000 worldwide!)

# ——— Choosing your medium ———

Deciding which medium or media to select for an advertising campaign can be a daunting task. Each working day, thousands of media salespeople contact companies trying to sell the virtues of a particular medium. Countless deals are struck offering everything from full-page discounts to discounts for multiple pages. So how do you begin to draw up a short-list of media?

The first place to look is your bank account. How much money can you invest in communicating your message? Next, return to your targeting parameters. Which media offer the greatest number of appropriate readers, viewers or listeners for the project? You have to remember that mass-market media like television or national press, may offer lots of readers or viewers. However, you have to ask how many of those people will actually be interested in your product or service. It boils down to quality as well as quantity. In terms of pounds per person, which media offer the greatest value for money?

The tighter your budget, the narrower your choice of media. Small budgets tend to direct advertisers towards concentrating all their buying power (often termed 'media spend') into one specific media title. The broader your budget, the wider your media potential. Often larger-scale advertisers with substantial budgets target media in funnel-like formation (see Figure 6.1).

The first advertiser to use the side of a space rocket was a Swedish firm called People Cellular and Computer. The rocket was launched just before Christmas 1995, and the advertisement measured 26 square metres.)

**Figure 6.1** Media targeting

Broad awareness is ideal to launch a product or to speak to the mass population. While the more that a budget is concentrated into one narrow target area, the greater the chance of making that area profitable. For example, Scotdale Northside may promote its range of coffees in a broad awareness campaign. However, it may promote its special 'Italian Super Strength' coffee to targeted coffee drinkers.

Each 'level' in the funnel (see Figure 6.1) complements the next. So a TV commercial may refer a consumer to a press advertisement or a press advertisement may refer the consumer to a sales promotion, and so on. In order to reinforce the strength of the message, creative elements used in one medium are often shared with another. For example, a poster may feature a specific scene from a television commercial. Through doing so, the power of the commercial is reinforced by the strength of the poster campaign and vice versa. (One reminds the consumer of the other.)

Getting the right mix of media is as essential as pruning the creative solution to its core benefit. After all, it would be fruitless to produce a stunning piece of creativity if it was communicated via an unsuitable medium.

Below is a summary of the creative pros and cons of the different forms of media available to you.

| Medium | Creative pros | Creative cons |
|---|---|---|
| Trade magazines | Relevant readership. Long shelf-life. | Danger of too many magazines in each sector, this dilutes your creative impact. |
| | Readers are searching for new ideas and announcements. | Some magazines lose editorial creditibility by featuring too many adverts – this affects circulation figures. |
| | Opportunity to be endorsed by a market's own official journal. | |
| | Opportunity to address decision makers in a market sector. | Danger of advertising perceived to be supporting favourable editorial write-ups. |
| | If the magazine is published monthly, you may possibly take advantage of extra time to  submit your final advertisement. | In comparison to some mainstream consumer magazines, some trade magazines may be hindered by inferior reproduction quality. |

| | | |
|---|---|---|
| | Often the chance to include loose leaflets, tax and mechanical restrictions permitting. (Ideal for copy to stand out from the crowd or when you have a longer 'story to tell'.) | In markets which are represented by one title alone, advertising costs can be relative high and creative use of space restricted. |
| Consumer magazines | Ideal for attracting consumer 'enthusiasts' such as car buyers, the health-conscious, fashion-conscious, and so on.<br><br>A chance to broaden your readership by advertising in magazines aimed at different audiences.<br><br>A chance to blend innovative copy with the latest trend-setting fads and styles.<br><br>Often good reproduction for photography.<br><br>The opportunity to include loose material. | Popular magazines may impose long-term copy dates (the time limit allowed for submission for advertisements.)<br><br>In comparison to newspapers, can be a costly way to reach an audience. |
| National press | Your message is reinforced by the credibility and urgency of news items.<br><br>Excellent national coverage.<br><br>High 'believability' factor.<br><br>A better chance of securing an innovative use of creative space on the page. | You're up against lots of other ads.<br><br>Depending on your design, creative impact can be enhanced or reduced by predominantly black and white advertisements.<br><br>Possible poor colour reproduction in the main newspaper. (As with all printing, make sure colour text on a colour background will be easy to read.) |

| | | Messages are 'flicked' rather than studied. (Unless, as in the case of weekend newspapers, when the reader takes more time to enjoy a newspaper.) |
|---|---|---|
| Local press | Good for targeting 'locals'. | Reproduction can be poor. |
| | Loyal readers. | Too many free circulation local papers hindering your message. |
| | Copy is often quite 'friendly' in its approach. | |
| | | Limited or non-existent use of colour. |
| | Adverts can be big on a page while economical in costs. | |
| | | Editorial is often 'light' in substance. (This has an adverse effect on the general creative quality of advertising.) |
| Television | Reaches people directly in their homes. | Production can be incredibly expensive. |
| | Viewers are usually relaxed and so 'open minded' to creative propositions. | Transmission airtime can be equally expensive (although the growth of cable and satellite channels is making it more financially viable). |
| | Excellent national coverage. | |
| | Thanks to satellite, excellent for international markets. | Can take several months to make a sustained long-term creative impact. |
| | Immediate short-term results. | |
| | Flexibility to target a commercial to appear at a set time and within a specific type of programme schedule (e.g. breakfast cereal commercials can be highly effective when shown during morning television programmes). | Creative messages have to be 'sensitive' to the greater viewing public who may tune in (e.g. children who may watch before the so-called 'watershed' at 9 p.m). |
| | | Open to the wide creative criticism. |

| | | |
|---|---|---|
| | A commercial can be shown regionally. | |
| | The greatest possible opportunity for 'all singing, all dancing' and especially creative communications. | |
| | Excellent for extending a creative theme into another medium. | |
| | Can refer to offers in other media (e.g. watch the commercial and 'clip' the coupon in the press, or e-mail on the INTERNET). | |
| Radio | Very loyal listeners.<br><br>Local and national coverage.<br><br>Marvellous creative possibilities using sound to stimulate the imagination.<br><br>Far cheaper than television.<br><br>Immediate impact.<br><br>Quick production times. | The danger of too many radio stations diluting the initial creative impact.<br><br>Short creative life.<br><br>Relies solely on one sense – sound. The listener can't actually see what you are offering. |
| Posters | Big, dramatic, colourful images.<br><br>Excellent for building awareness.<br><br>Copy can be reduced to one powerful headline. | You may have to book space several months in advance.<br><br>Apart from regular local traffic, you can never be 100 per cent sure who sees your creative message.<br><br>Image is often more important than copy. |

| | | You can't provide detailed copy on roadside posters.<br><br>Audience attendance is variable. |
|---|---|---|
| Cinema | Ideal for targeting the youth and younger adult market.<br><br>Good for attracting 'locals'.<br><br>Big screen excitement.<br><br>Ideal for reinforcing awareness to an audience in relaxed frame of mind.<br><br>Unique audience ambience. | You have to rely on a 'big' movie to pull in substantial audiences.<br><br>Production can be expensive. |

# The eight steps to effective media selection

Arguably, media selection is beyond the realms of responsibility held by a copywriter. However, given the fact that poor media selection can ruin a great piece of creative work, it is important to understand the basic process of media planning. That way you avoid pitfalls before they appear.

## 1  Will it enhance the creative work?

You should take the following into account:

- Is it targeted at the group that is addressed by the copy and visual?
- Does the medium allow for elements like colour or coupons?
- Will the general editorial style be in keeping with the copy 'tone of voice'?

## 2  Media penetration

Does the medium deliver more people who are likely to become customers?

## 3 Prove it

Consider the medium's track record. Have other advertisers who produce similar products used it? If so, and most importantly, if they consistently use it, the chances are strong that it is a good vehicle. You can track the type of advertisers who have appeared in a medium through contacting an organisation called The Media Register. It can supply relevant data showing who has advertised in which media, including television and radio as well as some overseas media.

## 4 What's the 'hit' rate like?

How often can your target audience see your advertisement? (Sometimes referred to as OTS – Opportunity To See.) OTS isn't a quality-led judgement. It doesn't ask whether an audience pays particular attention to the contents of a magazine and style of copy, for example. It is more concerned with the number of times the audience is able to see the advertisement. Specific interest would be governed by type of reader and whether that person identifies with the content and style of the magazine.

If you plan to write an advertisement to appear in a specific magazine, how often is it published? Is it the kind of magazine that is published only every now and again, but is constantly referred to by the readership? (Good examples of this are the magazines you find in a dentist's surgery – great for longer bodycopy where there is a captive audience!) Do you want your product to be seen repeatedly by an audience or is your message more suitable for a one-off appearance in perhaps a national newspaper?

## 5 Does it whisper or does it shout?

How targeted is the medium? For instance, if you are writing about vegetarian restaurant dining, would it be more appropriate to place an advertisement in a regional paper which covers the restaurant's locale. Or would it be better to place the advertisement in a magazine read by vegetarians?

## 6 Back to back who comes out front?

List the proposed medium's advantages compared with another kind of medium. (Don't get confused by comparing one magazine title against another.)

# 7 Describe the audience

Precisely who is the media targeted towards? List their ages, sex, income, job type and social grading (see page 58). You could take the media owner's word about the audience profile or you could also refer to figures supplied by organisations such as the Joint Industry Committee for National Readership Surveys (JICNARS).

You can find out more about media statistics in 'Further sources of media statistics', page 123.

# 8 Add more ingredients for success

You may wish to use more than one medium. Although your product is aimed at a particular person (user), the potential buyer may be someone else. For example, if Scotdale Northside wants to promote its own brand of healthy foods, it could place the advertisement in a woman's magazine, yet your copy would discuss the health benefits for men with high cholesterol.

Additional media also enhance the funnel effect discussed at the start of this section. So, in the case of the Scotdale Northside healthy-eating product campaign, during the course of a typical day the target audience may be exposed several times to a message via several media.

**Wakes up**
Hears a radio commercial
Sees a television commercial
Reads a press advertisement
Receives a direct-mail promotion

**Takes the kids to school**
Hears another radio commercial
Drives past a roadside poster

**Mid-morning**
Sees a television commercial
Hears a radio commercial

**Lunch**
Reads a magazine advertisement

**Afternoon**
Goes shopping and sees an in-store promotion

**Picks the kids up from school**
Hears a radio commercial
Passes a poster

**Evening**
Sees a television commercial
Serves the healthy meal

## *Further sources of media statistics*

If you need to find out more about your choice of media, you can refer to several key organisations. The Media Register and JICNARS have already been mentioned. Here are a few more.

### BARB

The Broadcasters' Audience Research Board (BARB) calculates terrestrial as well as satellite TV audience figures. It is based on a combination of special television-set monitoring equipment and diaries completed by members of households who make up the 'sample' audience. BARB takes into account video recording, sex, age (even including the age of any 'guest samples' who may visit the home of a 'main sample' person).

### TGI

The Target Group Index (TGI) is operated by the British Market Research Bureau. It draws upon the questionnaire that is completed annually by around 24 000 adults. It details demographic and media exposure information. The results highlight key data on around 500 product fields, ranging from washing-up liquid to beers.

### ABC

The Audit Bureau of Circulations (ABC) carries out audits on over 3000 UK and overseas magazines and newspapers. ABC certifies data monthly, bi-annually or annually depending on the type of publication. The ABC certificate carries details of the different types of circulation.

## VFD

Verified Free Distribution Ltd (VFD) produces figures for the majority of free newspapers. It is a subsidiary of the Audit Bureau of Circulations. The data shows the circulation of free newspapers which are delivered door to door to households. Bulk Verification Service (BVS) certification covers bulk dropped free circulation titles.

## Register–MEAL

Register–MEAL (Media Expenditure Analysis Limited) publishes monthly reports showing the estimated media spending on television, radio, cinema and outdoor media, as well as in the press. It estimates company advertising budgets and shows where advertising appears.

### Other media analysis data includes:

JICPAR – Joint Industry Committee for Poster Audience Research
OSCAR – Outdoor Site Classification and Research Advertising Association
PETA – Pan-European TV Audience Research
CAVIAR – Cinema and Video Industry Audience Research for cinema audience figures.

# 7

# THE PRESS
# UP CLOSE

This chapter deals with different aspects of specialised press advertising. The first is often much maligned by copywriters as not being 'creative' enough for their needs. However, it is surprising just how many 'great' copywriters started their craft in the recruitment advertising industry.

> The world's first-known agency was based in London in 1786. It booked advertisements in the provincial press, charging a handling fee of 6d or 1 shilling.

## ———— Recruitment advertising ————

'Person wanted' ads are more than simple employment announcements. They reflect a company's expansion plans. Every new job is another example of how the organisation is helping the community through recruitment investment for the future.

Recruitment advertising falls into four categories. First is the standard line advertisement which you often find towards the rear of publications. Second is the larger 'box' or classified ads which literally 'box-in' the copy, thereby giving the advertisement a much greater page presence. Third is the display advertisement. This provides the greatest creative opportunities – but at the greatest advertising placement cost. Fourth is the multi-media approach. This often utilises radio in addition to press advertising.

## Line ads

Line ads usually accommodate two to three lines (up to 30 words) of copy which describe the job opportunity. With such tight restrictions you have to make sure that your requirement is clear and to the point.

First, assuming that you have 30 words to work with, deduct the copy that provides response details (like your telephone number.) Never feature a lengthy address, as this is a waste of words, instead try to feature a telephone number. So, allowing for telephone codes, that reduces the words to 27. Is it essential that you include a name to contact? If it is, you have to deduct a further one or two words. Now you are left with only 25 words to convey your message.

Let's assume that Scotdale Northside is looking for a warehouse manager. Before you write any bodycopy, consider the main requirements that you are looking for in a candidate. For example:

- aged 25–50 years
- experienced
- qualified
- fit
- good manager
- available for shift duties

Now, of these six attributes, how many are essential for the job? Perhaps you are able to narrow the list down to:

- good manager
- aged 25–50 years
- available for shift duties

Next think about three key adjectives that describe the kind of person you want. For example:

- conscientious
- thorough
- cheerful

Finally, think of three key adjectives that describe the kind of work lifestyle that the warehouse manager would experience.

- hectic
- rewarding
- enjoyable

Combine the attributes:

> CONSCIENTIOUS, EXPERIENCED SHIFT WAREHOUSE MANAGER,
> AGED 25 TO 50, REQUIRED TO WORK IN A BUSY YET REWARDING
> SCOTDALE NORTHSIDE DEPOT. CALL 01234 56789.

The finishing touch is to embolden the job title and perhaps the contact number.

> CONSCIENTIOUS, EXPERIENCED SHIFT **WAREHOUSE MANAGER,**
> AGED 25 TO 50, REQUIRED TO WORK IN A BUSY YET REWARDING
> SCOTDALE NORTHSIDE DEPOT. **CALL 01234 56789.**

Often, publishers suggest that the first few words are emboldened. You could adapt the copy to allow for this. However, by featuring the emboldened job title a few words into the copy, you make the entire advertisement more effective.

If you simply cannot accommodate all your message in such a small space, you can either move up to a classified box advertisement size or opt for an alternative solution that is becoming popular. I call it the 'Read 'n' Ring' recruitment advertisement. Explained simply, your advertisement includes the most basic details and then invites the reader to phone a special number for a complete job specification. (This could be prerecorded – see page 160) For example:

> FOR A REWARDING **WAREHOUSE MANAGEMENT** OPPORTUNITY
> WITH ONE OF THE COUNTRY'S LEADING RETAIL CHAINS,
> **CALL 01234 56789** FOR A REVEALING WORD IN YOUR EAR.

## Box ads

These provide even greater impact on the page. Although they allow for more words, they are best managed by using their extra space through incorporating fewer words. Remember, you have to be clear about the job title and precise about the candidate profile.

---

**WAREHOUSE MANAGER**

CONSCIENTIOUS,

EXPERIENCED, AGED 25 TO 50,

REQUIRED TO WORK IN A BUSY

YET REWARDING

SCOTDALE NORTHSIDE DEPOT.

*CALL 01234 56789.*

---

Notice how fewer words makes greater use of the box's available space.

---

**WAREHOUSE MANAGER**

AGED 25 TO 50

FOR A BUSY YET REWARDING

SCOTDALE NORTHSIDE

DEPOT.

*CALL 01234 56789.*

---

## Display ads

Display recruitment advertisements provide the space, scope and positioning to make the maximum impact on a recruitment page. This gives candidates, as well as any competitor organisations that may see the advertisement, a favourable impression of your company.

The display advertisement features three essential ingredients for success:

1 consistent and dynamic borders
2 relevant graphics
3 succinct copy

## Borders

Consistency in borders is particularly relevant in recruitment advertising which has to make each display format advertisement achieve several tasks. (Advertise the job vacancy, as well as reinforce presence in the market place and – in some cases – demonstrate to shareholders and the public that the organisation is prospering.)

Borders can incorporate logos and, as long as they operate within the permissible space on the page, borders can be stretched to the limits of your imagination. Likewise, in order to make a recruitment advertisement as distinctive as possible, always try to use typography creatively.

## Relevant graphics

Poor use of graphics can spoil an otherwise well-planned display advertisement. A common mistake is to show people at work. It is obvious that people work at the organisation, so instead, why not show a detailed specialised aspect of their work or the professional camaraderie enjoyed? Perhaps you could highlight some of the other job benefits the candidate will enjoy.

## Succinct copy

As in most ads, copy needs to be succinct. Traditionally, display recruitment advertising follows a formal order of contents:

1 Headline featuring job title, geographic location of office and, depending on the salary, salary level. Usually, the bigger the financial reward the greater the need to include it in the headline;
2 Introduction paragraph of about 40 to 50 words about the company and its caring attitude towards employees, as well as its success story to date;
3 Who the candidate reports to and who in the company reports to the candidate. This provides an idea of seniority of the role;
4 What the key tasks involve;
5 What key attributes are needed to perform the tasks;
6 How the job will help the candidate achieve something personally as well as contribute something corporately;
7 A summary of the required educational, work experience and personal qualifications.

8 Instructions regarding who to contact and where to send a CV;
9 The contact address details.

## Multi-media approach

This approach combines press advertising and radio commercials. Depending on the general state of the economy, this kind of recruitment advertising falls in and out of fashion. Chapter 12 deals with radio commercials and provides more comprehensive details about producing an effective radio commercial. The main point to bear in mind when creating a recruitment radio commercial is that it should work in tandem with the press advertisement. So the 'close' of the commercial should refer the listener to the appropriate advertisements in the press. The copy technique applied in the press advertisement should also be applied on the radio, namely:

- who is wanted...
- where...
- for what reward?

# Recruitment advertising quick tips

- State the job title clearly in the headline.
- Refer to salary, experience and qualifications.
- Make sure your copy is non-discriminatory against sex, religion or race.
- Consider 'testing' your advertisement in several media.
- Monitor which media produce the best response (you can achieve this by incorporating a code on the advertisement).
- Make your copy sound appealing and enthusiastic.
- Highlight the company's achievements and goals.
- Set out potential employee's long-term career and additional financial benefits.

# Over to you

1 Write a recruitment advertisement for a prime minister.
2 What does VFD stand for?
3 Name one advantage and one disadvantage of television advertising.
4 What are the three media territories of the advertising industry?

# Business-to-business press advertising

Business-to-business advertising is a vast subject that justifies an entire Teach Yourself book to itself. However, for now, it is worthwhile assessing its role in the business media perspective.

There are hundreds upon hundreds of specialist trade publications dealing with everything from Accountancy to Zoo Management. Each provides the opportunity to address very specific areas of interest. Many trade titles feature international publications that offer even greater business opportunities overseas. Likewise, many trade magazines sponsor specialist trade exhibitions – another showcase for your creative message.

## Who uses trade publications?

Business-to-business advertisers who use trade publications fall broadly into three categories.

### Sellers of materials, products or equipment

Those who sell materials, products or the equipment to process those materials use business and industry-specific magazines to either highlight a new product or endorse the credibility of an existing one. This kind of advertising can be used tactically to influence a specific professional sector. Once you can prove that those within an industry choose your product or service above another, you can manipulate this information to influence others such as distributors and retailers as well as the end consumer.

### Sellers of services

These services include software, accountancy, office equipment, etc. Those who wish to sell services to help run a company's operations employ business magazines to inform one industry sector about another industry's products or services. For example, a financial software company advertises an accountancy computer program in the relevant business press for accountants.

## Distributors of products or services

Those who distribute or resell a product or service for direct profit are your 'front-line' interface between you and the ultimate consumer. Therefore, from a copy view, your creative message has to incorporate product enhancements as well as encourage loyalty through ongoing promotions.

# Addressing response

Highly targeted business-to-business campaigns often feature direct mail. This is because direct mail is such a precise form of targeting a message and has the added bonus of being something that can be 'filed away' by a potential customer, for future reference. However, trade magazines perform an equally important role. Through them, you are able to create awareness, and invite a response for further information. The response will be sent via either a coupon or telephone response device.

## Keep an 'I' on business copy

In order to solicit an appropriate response, your copy has to:

- Influence the decision makers;
- Inform those people about your product or service benefits;
- Instruct those people on how to contact you.

One of the main purposes of trade advertising is to encourage distributors and retailers to specify *your* brand. On the whole, trade advertising requires copy that 'pushes' one of the following elements: the commodity or product; the promotional offer; the bottom-line profit margin.

# 'I' want, you supply

Typically, business-to-business advertising copy addresses one of three categories of people, namely:

- Users, like secretaries or mechanical operators who want to try out a product; they want to read copy that shows how the product works;
- Choosers, like purchasing managers empowered to place an order – they want to read copy that demonstrates affordability and effectiveness;

- Proprietors, like directors who have the authority to sign the cheques – they want to read copy that highlights trust and integrity.

There is also a fourth category: investors, like shareholders who are addressed in corporate advertising. They want to read copy that assures them that the company is making the right profit-driven decisions.

This is summarised in the following table.

| Job title | Target group | 'I' want | Your copy offers |
|---|---|---|---|
| Secretary/ Administrator | User | efficiency supply reliability | competence willingness trust |
| Salesperson | User | support results credibility | encouragement reassurance qualification |
| Technician | User | performance adaptability maintenance | demonstration tailor-made for you guarantees |
| Manager | Chooser | service speed economy | dependability proficiency competitiveness |
| Director | Proprietor | trust stability control | integrity certainty character |
| Shareholder | Investor | experience direction profit | knowledge objectivity optimism |

The smaller the business, the greater the chance that Users are also Choosers. The overwhelming difference between trade and business advertising when compared with consumer advertising is that your copy has to indicate 'what profit is in it for me'.

For example, PenPod want to produce a glitzy television and press campaign at consumers.

PenPod's USPs include:

- portability
- durability
- convenience

These are all of interest to the retailer, wholesaler or distributor. Of greater relevance, however, is the anticipated customer demand generated from such a celebrated campaign. Or it could be the special financial incentives that the retailer will enjoy by encouraging sales.

The creative challenge of this type of trade advertising is to combine the 'hard commercial messages' with softer mass-market appeal.

Therefore, the headline:

**PENPOD MEANS BUSINESS**

offers a promise of further business for the industry, but it still lacks direct association with a specific promotion.

**PICK UP A PENPOD**

may be a neat message for the ultimate user, but it isn't really that relevant to the retailer.

However...

**BUSINESS PICKS UP WITH PENPOD**

offers one route by which you can combine the two messages and at the same time stimulate the retailer.

Let's stay with this headline for a little longer. Now that you have captured the trade's interest, you need to plan how to structure your copy effectively.

Even if you do managed to write a piece of copy that compliments the consumer campaign, don't leave it at that. In terms of creative quality, there is no real reason why a trade advertisement should have less time and effort spent on its production than a consumer advertisement. Show the industry that you mean business in *every* aspect of your work.

One of the creative danger signs to watch for when writing a trade-press advertisement is to avoid falling into an open trap. Just because you or your client may spend a great sum of money directing your advertising towards the consumer, via, for example, television or the press you can't ignore trade advertising. The trade is your support. Remember, it is the people behind the counter who ultimately can sway the people in front.

Another important factor to bear in mind when writing for the business-to-business sector is that your reader may know more about the subject than you, despite your extensive research. More often than not, this kind of advertising involves considerably more investment on behalf of (for example) the wholesaler or retailer than that of the consumer. Every sentence you write will be studied in detail. Each fact will be checked for accuracy. Of course, if as a copywriter you knew everything there was to know about every single subject you ever wrote about, you would probably be in line to pick up some sort of a Nobel Prize. Instead, simply carry out as much research about the subject in question as reasonably possible and never be afraid to seek further information. Nine times out of ten, people will respect you for asking and dismiss you for not. The worst thing you could do is to try to 'fob off' the trade reader with clever prose when commercial facts will suffice.

## Meet the cogs that turn the wheels

Apart from studying the available documentation about a product or service, it is a sensible step to meet the manufacturers, sales staff and buyers. Justify for yourself what the product or service claims to offer.

### You'll be wanting the shop next door

There is an old joke concerning a man who went into a shop and asked, 'Do you take anything off for cash?' The shopkeeper replied, 'Sir, I think you have the wrong shop – you want the striptease joint next door.'

The point of this (let's face it not so 'rib-ticklingly' funny) story is that, as with all forms of copywriting, you have to understand the language of the business sector you are writing for. More importantly, you have to be sure that the sector will understand the jargon. Each business sector has its own vocabulary. Professionals within a specific sector prefer their particular industry language. Nevertheless, however much jargon you use, always balance it with user-friendly copy. (Within the sector's acceptable creative bounds.)

Pictures and illustrations should also be industry-friendly. Only show what is relevant to your message. If, for example, you want to demonstrate a printing machine to a printer, feature graphics that highlight the mechanics and printed results rather than the gleaming bodywork. (Sparkling machines don't necessarily add up to sparkling results.)

## Keep your business copy 'human'

If you recollect, earlier I told you about the virtues of using 'you' in your bodycopy – especially for bigger companies requiring corporate-type advertising.

However, there is also an argument for 'toning-down' the use of personal language. Indeed, making a point to write in an impersonal style. Often corporate-type business-to-business advertising is directed to a person who, if at all interested in what you are saying, will pass it to a colleague whose job is to delve further. *They want facts not chat*: which is one reason to avoid humour in business-to-business advertising. (The other is because, if you can't take your own product or service seriously, how can you expect anyone else to take you seriously.) My personal feeling, however, is to balance a friendly tone of voice with a powerful and convincing fact-led commercial proposition.

Good examples of specific vocabulary used within specialised industries include the financial sector, the medical sector, the armed forces, government institutions, the legal profession, chemical and mechanical engineering, and information technology.

The key to writing for each of these sectors is to allow your creative language to enhance rather than engulf a factual message. For example, a chemical manufacturer requires an advertisement directed towards doctors treating asthma.

Headline (creative approach):

## ASILAZ
### A BREATH OF FRESH AIR FOR DOCTORS.

Bodycopy (*factual*):

THE COMBINED ACTIVE INGREDIENTS OF SILBUTALMOL,
BRICANONTL AND SODIUM CROMOGLYCATE IN ASILAZ DELIVER
IMMEDIATE RELIEF FOR ASTHMA SUFFERERS.
RECENT TESTS CARRIED OUT BY THE BRITISH MEDICAL ASSOCIATION
SHOW THAT WHEN COMPARED TO TRADITIONAL ASTHMATIC
TREATMENTS CONTAINING COMPOUNDS SUCH AS DROXY 7
OR BETAMAC, ASILAZ DELIVERS A RELIEVING 20% IMPROVEMENT
IN BRONICHAL CONGESTION.
AS WITH ALL SIMILAR PRODUCTS, IT IS RECOMMENDED
THAT PATIENTS FOLLOWS DOSAGE AND
TREATMENT INSTRUCTIONS AS SPECIFIED ON THE LABEL.

(Logo)

ASILAZ

RECOMMENDED DOSAGE – ONE SPRAY TWICE A DAY.

Strapline (*creative*):

DELIVERING RELIEF.

## Time is money

Business people remain so by making money. That requires an investment in time and effort. Time the immediacy of your message to fit in with a business person's busy lifestyle. Don't waste people's time trying to understand 'clever' headlines or subheads which are 'clever' for the sake of it. Get to the point. If your proposition is relevant, then and only then, will the reader consider investing the time to study your copy. Once such a commitment has been made by the trade reader, you will discover that he or she is much more willing to extend that investment by reading longer copy than the average consumer.

## Turning business around

Trade advertising can be used to combat declining sales. For example, toothpaste manufacturers are constantly having to improve their products. It is not uncommon for one brand of toothpaste to be found less effective than a newer brand. Sales decline. Market share begin to decay (see also page 42). In terms of copy, what should the manufacturer do to address this?

Well, one way is to challenge indirectly the findings of the newer brand by organising an independent research project. Here, the manufacturer could inform the trade that latest tests prove the effectiveness of brushing with the original brand as opposed to the new brands. (Of course, the research has to be conclusive and indisputable.)

If you can't beat 'em... another way to challenge falling sales is to announce a modified toothpaste.

Headline:

> **NOW WE'RE SET FOR AN
> EVEN BIGGER BITE OF THE MARKET.**

(The bodycopy explains how the company has improved the toothpaste's ingredients as well as offering greater trade incentives.)

Now that you have relaunched the toothpaste, you can adapt the new USP (in this case unbeatable cleaning power, better trade discounts) into an entire trade campaign. This could include point of sale material such as cardboard cut-outs, price reduction coupons for distribution to the public, and so on.

When the product in question doesn't have that much to differentiate itself from other similar competitive products, sales promotion and alternative forms of trade support play a lead copy role. In such a case (again, let's use toothpaste as an example), you can concentrate your copy on all the various forms of incentives and display material that the manufacturer offers the retailer.

(Leaflet to trade)

> **10% MORE IN EVERY TUBE**
> **FOR YOU *AND* YOUR CUSTOMERS.**

(Point of sale for the counter)

> **10% MORE IN EVERY TUBE.**

On the other hand, the toothpaste may be just one of literally scores of products produced by a company. Advertising each brand separately in the trade press would be costly and, quite frankly probably a waste of those invaluable business commodities – time, effort and money.

Instead, why not consider advertising the umbrella brand of which the toothpaste is a successful product in its own right. That is not to suggest that you write copy only relating to the umbrella brand rather than individually successful products. Try to position the product as part of a bigger picture.

> **TINGLE TOOTHPASTE –**
> **FROM SCOTDALE NORTHSIDE – THE PEOPLE'S CHOICE.**

At this point you may be scratching your head, concerned that your own product is neither part of a multinational company's portfolio of brands nor fits neatly into the category of 'me too' types of products. We can use PenPod as an example of this. In this case, the trade needs to be reassured that apart from being innovative, the product has distribution and marketing support to make it a viable product to stock. Above all, you need to produce trade advertising that anticipates genuine potential profit.

Headline:

> **PENPOD. WE'RE INVESTING £250,000 WORTH OF MEDIA**
> **SPENDING TO GET YOUR CUSTOMERS WRITING OFF FOR MORE.**

You need to keep your copy one step ahead of your reader by tackling difficult questions before they even arise. This technique is particularly helpful when you want to placate the worries of the business user. Your ultimate customer may be concerned with everything from security to durability. You can address these concerns effectively by highlighting a possible problem upfront.

Headline:

> **INFERIOR COMPUTER BACK-UP DISCS CAN CAUSE YOU TO LOSE MORE THAN A GOOD NIGHT'S SLEEP.**

Subhead:

> **XYZ DISCS ARE GUARANTEED NEVER TO LET YOU DOWN.**

Bodycopy:

> **LOSING DATA IS A NIGHTMARE. NOW YOU CAN SLEEP EASY.**
> **XYZ HAVE PRODUCED THE MOST EFFECTIVE BACK-UP DISCS EVER.**
> **THEY ARE CERTIFIED 100% ERROR FREE**
> **BY OUR 10 YEAR WARRANTY...**

## More from the 'room at the top'

Often, a dynamic corporate press advertisement can be wiped out by overly cautious company legal teams. The thing to bear in mind is to use corporate-style copy that leaves a warm glow as long as the company doesn't get its fingers burnt. Corporate advertising has to achieve much more than just announce products or educate a market about product use. It may need to:

- explain a company's policy direction
- endorse sub-brands
- instil confidence
- show ability
- empathise with a business person's own goals and concerns

## Explain direction

It may be important to demonstrate a company's open culture of discussing its exciting plans for ever-expanding market penetration with the people who will be responsible for helping the organisation to implement those schemes. (Retailers, wholesalers, distributors, and so on). Sometimes, through keeping people in touch with your business objectives you can encourage them to keep the ultimate consumer in touch with you.) In other words, it pays to keep in touch.

New directions may involve new markets. It may entail announcing joint ventures with companies that produce complementary products to the ones that you or your client already produces. (A classic example of this would be a camera manufacturer who links up with a photographic film manufacturer.) You may plan to expand into new markets by enhancing the features of your existing product or service. For example:

*Teach Yourself* Books (Professional division)
*Teach Yourself* Tapes
*Teach Yourself* Kits
*Teach Yourself* Away Days
*Teach Yourself* CD-ROMs

## Endorse sub-brands

In 'Make your 'G' spot into 'G' force', page 40) I told you about the use of 'umbrella brands' to endorse individual product lines. This is where creative corporate endorsement copy comes into its own. Such advertisements need not be directed solely at the trade.

Headline:

SINCE OPENING OUR FIRST SHOP **100** YEARS AGO,
WE'VE ADDED A FEW EXTRA PRODUCTS ON TO OUR SHELVES.

(Picture of original interior of small Scotdale Northside corner shop with proud shopkeeper in front of shelves stocking a couple of dozen products.)

Lead-in bodycopy:

> TO BE EXACT, 37,481 OWN BRAND PRODUCTS...

Instil confidence

There are numerous creative messages that can instil confidence. One is to discuss outstanding levels of service. For example, an advertisement for PenPod.

Headline:

> AFTER 9 DAYS, 2 CARTRIDGE REFILLS AND 2.7 MILES OF INK,
> BOB DECIDED TO EXCHANGE HIS PENPOD FOR ANOTHER MODEL
> (FREE OF CHARGE).

Bodycopy:

> BOB LOVED USING HIS PENPOD. YET, EVEN WHEN HE BROUGHT IT, HE WAS NEVER SURE WHICH MODEL HE LIKED BEST — THE 'SLEEKER', THE 'STYLER' OR THE 'GRIPPER'. THANKS TO OUR NO-NONSENSE 10 DAYS MONEY BACK GUARANTEE PROMISE, BOB WAS ABLE TO SWAP HIS PENPOD FOR ANOTHER WITHOUT ANY PROBLEM.
>
> IF, AS INDEPENDENT RESEARCH PROVES, AFTER 10 DAYS, LIKE 99.9% OF PENPOD USERS, BOB WOULD HAVE BEEN 100% HAPPY WITH HIS PURCHASE, HE COULD STILL TAKE ADVANTAGE OF OUR UNIQUE EXPRESS CARTRIDGE SERVICE THAT DISPATCHES BOXES OF NEW CARTRIDGE REFILLS DIRECT TO A NOMINATED RETAILER WITHIN 24 HOURS. (IT'S ALL PART OF THE SERVICE.)

Another method is to discuss a company's excellent track record. For example, an advertisement for Scotdale Northside.

Headline:

## 1927

**EDNA SMITH INSISTS ON DOING ALL HER SHOPPING AT SCOTDALE NORTHSIDE.**

(Picture of Edna Smith in 1927, shopping at her local Scotdale Northside corner shop.)

## 1997

**JEAN SMITH CAN'T FIND ANY REASON TO CHANGE A FAMILY TRADITION.**

(Picture of her young girl in 1997 shopping at her local Scotdale Northside superstore.)

Lead-in copy:

**THE SMITHS HAVE ALWAYS SHOPPED AT SCOTDALE NORTHSIDE.**
**TRUE. OVER THE YEARS, OUR PRODUCT RANGE AND STORE DESIGN HAVE CHANGED RADICALLY.**
**HOWEVER, SOME THINGS ARE THE SAME TODAY AS THEY HAVE ALWAYS BEEN:**
**GREAT FOOD, DISCOUNT PRICES, TERRIFIC SERVICE...**

## Show ability

Your copy needs to prove that when the going gets tough, a company gets going. Copy can demonstrate how a company professionally fulfilled the tallest of orders, for example, this advertisement for PenPod:

Headline:

> **WHEN THE BRITISH ANTARCTIC TEAM ORDER PenPods**
> **THEY DON'T WANT TO BE LEFT ON ICE.**

Lead-in copy:

> **ON 9TH FEBRUARY 1997, WE RECEIVED AN E-MAIL FOR 50**
> **PenPods TO BE DISPATCHED POST HASTE TO THE NORTH POLE.**
> **IT WAS FROM THE BRITISH ANTARCTIC TEAM. THEY CHOSE**
> **PenPod BECAUSE OF ITS PROVEN RELIABILITY, EVEN AT –60°F.**
> **CAPTAIN JOHNSON, THE TEAM LEADER, NEEDED SUPPLIES WITHIN**
> **48 HOURS. HE DIDN'T WANT EXCUSES.**
> **WE MET THE DEMAND...**

Another example – an advertisement for Scotdale Northside.

Headline:

> **EVERYTHING IS CHECKED-OUT PERFECTLY –**
> **JUST ASK SANDRA.**

(Picture of customer at check-out with 'Sandra' the check-out assistant.)

> **EVERY DAY, EXPERIENCED ASSISTANTS LIKE OUR SANDRA**
> **GET TO MEET HUNDREDS OF CUSTOMERS WHO PASS THEIR WAY.**
> **IT'S SANDRA'S JOB TO ENSURE THAT THE GROCERIES**
> **ARE SPEEDILY AND EFFICIENTLY PRICE CHECKED AND PACKED,**
> **SAVING TIME AND HASSLE.**

## Empathise with a business person's own goals and concerns

Business people are beset by daily challenges. Ideally, each problem has to be turned into an opportunity. On behalf of your client, your copy has to demonstrate how a product or service can help turn those opportunities into profits.

| Most business people want to be... | Creatively, your message should demonstrate |
| :---: | :---: |
| rich | financial credibility |
| efficient | business support |
| confident | the ability to meet deadlines |
| respected | a tried and tested heritage |
| innovative | investment in the future |
| competitive | market understanding |
| a leader | the 'choice' of the professional |
| successful | a sound track record |
| popular | the preferred choice |
| technically competent | leading edge products or services |

Typical key creative corporate 'feel-good' phrases would include:

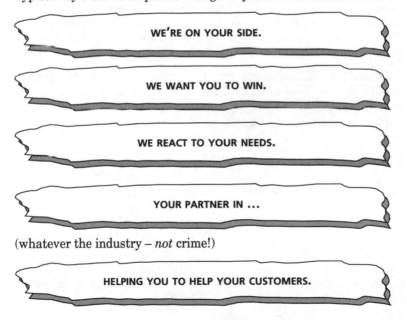

**WE'RE ON YOUR SIDE.**

**WE WANT YOU TO WIN.**

**WE REACT TO YOUR NEEDS.**

**YOUR PARTNER IN ...**

(whatever the industry – *not* crime!)

**HELPING YOU TO HELP YOUR CUSTOMERS.**

BY YOUR SIDE.

THE RIGHT CHOICE.

COMMITTED TO YOUR SUCCESS.

JUST CALL, WE'LL ANSWER.

## *Writing for the executive market*

Another field of business-to-business advertising is the executive and management sector. In terms of creative copy tone of voice, this market is much closer to the style that you adopt when addressing the consumer market. A manager has to show professional competence to help run a successful business. It is up to him or her to ensure that the right resources are used to enhance specific opportunities related to employers, administration, operations or tactical corporate plans.

One familiar commodity remains top of the list to aid the effective performance of management duties: time. All managers need the appropriate tools to help manage time and so fulfil their responsibility. Typical products or services that are targeted towards managers include:

| | |
|---|---|
| Banking | (24-hour, fast-to-react business account managers, and so on) |
| Business information services | (What's happening, where and when |
| Calculators | (reliable accounting, portable) |
| Cars | (Get you from A to B in style) |
| Cases | (Efficiency with character) |
| Computers | (Gets the job done in a fraction of the time – even portable) |
| Courier services | (When one hour late may be too late) |

| | |
|---|---|
| General transport such as airlines or trains | (Arrive in better shape for business) |
| Insurance | (What if your time and effort is wasted?) |
| Pagers | (You can't afford to be out of touch) |
| Pens | (Status symbol, yet essential business tools) |
| Phones | (Mobile, cost effective, able to handle the communications traffic) |
| Time management equipment such as diaries | (Manage your time to give you more time) |
| Travel services | (Reliable, ready to deliver the tickets to you, and you to your destination) |
| Watches | (More than a timepiece – a style statement on your wrist) |

and so on.

## You've got time so what else is news?

Managers are notoriously busy people. They have a strictly defined agenda to meet deadlines and make deals. In order to satisfy commercial demands they need to be worldly wise. They have to keep in touch with industry news as well as international news. They listen while travelling, often to news-based radio stations. They read leading newspapers as well as trade journals. They are influenced by trends. They like to set standards.

Accordingly, your copy has to be sharp, appreciative of their needs and modern in context. Visuals can be dynamic, people-centred affairs. Bodycopy content frequently incorporates a promise of achievement; to become the all-round totally 'professional' person (thanks to whatever your product or service may be). Management and executive-targeted copy needs to demonstrate that you are on 'their' side without sounding grovelling or insincere. It has to present a goal and provide the facts via the product or service features and benefits.

(Picture of luxurious executive car cruising along a motorway at sunrise).

Headline:

> THE MEETING IS AT 7.30 A.M.
> FOR THE DISCERNING FEW, THE RIDE AHEAD
> WILL BE EXCEPTIONALLY SMOOTH.

Lead-in sentence:

> HOWEVER TURBULENT THE MEETING AHEAD,
> THANKS TO YOUR NEW TURBO POWERED PASTICHE 200
> YOU CAN FACE THE MUSIC IN CONSIDERABLE STYLE.

Bodycopy:

> *CAR CHOICE* MAGAZINE DESCRIBED THE NEW PASTICHE
> 200 SERIES AS 'THE ULTIMATE EXECUTIVE CAR'.
> EVERYTHING ABOUT IT IS SPECIAL. BENEATH THE BONNET
> SITS A RAZOR SHARP 2.3 LITRE MULTI-VALVE ENGINE.
> IT 'PURRS' A PANTHER-LIKE PERFORMANCE, WHICH IF THE
> LAW PERMITTED, COULD POUNCE AT EXHILARATING SPEEDS
> OF UP TO 130 MPH WITHIN A CAT'S WHISPER OF 0–60 IN
> 8 SECONDS. YET UNRUFFLED ACCELERATION IS NEVER
> COMPROMISED BY AMBIENT NOISE. FUEL IS 'SIPPED' NEVER
> GUZZLED – PROVIDING AN ASTOUNDING 61.2 MPG AT A
> STEADY 56 MPH, EVEN WITH ITS CATALYTIC CONVERTER.
> STEP INSIDE AND RELAX IN ONE OF THE LUXURIOUS LEATHER
> UPHOLSTERED, COLOUR CO-ORDINATED SEATS.
> EACH FEATURES COMPUTER CONTROLLED, AIR-SPRUNG
> CUSHIONED SUPPORT AS WELL AS SIDE IMPACT

AIR CUSHIONS – TESTED TO STANDARDS WHICH FALL WELL
WITHIN THE LEGAL MINIMUM REQUIREMENT. SO YOU CAN
ENJOY COMFORT WITH PEACE OF MIND.
THE DRIVER'S CONSOLE IS CLEARLY DEFINED, COMBINING
HI-SPECIFICATION FEATURES LIKE AIR CONDITIONING,
MULTI-PLAY ALL-ROUND SPEAKERS, CD DRIVE, CENTRAL
DOOR LOCKING AND ELECTRIC WINDOW POWER –
ALL AT FINGER-TIP REACH.
YOUR PASSENGERS WILL FEEL EQUALLY AT HOME WITH
ON-BOARD INTEGRATED SEAT MOUNTED TELEVISION. THERE
IS EVEN A FOLD-AWAY COURTESY WORK DESK FOR ANY
LAST-MINUTE PAPERWORK.
OTHER CAPTIVATING FEATURES INCLUDE ALLOY WHEELS,
HEAT-SENSITIVE ELECTRONIC SUNROOF AND ABS BRAKING
– ALL FITTED AS STANDARD.
WHY NOT ARRANGE FOR A TEST DRIVE TODAY?
JUST CALL 0800 00 200. IT COULD BE ONE OF THE
SMOOTHEST MANAGEMENT DECISIONS YOU'VE EVER MADE.

This type of 'tough' management creative approach was particularly popular in the 1980s. During the so-called 'caring Nineties', management attitudes changed radically. Expressions like 'hands-on management', meaning a manager who gets physically involved with a business at all levels, were replaced with terms like 'hands-off management', where everything is delegated to someone else. Advertising reacted by addressing issues in a different light. For example, a sacked manager was, 'indefinitely idle'. Of course, copywriters never took this too far or the copy would sound 'suboptimal' (lousy). The serious side of all this is that the 'caring Nineties' was a typical example of creative advertising following, rather than setting trends.

Returning to the example advertisement overleaf aimed at the busy manager on the way to a hectic meeting, during the early 1990s, the headline may have altered to something like the example below.

Headline:

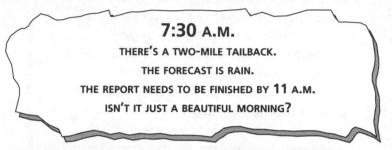

**7:30 A.M.**

THERE'S A TWO-MILE TAILBACK.

THE FORECAST IS RAIN.

THE REPORT NEEDS TO BE FINISHED BY **11** A.M.

ISN'T IT JUST A BEAUTIFUL MORNING?

(The copy proceeds to describe the relaxed state of mind enjoyed by the manager, after all he or she drives a Pastiche 200 series executive car.)

## *Business-to-business quick tips*

- Trade magazines can help create awareness and provide an educational platform.
- Copy needs to 'push' the product, 'push' your offer and 'push' your client's own profits.
- Always ask yourself, 'What's in this offer for my clients?'
- Never assume that consumer advertising alone will satisfy the business market?
- Try to get out and actually meet the people who sell your product or service to the customer.
- Make time to understand the business language and jargon of a specific business sector.
- Remember, you are dealing with business *people*. Keep your copy professional but 'human'.
- Never allow your creative message to dilute your product or service facts.
- Get to the point.
- Use research to substantiate claims – especially when you want to re-establish a product's or service's credibility.
- Always stay one step ahead of your buyer's questions.
- Reward managers with the tools to save time and earn respect.
- Positively address declining sales.

# 8

# OFF-THE-PAGE ADVERTISING

As you enter the world of off-the-page advertising, you leave the world of general informative or announcement copy dealing purely with issues such as branding and image. You enter a completely different dimension. Your words need to leap out of the page to pull customers all the way to your doorstep. You are in fact about to enter the interactive world of direct marketing.

In this different world, customers are able to look at advertisements and react immediately by contacting a company through a response device such as a coupon or telephone number. Here, advertising can be likened to a sign outside a kitchen which reads 'Come and Get It'. All the customer has to do is open the door, step in and enjoy it.

Off-the-page advertising enables you to actually sell something off the printed page. This makes it highly popular with a small business wanting to produce advertising that pays for itself. One thing to bear in mind when measuring advertising that pays for itself is to consider the cost of placing an advertisement, as well as the cost of producing it, and fulfilling an order, *before* assessing its value rate-card. Then you have to consider the longer-term enhanced value that one off-the-page advertisement has in relation to a future advertisement. The would-be buyer sees the first advertisement but doesn't make a purchase. However, when the second new advertisement makes an appearance its copy and contents, along with the credibility derived from seeing that the advertiser is an ongoing advertiser, enhance the eventual decision to buy.

In the past, some 'shady' advertisers have used off-the-page advertising to sell dubious products and services. The Mail Order Protection Scheme helps to protect both publishers and readers from disreputable traders. Copy that is approved by the Mail Order Protection Scheme reassures the readers that even if the company was unable to meet the orders generated by a campaign, there would still be some financial compensation.

# Completing the off-the-page sales cycle

Off-the-page selling offers you a choice of two creative copy steps towards securing a sale. The first is when you make an offer, ask for payment and then despatch the product. The second is when you make an offer, provide some outline details of the actual product or service, and then offer to mail back even more information. The final purchase is made either via mail order or another avenue of distribution. Examples of this include:

- Selling property off the page – read the ad, ask for a brochure, see the property, sign the contract.
- Selling insurance off the page – read the ad, call for advice, request more details (a standard legal requirement), (see your financial advisor), sign the contract.

Even if your copy is persuasive enough to generate a sale from your advertisement, that doesn't necessarily mean that you have created the ideal self-financing advertisement. Likewise, never be fooled into believing that all that is needed in order to produce a powerful off-the-page advertisement is the inclusion of a response device.

The real 'acid test' to measure the effectiveness of an off-the-page advertisement is if the advertisement generates a sale *and* encourages continued future purchases from the same buyer. ('Buy this product and start a collection'.) To achieve this fully, you need to venture even further into the world of direct marketing (which we'll do in Chapter 9). However, for now, let's concentrate on the copy features that will encourage your customers to 'come and get' what you have on offer.

By now, you should have a good idea about how to create a high-impact headline and maintain that impact through carefully crafted bodycopy.

## *Describe everything*

A couple of extra bodycopy points to keep in mind are related to collectables off the page (such as plates, record compilations, pictures, and so on). As with all direct marketing copy, always provide as many descriptive copy details about the collection as possible. If you are advertising a record collection, somewhere in the copy leave space to list every single track. Believe me, someone somewhere will want to buy the collection just because of 'that special track'. If you are writing about a dress, discuss its texture, how it flows, how it feels, the rich colours, and so on.

> ITS PRETTY PASTEL COLOUR IS AS DELICATE
> AS THE SILK THAT WOVE IT.

If you are selling something that is big, explain just how big, big really is...

> THE TRAVEL BAG CAN CARRY TWO SUITS, THREE DRESSES,
> SIX PAIRS OF SHOES, TWENTY SHIRTS, THREE SCARVES ...

Likewise, if the product is small, describe just how small, small is.

> IT'S SO TINY THAT ONLY YOU WILL EVER KNOW IT'S THERE.

(A good copy line for a hearing aid.)

If you are selling an artistic collection like bone china plates, provide details of actual size, the work that went into crafting the piece, and so on.

> THIS BEAUTIFUL COLLECTOR'S PIECE HAS BEEN SPECIALLY
> COMMISSIONED BY LEADING ARTIST BOB JONES.
> EVERY PLATE IS HAND MADE. EACH FLOWER, HAND PAINTED.
> SO EACH PIECE IS UNIQUE.

If you are selling electronic home entertainment products, provide details of things like accessible controls or sound wattage.

> A THUMPING GREAT 35 WATTS PER SPEAKER.

Does the product come complete with everything you need to switch on and go? Yes? Then say so: even the plug can be a selling aid.

For greater urgency, consider the 'limited edition' technique.

> ONLY 1000 EVER MADE.
> YOUR PIECE IS INDIVIDUALLY NUMBERED.
> ONCE WE'VE SOLD THE 999TH PIECE, WE'LL BREAK THE MOULD.

Next, you need to consider how to turn an interest into a positive response.

## The role of incentives

Before anyone 'splashes out' he or she has to take the plunge. Once a prospect has read about your many product benefits and features, he or she may still need one final creative 'push' before 'taking the plunge' and responding to you. This could call for incorporating some kind of reward for prompt action. Your copy can accommodate this by combining the reward with the instruction to respond so, for example:

> ANSWER IN 10 DAYS AND CLAIM A FREE GIFT.

REPLY TODAY AND SAVE **10%** OFF YOUR BILL.

RESPOND NOW AND YOU COULD WIN A HOLIDAY FOR TWO.

REPLY SOON AND *WE'LL* PAY YOUR FIRST MONTH'S INSURANCE PREMIUM.

Another 'plunge making' technique is to feature a time limit.

HURRY. THIS OFFER ONLY LASTS **5** DAYS.

HURRY. STOCKS ARE LIMITED.

HURRY. FIRST COME, FIRST SERVED.

HURRY. AVOID DISAPPOINTMENT BY REPLYING TODAY.

HURRY. THERE ARE ONLY **20** SHOPPING DAYS 'TILL XMAS.

These 'plunge makers' can be further enhanced by featuring them as flashes.

Only 12 remaining!

Buy one
get a
2nd
FREE!
OFFER ENDS FRIDAY

Generally speaking, there are two popular response options available to you: coupons, and telephone. Whichever route you decide to take, always remember to make it as simple as possible for a prospect to get in touch.

## Coupons

Strategically, your copy should refer to how easy it is to use a featured coupon. The closer the prospect gets to the coupon, the greater the creative emphasis given to simplicity. Coupons often have specific captions that reinforce the easy buying process, as well as urging fast action. Over the years, designers have tried various ways to balance urgency with style. Coupon captions have been reversed out of boxes, run along the coupon's edge, 'splashed' with colour, enlarged, reduced… the list is endless. Like many aspects of creative copy and design, as long as you try to tone down the trite and keep everything 'sounding' as well as looking credible and in keeping with the overall creative tone, your coupon should get 'clipped'.

Typical coupon captions:

CAN YOU ANSWER 'YES' TO THESE QUESTIONS?

COMPLETE AND REPLY TODAY.

HURRY. **14** DAYS TO RESPOND.

ORDER TODAY.

ORDER NOW.

CUT OUT THE WAIT. CUT OUT THE COUPON.

ALL YOU NEED TO DO IS SIGN.

RESERVE YOUR ORDER NOW.

SECURE YOUR ORDER WITHOUT DELAY.

THIS COUPON SAVES YOU MONEY.

IT TAKES JUST A COUPLE OF 'TICKS' TO REPLY.

## Making coupons user-friendly

I have always been suspicious about people who enjoy completing coupons. I can understand the desire to send off and win or order something. However, the thought of actually enjoying the process of filling in tiny, often badly designed boxes for the sake of it, amazes me.

A good coupon should be simple: not just for the benefit of the person who has to complete it, but also for the benefit of the person who has to process all the information. Wherever possible, guide the prospect to completing things in legible CAPITAL LETTERS. One question should follow the next. Consider the person in the 'back room' who physically has to process all of these coupons.

In addition to receiving what will hopefully be sacks full of coupons, someone has to gauge the effectiveness of the media where the coupons appeared. So, incorporate a discreet publication code that indicates a publication's title and date. (Also used in recruitment copy – see page 130.)

Another 'sneaky' way to track the effectiveness of publications is to create an artificial order department. One publication features coupons addressed to a certain department, while another features a different department. (This is useful for large-scale, even international campaigns.)

Coupons should be positive pieces of communication.

> **YES! I AM INTERESTED IN WHAT YOU HAVE TO OFFER.**

They should minimise laborious detail writing.

> **ORDERING IS AS EASY AS 1.2.3.**
> **1. WHAT IS YOUR NAME?**
> **2. WHAT IS YOUR POSTCODE?**
> **3. HOW MUCH WOULD YOU LIKE TO SPEND?**
> PLEASE SEND ME A:
> **RED**  ☐
> **PINK**  ☐
> **BLUE**  ☐
> DRESS. (JUST TICK THE RELEVANT BOX.)

> **PLEASE CHARGE MY VISA** ☐
> **ACCESS** ☐
> **CREDIT CARD.**
> **MY ACCOUNT NUMBER IS** ...................................
> **THE EXPIRY DATE IS** ...................................

and so on...

Explain what happens after the person sends back the coupon. How long will it take to process the order? How much time should be given for postage?

One completed coupon shouldn't just mean one completed sale. The information can be used again and again for selling other products or services in the future – a technique called 'cross selling'. However, it is illegal to pass on the information contained within the coupon to another company without permission. If you think that you may need to do this, always inform the prospect using copy along the lines of:

> **MAY WE PASS YOUR DETAILS ON TO OTHER SUPPLIERS**
> **WHO COULD BE OF INTEREST TO YOU?**

or...

> **WOULD YOU LIKE TO BE KEPT IN TOUCH WITH FUTURE OFFERS?**
> **IF NOT, PLEASE TICK THE BOX.**

Notice that the copy read: '**if not**'. This is a tried and proven technique to secure more 'YES' answers. It is easier to ignore a box than tick it.

Finally, think about the confidentiality of the information contained within the coupon. People don't like to send their address details 'open' and ready for anyone to read. To get around this, offer a Freepost address in which you pick up the postage costs. All the prospect has to do is pop the coupon in an envelope and then post it.

## Call now! – telephone response devices

The second response mechanism often featured in off-the-page press advertisements, is the telephone. Telephone response advertising adds even greater urgency to a creative message than coupons. A strong telephone graphic accompanied by copy such as:

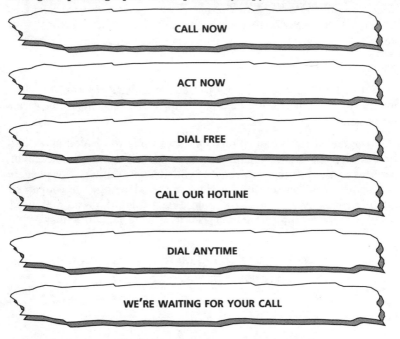

**CALL NOW**

**ACT NOW**

**DIAL FREE**

**CALL OUR HOTLINE**

**DIAL ANYTIME**

**WE'RE WAITING FOR YOUR CALL**

tells your prospects that you mean business and are ready and waiting for their call. This can be essential for organisations such as charities which need to raise money quickly.

**ONE PHONE CALL CAN SAVE THIS BOY'S LIFE.**

**TO SAVE HER THE TEN-MILE TREK FOR A CUP OF WATER,
JUST WALK TO THE PHONE.**

**YOUR PHONE IS HER LIFELINE.**

You'll notice that one of the copy lines above includes the word **'Hotline'**. Hotlines, are nothing particularly new. However, their implied exclusivity, is a valuable tool to include in telephone response-led copy. Many companies use the Hotline technique to imply even greater specialisation and expertise of a given product or service. How?

| Forecast growth in European teleshopping 1992–2000 ($m) | | | | |
|---|---|---|---|---|
| | 1992 | 1994 | 1996 | 1998 | 2000 |
| Germany | 0 | 15 | 110 | 626 | 2,317 |
| Netherlands | 0 | 4 | 24 | 115 | 385 |
| France | 0 | 2 | 13 | 85 | 380 |
| Belgium | 0 | 3 | 17 | 84 | 280 |
| UK | 0 | 10 | 35 | 100 | 256 |
| Total | 0 | 34 | 199 | 1,010 | 3,618 |
| (Source: Datamonitor) | | | | |

Easy. They drop the first syllable, 'hot' and replace it with the product name or company name. So, in the case of PenPod, variations could include:

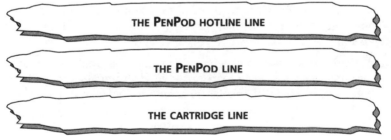

THE **PENPOD** HOTLINE LINE

THE **PENPOD** LINE

THE CARTRIDGE LINE

If Scotdale Northside wanted to promote a particular own-brand (say nappies) service and sales line they could call it:

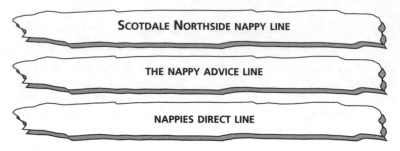

**SCOTDALE NORTHSIDE NAPPY LINE**

**THE NAPPY ADVICE LINE**

**NAPPIES DIRECT LINE**

and so on.

Another neat idea is to use 0800 or 0500 numbers. In addition to being free-of-charge calls – so attractive to callers – these are particularly effective if your product features a number in its name. Another variation is 0990. It is not free of charge but a useful, easy-to-remember number that can be dialled nationally.

For example, a Jumbo jet passenger service may have a telephone number like:

**0800 00 0747**

*Lo call* 0345 telephone numbers can also feature key numeric sequences but are not as attractive as free-of-charge numbers because they still cost the caller some money for each call (if only the price of a local call). (Incidentally, according to a 1993 study carried out by British Telecom and UK's Channel Four TV station, using an 0800 number on television is 33 per cent more effective than 0345 numbers.)

Another idea is promote a Freephone number. The creative benefit of this is that you are able to feature the product name as part of the Freephone response mechanism. For example, PenPod could have:

**FREEPHONE PENPOD**

The copy would read:

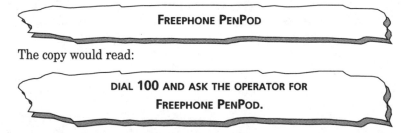

**DIAL 100 AND ASK THE OPERATOR FOR
FREEPHONE PENPOD.**

Creatively, the drawback to this approach is that it can slow down response as the caller will have to dial via an operator. However, it means that the caller doesn't have to remember so many numbers.

Fax Back is an interesting UK response development. By dialling a special number on a fax machine, a respondent is redialled with a printed fax sheet(s) or relevant information. This is useful for companies wishing to send extra details of a product or service. Restaurants, for example, to send menus. Holiday companies could use this facility to send details of last-minute bookings, and so on. A further variation, Standard Fax Back is a multiple Fax Back that can send multiples of pages selected from a large database. This is ideal if, for example, you wish to fax travel information concerning various destinations. So a traveller could request travel details about Rwanda, Brazil and Portugal on one fax.

A further creative way to include a telephone response number is to use an existing enquiry line that caters for lots of companies all on one heavily promoted number.

Finally, there is the option to promote a telephone number that features a relevant numeric sequence (as in the example of the Jumbo jet 747) but is actually a prime-rate telephone number which pays the advertiser each time the number is dialled (for example, 0891 telephone numbers). The down side of this approach is that people know that the call is costly, so, by law you have to include a line of copy that details the cost of the call. It can also be seen as irresponsible – especially when the product encourages the young or vulnerable, to call.

The up side of using 089 numbers is that they can be great money-earning devices. In 1994/5, 787 million 0800 and 0345 calls were made in the United Kingdom. (Source: BT.) Excluding set-up costs, this is what each number pays *you*.*

**0891**  24.78 pence per minute.
**0894**  Up to ten seconds, 8.5 pence per call.
Between 10.1 seconds and 40 seconds, 16.3 pence per call.
After 40 seconds the revenue decreases to 0.25 pence per second, until the revenue is eroded and you start paying for the call at 0.25 pence per second. (There is another slight variation to this particular number scheme.)

**0897** Costs the caller £1.50 per minute, but you receive 97.2 pence per minute.

**0898** Costs the caller between 39p per minute and 49p per minute.

(*Figures supplied by British Telecom. Based on 1995 prices.)

Other UK premium-rate numbers include:

| | | | |
|---|---|---|---|
| 0881 | 0839 | 0660 | 09911 |
| 09919 | 08364 | 0336 | 0331 |
| 0930 | 0338 (Adult service) | | |

All UK premium-rate numbers are regulated by the Independent Committee for the Supervision of Standards of Telephone Information Services (ICSTIS).

Telephone response devices can also be extended to cover *Order by Fax* techniques, as well as order via the INTERNET (this is discussed in Chapter 15).

## Combining coupons and telephone response

If you cannot decide between featuring a telephone or coupon response, you could always feature both.

**CLIP THE COUPON**

**OR FOR AN EVEN FASTER SERVICE**

**CALL NOW ON 0800 00 0123**

Whichever route you choose, ensure that you or your client is able to handle the anticipated response. There's not much point in producing a great advertisement if the consequential enquiries are ignored.

As I mentioned, not all off-the-page advertisements complete sales transactions immediately off the page. For example, medical or financial services may require further information. High-priced items may call for further creative reassurance than can be provided only either by a salesperson or, as a next step, a brochure. Getting your prospect to make the next step often relies on the only form of advertising which offers the creative opportunity to be as intimate as the law allows with your target audience... selling through the letterbox (see Chapter 9).

# Off-the-page quick tips

- Decide whether you want to sell directly or indirectly off the page.
- Encourage future as well as immediate sales. (Buy today and start a collection.)
- Describe everything about your product from its size to its material, even down to the plug, if applicable.
- Reward response (e.g. discounts).
- Feature a time limit on responses.
- Endorse the simplicity of responding.
- Keep coupons concise and easy to complete.
- 'Track' the effectiveness of a publication by incorporating a special coupon code.
- Encourage action with command headlines.
- Add urgency with 'Hotlines'.
- Test response by telephone or coupons or both.

# Over to you

1 Design and write a coupon used in an off-the-page advertisement for PenPod.
2 List 12 different 'jump-to-it!' headlines.
3 List six business benefits offered by a photocopier machine.
4 Write an advertisement that highlights the business benefits of an old second-hand car.
5 Write a headline that announces a business merger to:
   a) Users
   b) Choosers
   c) Proprietors
   d) Investors
6 PenPod has a big competitor with a better product, write an advertisement which supports PenPod's position.

# 9

# SELLING THROUGH THE LETTERBOX

Above-the-line advertising helps you get a strong hold on a market (i.e. increase your market share). Direct marketing helps increase your share of the individual's buying decisions. For example, a prospective client may decide to take three holidays. You need to demonstrate why your holiday company can accommodate specific holiday needs at any time of the year. To achieve this, you need to know as much as possible about your client – more than why a buying decision is made. This requires extensive data, which is why direct marketing is sometimes referred to as 'database marketing'.

Direct marketing, using direct mail, enables you to reach a client through the letterbox and lead him or her to your point of sale. Reaching the appropriate letterboxes calls for accurate lists. These can be purchased from list brokers (see page 170) or generated à la carte from completed sales promotion coupons, press advertising coupons, telephone research or even questionnaire mailings.

Direct marketing increases the chances of a person choosing your product or service. It also encourages a developing relationship between you and your customer. (This is why direct marketing is sometimes referred to as 'relationship marketing' or 'one-to-one marketing'.) This relationship can be so strong that eventually, by keeping in touch at appropriate times with relevant information and incentives, the customer will remain loyal and recommend your company to others. In doing so, the person's value to your company is increased with every new customer he or she introduces.

This is demonstrated in a classic sales model used throughout the advertising and marketing industry, devised by American salesman Ray Consada (see Figure 9.1).

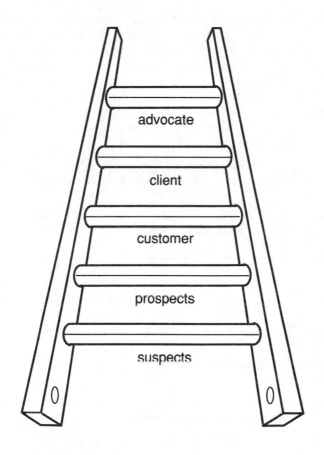

**Figure 9.1** The Loyalty Ladder

Direct marketing establishes a direct relationship between you and your customers as individuals so that they remain loyal and provide a lasting valuable asset as distinct from a casual one-off sale. Direct marketing is not just confined to direct mail. It includes virtually any marketing activity where your prospect responds to you directly.

# Open the envelope, pull out a benefit

Direct mail is sometimes referred to as 'junk mail'. This is actually quite unfair especially when you consider the volume of direct mail used in the United Kingdom. Such volumes are justified by sales results. Which is why all kinds of businesses rely on direct mail as a cost-effective method of communication. In the United Kingdom, the average household receives 6.6 items of direct mail every four weeks. According to the Direct Mail Information Service 2730 million items of direct mail were sent in 1994: 2015 million of these were consumer and 715 million were business-to-business.

Mail received by type of household
(Number of items – average four-weekly receipt, 1994)

| Type of household (socio-economic grading) | Free newspapers | Leaflet/ coupons | Personal mail | Direct mail | Total |
|---|---|---|---|---|---|
| All | 4.6 | 8.2 | 18.4 | **6.3** | 37.5 |
| AB | 4.6 | 9.7 | 25.8 | **9.0** | 49.1 |
| C1 | 4.9 | 10.1 | 20.3 | **7.3** | 42.6 |
| C2 | 4.0 | 5.8 | 16.5 | **5.4** | 31.7 |
| DE | 4.8 | 7.8 | 14.3 | **4.7** | 31.6 |

Source: Direct Mail Information Service/Royal Mail Consumer Panel.)

So what exactly is direct mail? Simply, it is postal advertising. When correctly implemented, direct mail can:

- Target a message in a controlled campaign;
- Personalise a message to a specific audience;
- Prioritise a message by delivering it directly into the hands of a specific audience;
- Time a message to arrive at a specified time – day, week, month, occasion;
- Explain a message in detail by including enclosures such as brochures and leaflets;

- Offer confidentiality when a message is sensitive;
- Hasten a message through first class postage;
- Stimulate sales leads by 'following-up' messages by phone or post.
- Offer outstanding value in terms of cost per reply when compared to other media, such as pure awareness advertising;
- Test the effectiveness of a message by segmentation of your mailing's distribution;
- Update your message by content or distribution;
- Allow for unusual formats such as pop-ups, video mailers, large or small size envelopes, and so on;
- Keep customers in touch with company developments and so stimulate interest in future offers (perhaps through a newsletter);
- Ask customers for views and opinions;
- Stimulate sales by offering special vouchers against new or ageing products;
- Fight competition quickly by promoting revised prices;
- Increase store traffic by inviting consumers to special retailer or distributor events;
- Tie in with other media such as the press who may feature an awareness/information-type advertisement;
- Cross sell with other direct mail users, (for example, the Scotdale Northside restaurant – Directions – could share a mailing list with a restaurant guide publisher);
- Cover sales not readily accessible by sales staff.

## —— Is there anybody out there? ——

In a word, YES. Lists, either business lists or consumer lists, can help you pinpoint target areas with amazing accuracy. The importance of an accurate or 'clean' list in direct marketing can never be over stressed. Good copy without a suitable 'clean' list isn't even worth the stamp on an envelope.

The best source of lists is a client's own customer database. Every coupon returned, even those with a 'no' reply, is worth its weight in gold. Every list generated by distributors or agents should be used. Every lead followed up by sales teams is vital. From a creative copy view, you must always design your direct mail to sell a product or service *and* provide an opportunity to capture data – including data about other potential future clients (see 'Member-get-member mailings, page 192).

Once a suspected customer has become a prospective customer and then an actual customer, you can spend less time crafting your copy to sell a proposition and more time crafting your copy to encourage your customer to become a regular client.

## Where's the list?

There are several sources of lists, namely:

- Lists belonging to other companies whose product or service complements your product or service. These are called affinity mailings;
- A list broker, list manager, list compiler;
- An existing list can be purchased that targets people by geographical area, type of household, zip or postcodes, size of business, types of interest, purchasing patterns, financial status, information based on national censuses, and much more besides. In all these cases the key questions to ask a list broker are:
  1 When was this list last updated?
  2 How was it compiled?
  3 How many other companies use the list?
  4 Of those companies, how many offer the same or similar message?
- Build your own list by carrying out research via the mail and telephone lists.

# ———— Direct mail contents ————

## Envelopes

Once your mailing hits the doormat, it still has to compete with many other enveloped pieces of information ranging from utility bills to letters from friends or relatives. Your envelope should indicate at a glance that its contents are interesting, relevant, and worth the effort to open the envelope.

Above all, your mailing has to be *involving*. The more you can involve readers with your creative proposition, the higher the likelihood that they will follow your copy all the way to a sale (if you are selling). The envelope's copy and design needs to reflect the mailing's contents. Never be afraid to use colour – even photography – on the envelope if, and only if, it is relevant to the enclosure. Envelope copy needs to entice the reader. One of the strongest words you can incorporate is 'FREE'. For example:

OPEN NOW FOR DETAILS OF A **FREE** GIFT.

(An implied variation…)

OPEN NOW AND SAVE **25%** OFF YOUR NEXT GROCERY BILL.

Another technique is to give the recipient a 'peek' of what's inside the envelope. This is achieved by adding one or more transparent 'windows' on the envelope. One window may show part of a picture from the brochure inside, while another window shows part of the message on a sales letter – such as details of a cash prize.

Why not use a 'zipper' envelope? Here the recipient is asked to pull a tab on the envelope which 'zips' it open. As the tag is pulled, so a message is revealed on its reverse side. For example:

PULL OPEN FOR GREAT NEWS.

EXERCISE FOR A HEALTHIER LIFESTYLE.

START BY PULLING OPEN HERE.

A further idea is to announce that there is a secret message inside. For example:

ARE YOU A MILLIONAIRE?

INSIDE THIS ENVELOPE IS YOUR KEY TO SUCCESS.

CAN YOU FIND THE HIDDEN MESSAGE WORTH **£500,000?**

You can personalise an envelope with the recipient's name. For example:

> **YOUR TABLE IS WAITING, MR JONES – AT DIRECTIONS...**

> **SOMEONE SHOULD GIVE MR JONES A MILLION POUNDS...**

(Pull a 'zipper' tag.)

Copy on reverse of tag:

> **SOMEONE LIKE US.**

Envelopes are ideal vehicles for short 'teaser' copy lines. Such copy lines are particularly effective when you do not want to plaster your envelope with brash illustrations or use unusually large-sized envelopes which may otherwise give the appearance of tacky 'junk mail'.

Teaser envelope copy lines are invariably unanswered questions – to find the answer, the recipient is forced to open the envelope:

For example, Scotdale Northside is promoting their new restaurant, Directions.

> **WOULD YOU PREFER A CREAMY PRAWN COCKTAIL**
> **OR A FILLING MINESTRONE SOUP?**
> **DOES £9.99 SOUND APPETISING FOR A THREE-COURSE MEAL?**

Another example, this time for PenPod's business-to-business mailing.

> *Isn't it annoying when your pen runs out just as*

People often open envelopes from the back rather than the front. So use the reverse side as well. The minimum you can do is feature a return address if the mailing is undelivered. The maximum is to strengthen the offer by featuring further details about the product or service inside. Alternatively, you could highlight a free incentive – such as a holiday weekend or complementary travel bag.

According to research carried out by The Direct Mail Information Service, the best way to get someone to open an envelope is to feature a hand-written address; this is up to fifteen times more effective than using a 'confidential' or 'urgent' type stamp. The second most effective effective technique is to feature a thick package. In the United Kingdom 83 per cent of consumer direct mail is opened by the recipient, 68 per cent is opened **and** read, 31 per cent is passed on to someone else. Of business direct mail, 84 per cent is opened, 17 per cent is redirected to a colleague, 13 per cent is filed or responded to.

Finally, consider affixing a real postage stamp on your envelope – or at least a smart pre-printed 'postage paid' emblem. Barcodes and other forms of electronic postal tagging make it clear that a piece of direct mail is just that.

---

The world's first pre-paid envelope was issued on 1 November, 1838, by the New South Wales Post Office in Australia.

---

## The letter

There are scores of copywriting techniques that can help improve the effectiveness of letters. If I was to sum up all these methods into one it would be: *write to a person as you would write to friend or colleague – formally enough to be credible yet informally enough to be sincere.*

Letters should be as long as it takes you to write them. By this, I mean either until you run out of permissible space (for example, one side of A4 paper) or until you have nothing else to discuss.

Long copy letters take time to read but short copy letters may not be adequate. The ideal compromise is to structure your letter copy with several 'entry points'. Whether your copy is long or short, it means that the reader can 'dip in' at reference points. If your message is interesting, the reader will read on or return to the letter at some later stage. Just because you sent a direct mail piece by first class mail, it doesn't necessarily follow that it will receive prompt attention.

## Letter entry points

Possible 'entry points' include:

- headlines
- subheads
- captions
- panels
- illustrations
- photographs
- diagrams
- bullet points
- underlined words
- words highlighted or in capital letters
- handwritten sections
- ticks
- arrows
- reverse printing (white out of black)
- PSs
- margin notes
- boxed or shaded-in copy (originally termed a 'Johnson box')
- tables

## A step-by-step guide to letters

*Overall appearance*

Your letter should be clearly laid out on good quality paper. A company logo helps add to the overall credibility as well as increasing recognition. (However, the heavier your paper, the more costly your postage.) It is not necessary to force all your text onto one sheet of paper. If your letter is particularly long, you may have to 'spread' your message over two or more sheets.

> Wherever possible, give your copy the space to breathe. Crammed sentences look messy and are very difficult to read.

Type styles should also be easy to read – save the creative flourishes for your message

*not the typeface*

Letters that are set in a typeface, such as this one, with a serif – the small stroke at the end of the main terminal stroke of a letter:

T

...are easier to read than so-called sans serif typefaces

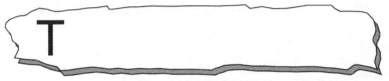

T

Think about how the eye tracks your letter. It's fine to feature a serif typeface to aid reading, but if your layout is generally quite messy, the whole thing could be a fruitless exercise. Eye-tracking is an easy technique to pick up. Unless you are writing for the Middle East market – which reads from right to left – or the Far East market – which reads from top to bottom – base the structure of your letter with the headline and any subheads or illustrations leading top left. Then flow the copy neatly left to right with your final 'push' at the bottom right-hand side of the page (but remember, this is only a basis for your letter layout, not the template for *every* letter).

Don't staple your sheets of paper together. This can tear the letter and get caught on fingernails.

Your letter is a person-to-person affair. Make it appear as personal as possible. Photocopied letters look and feel tacky. Printer typeset letters look like printer typeset letters. It would be wasteful to have spent so much time and effort posting a letter to a named person just to wipe out all elements of individuality in one clumsy sweep.

*Dear...*

Address your reader by his or her name. (Remember that direct mail, as part of direct marketing, is also called 'one-to-one' marketing.) Check that you have spelled the recipient's name correctly and included the correct address details. If you don't know the person's name, address them by job title; if this isn't possible, address them by category (e.g. Dear Diner; Dear Shopkeeper; Dear Fellow Director...).

*Headline*

Where possible, try to encapsulate your main proposition in a headline. When you write such a headline, try to include copy words that stimulate involvement or action. For example:

> At last here's a restaurant that
>         caters for all the family.

> Announcing a brand new
> Scotdale Northside store.

> 12 reasons to pick up a PenPod.

> Don't buy anything until
>         you have read this

> Yours free...

> Everything you ever wanted
>         to know about...

*Opening paragraph*
If you haven't yet included it, now is a good time to use the word, 'you'. (Remember, direct mail is a personalised, targeted form of communication.)

You are obviously a person who appreciates the finer things in life...

Our records show that you are a keen reader of **Teach Yourself** books. You already know how the series features fascinating insights into everything from public relations to writing for children. Each title is written by a respected expert in his or her field.

Now you can extend your library knowledge by taking advantage of our exclusive reader's **Teach Yourself** book club.

Each month you can select another Teach Yourself title that will be sent direct to your home at a price that is guaranteed to be at least 25% off our recommended retail price.

Just think. All that invaluable information available when you want it.

School projects are made even more fascinating. Hobbies come to life...

Your opening paragraph needs to grab a reader's attention quickly and succinctly. Opening paragraphs should contain no more than six lines of provocative copy. In general, try to keep all your paragraphs reasonably short so that the copy looks lively on the page. Overloaded copy can lead to overloaded readers. One paragraph should lead to the next. Use the technique of asking a question and then following on with a reply within the body copy of the next paragraph. Or why not really get your reader involved with something in the last paragraph on a page...

...and then complete the message on the next page? Alternatively, introduce a fresh idea into the end of each paragraph.

*Benefits*
Hammer home your benefits. Tease your reader with further details of such benefits (for example, a free mystery gift) which will be revealed at a later stage within the copy. Highlight your benefits with bullet points. Stress the benefits.

> Believe me when I say...
>
> When they told me, I couldn't believe it. What do you think?

Incorporate benefits in captions...

(Picture of PenPod)

> Stainless steel casing, tungsten tip and tested to write for miles and miles.

Explain why the reader needs the product or service. Show examples of how the product or service can enhance his or her life.

> Compared to many other credit cards, the Scotdale Northside credit card can save you up to 25% off purchases and an additional 5% off every bill totalling over £50 each and every time you shop at Scotdale Northside.

### Feature the three Ws

- What is it?
- What does it offer?
- Wow!

For example:
What is it?

> **PENPOD IS THE WORLD'S FINEST INDESTRUCTIBLE PEN.**

What does it offer?

> **EACH CARTRIDGE PROVIDES UP TO TEN MILES OF INK.**

Wow!

> **SO YOU CAN WRITE ABOUT EVERYTHING FROM ANTS TO ZIP CODES AND STILL HAVE MILES MORE IDEAS FOR THE ROAD AHEAD.**

Another way of highlighting benefits is the 'Grim Reaper' approach. Rather than stating the positive benefits of buying your product or service, discuss the consequences of *not* making a commitment. Life assurance companies use this technique...

> Should the worst happen, your dependants could be left to cope with financial burdens such as funeral expenses and mortgage repayments.
>
> The Protection Plan helps to ensure that even if your existing life policies have matured or been cashed in, you can still leave a significant cash sum to the ones you love.

or

> Nobody plans to be stranded in the dead of night in a car that's broken down – miles away from a public phone box. But you can take sensible precautions with an emergency mobile phone from Mobile Inc.

*It pays to reply today*
Offer an incentive for a quick response. This can be anything ranging from a money-off coupon to a service incentive. Whichever incentive you use, as with the rest of the copy, describe it in full.

It pays to reply today because:

✓ We can't hold this price forever.
✓ Stocks are low.
✓ We'll give you a 'cashback' for your old product.
✓ The bigger your order, the more you save.

✓ We'll refund the cost of your entire purchase when you place your next order.
✓ We want to demonstrate it in the comfort of your own home.
✓ This offer is exclusive to you.
✓ We want you to try it before you buy it.
✓ We want to offer you a personalised quotation.
✓ This is only a small sample of something even better.
✓ If you buy it we'll give you a second one free.
✓ If you buy the bread, we'll give you the butter.
✓ We want to explain it to you in person at a convenient time and date.
✓ If you don't like it, you can exchange it for something else.
✓ It's delivered free.
✓ We don't want your money until next year.
✓ We're always here to service it.
✓ You can sample the entire range for a special price.
✓ You have our guarantee on it.
✓ Buy it today and we'll extend our guarantee.
✓ We'll also send one to your friend.
✓ We'll enter your name into our prize draw.
✓ Every applicant wins a prize.
✓ We'll match every penny with a donation to charity.
✓ We'll pay the extra costs.
✓ We'll eat our hat if you don't like it.

*Guarantee your guarantee*
Don't just make an ordinary guarantee: offer an extraordinary level of assurance – after all such an amazing product or service as yours is perfect.

# GUARANTEED 3 WAYS

**14 DAYS NO QUESTIONS ASKED MONEY BACK GUARANTEE**
**365 DAYS NO QUIBBLE SERVICE GUARANTEE**
**10 DAYS PART-EXCHANGE GUARANTEE**

> ### *GUARANTEED* **FOR LIFE**
>
> - **Up to £10,000 BIG value life insurance** *GUARANTEED*
> - **From just 30p a day** *GUARANTEED*
> - **No intrusive health questions** *GUARANTEED*
> - **Up to £50 *cash back* on your**
>   **first month's premium** *GUARANTEED*

### *Save the best till last*

Save your most exciting benefit till last. Just as the reader thinks that you couldn't possibly offer more – bang! You fire off your dynamic closing shot. Urge the reader to 'act now' quick! Before it's too late!

### *It's so easy to order*

Nothing could be easier than saying 'yes' to your terrific offer. All the reader has to do is complete the simple reply device that is either attached or found in the mailing package.

### *Yours sincerely*

Every letter should be signed, if not in person, at least the signature should be printed in blue ink – as it would if it was individually signed.

### *PS. Don't forget the PS*

The PS is your last opportunity within your letter to reinforce your sales argument. You can use it in a number of ways including adding a last-minute benefit, reminding the reader about a special free gift or drawing the reader's attention to one of the key points made within your copy.

### *PPS – Just in case you didn't hear me the first time*

The postscript (which actually means 'after writing') is one of the most powerful creative elements in a letter. Keep your postscript short. Response may be even further increased if your postscript is in a handwritten typeface.

### *The optional gizmo*

Like them or loathe them, direct mail gadgets can be effective. Gadgets help give a mailing an extra creative dimension. For example, you could include a gadget such as a pair of 3-D glasses to view a specially printed leaflet. Or a pen to sign the order form. One interesting idea is to attach a penny to your sales letter – then ask the reader to use it to scratch out a panel revealing whether or not a prize has been won. This technique is sometimes called 'coin rub'.

The 'OK guidelines' of including gadgets are:

It's OK to... attach your gadget to one secure spot.
It's OK to... try to tie-in your gadget with the copy.
It's OK to... strengthen your envelope so that the gadget doesn't rip it to bits.
It's *not* OK to... include anything than can be squashed or melts in the post.
It's *not* OK to... including anything that's perishable.
It's *not* OK to... include a gadget that can offend (e.g. a key ring holding a condom)
It's *not* OK to... include a particularly bulky or heavy gadget.
(**NB**: Although not a gadget, don't treat live animals as such. *NEVER include anything that's live.*)

## Putting it all together

Let's see how some of the above techniques can be incorporated into the copy text of a typical direct mail letter.

*Relevant gadget*
(Packet of seeds stuck to the letter)

> Cultivate these seeds for
> a beautiful display of flowers.

*Strong headline*

> **BUY THIS BOOK AND CULTIVATE YOUR GARDENING KNOWLEDGE**
> **AT A NEVER-TO-BE REPEATED PRICE**

*Personalised salutation*

> Dear Mr Jones

*Intriguing opening paragraph*

> John Willis once said that the
> 'essence of caring for and
> understanding a garden starts with
> appreciating the simple botanical
> make up of a seed'.

(Now show how all of this is directly relevant to the reader...)

> In fact, you will probably agree
> that the longer you spend caring and
> nurturing a garden, the greater your
> horticultural knowledge becomes.
>
> Now, you can develop your
> understanding and so gain even
> greater satisfaction from gardening.

(Note the use of words 'you' and 'yours'.)

*Now introduce the three Ws*
**W**hat is it?

> The Gardening Almanac is the
> most authoritative work of its
> kind ever published.

## What does it offer?

It draws on the highly respected experience of over 100 of the world's leading botanists and horticulturists. Their combined knowledge means that this book sets the plant classification standards which are practised internationally. The <u>Gardening Almanac</u> classifies and describes practically every plant species available to gardeners the world over.

## Bullet point benefits:

<u>Everything you'll ever need in one volume</u>
- Over 10,000 ornamental and economic plants.
- 350 specially commissioned, beautifully accurate line drawings.
- In-depth facts that help you identify and name even the rarest plants accurately.
- Practical guidelines that will help you achieve spectacular results with your own plants.
- The 'inside secrets' of creating spectacular urban landscapes such as rock gardens, water gardens or even coastal gardens.
- Revealing explanations of the world's great gardening traditions.
- This is just s small example of how the extraordinary <u>Gardening Alamanac</u> deals with all your gardening questions.

## Wow! – Save the best until last

> You can own this outstanding work at an
> exclusive price. Just £99.99
> for more than 2,000 pages.
> <u>That's a saving of £60 off the
> recommended retail price</u>.

## *It pays to reply today*

> **An extra 'thank you' with our compliments**.
> However, you must place your order before
> 31st May. Please do so and, as a token of
> thanks, we will send you a complimentary
> copy of <u>Gardening Secrets</u>.
> This is an essential reference that is
> packed with tips on how to make
> your garden bloom.

## *It's easy to order*

> Ordering your <u>Gardening Almanac</u> is easy.
> Simply complete the enclosed order form and
> return it to me, with payment in the prepaid
> envelope provided. Alternatively, you can
> order with your credit card. Just call our
> 24-hour customer Hotline on 01234 56789,
> quoting reference number '1'.

> I look forward to sending your <u>Gardening Almanac</u> and
> hope you enjoy the complimentary packet of seeds.
>
>     Yours sincerely,
>     [Name]
>     [Title]

*Don't forget*

> **PS** Remember, this offer will never be repeated.
>     You must respond before 31st May.

## Other elements

### Leaflets

Although the sales letter plays a key role in communicating your message, it is rarely the only content. Leaflets, for example, explain benefits in greater detail. Moreover, leaflets don't restrict your creativity to text. Illustrations can show how a product processes something. As long as the leaflet fits into the outer envelope, size can be made to work for you.

Common leaflet formats are 'roll folds'. This type of leaflet is folded up to eight times. As the reader unfolds each page, so the creative message is explained in greater detail.

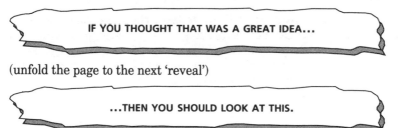

> **IF YOU THOUGHT THAT WAS A GREAT IDEA...**

(unfold the page to the next 'reveal')

> **...THEN YOU SHOULD LOOK AT THIS.**

As with advertisements, allow subheads to direct the reader through your leaflet copy. If the product is particularly technical, you may like to consider including a question-and-answer panel towards the end. Question-and-answer panels help to address legal requirements: how long a product or service will operate, who is eligible to apply, and so on.

Another kind of leaflet is the one-page leaflet. This encapsulates your benefits on to a double-sided (often A6 paper size) sheet of paper. One-page leaflets are ideal for recapping the benefits of an early reply. For example:

Headline:

> **REPLY EARLY AND YOU CAN RECEIVE A**
> **FREE TRAVEL HOLD-ALL.**

> **YOURS FREE IF YOU APPLY IN 14 DAYS.**
> **THIS HANDY TRAVEL HOLD-ALL DOESN'T ONLY LOOK GREAT, BUT WILL**
> **HELP LIGHTEN THE LOAD WHEN YOU'RE OUT ON YOUR TRAVELS...**

(One-page leaflets detailing incentives should always feature a picture of the incentive and, if practicable, close-up pictures of certain special details – in the case of the travel hold-all double zips, hidden pockets, rubber-grip handles...

## Lift letters

Give your copy a little lift with lift letters. These are small note-like memo letters that can help enhance a sales message or reassure the reader of a purchasing choice. Often, such lift letters appear to be written by someone other than the writer of the main letter copy. This has the effect of an individual endorsement.

Dear Mr Jones,

Can't make up your mind?

When I first looked through the <u>Gardening Almanac</u> I was amazed at the kind of detail that each entry goes into. The illustrations are, to say the least, impressive. The technical data reveals fascinating facts that will help you get the most from your plants and flowers.

Best of all, the price of just £99.99 means that you save £60 off the recommended retail price.

Take it from me, if you only ever buy one gardening reference book in your lifetime, make sure it's the <u>Gardening Almanac</u>.

   Yours sincerely,

## *The reply device*

Like coupons in press advertisements, the mailing reply device, needs to be clearly designed. Be sure to include details such as your fax number or telephone number *for an even quicker response*. You could also consider completing a sample order form in handwriting. Always repeat the response incentive offer if only in a couple of key words.

You could consider including a YES and NO sticker for your reply device. This is a great involvement device that encourages the reader to select either the YES sticker or the NO sticker and then adhere it to the response device. Research shows that if, in the case of a free prize draw, you offer people the choice of a YES and NO sticker, people feel obliged to use the YES sticker in preference to the NO sticker as it appears to influence their chance of winning in the draw. (Of course, this is not true.)

Alternatively you could always include a MAYBE sticker. This half way compromise retains interest and, if you ask for a day time number which is followed up quickly by a phone call, you could 'convert' a MAYBE to a YES. MAYBE can also be passed on to other departments within the company who could offer the respondent an item that is more suitable to their needs.

Finally, try to include the powerful YES word within the copy of the reply device:

## YES – I WANT TO KNOW MORE.
## YES – SEND ME MY ALMANAC TODAY.

# — Twenty-six creative mailing ideas —

### 1 Envelopes with 'peal off' stickers

Stickers add intrigue and involvement. They are infinitely versatile. Peel the sticker and you can reveal part of the contents of the package. Or why not give the sticker additional value by asking the recipient to use it on a free-gift voucher.

STICK THIS ON TO THE COUPON INSIDE
AND YOU COULD WIN A
FREE HOLIDAY TO CAIRO.

### 2 Round envelopes

Unusually shaped envelopes help make your mailing more distinctive. However, circles can be quite expensive to produce as they take up a lot of paper stock. Other ideas are triangular-shaped envelopes, extra large envelopes, extra small envelopes...

### 3 Card decks

(Also known as 'postcard decks' or 'foil card decks') Card decks involve you sharing a mailing with other advertisers who have contributed special cards that fit either in a foil pouch or a clear plastic pouch. Your product details are presented in the form of a postcard. One side details the product while the other features a response device. A variation of this is a 'postcard' that is distributed to hotel, cinema or restaurant chains. Tourists pick up a complimentary postcard and, by doing so, mail your message – usually featuring an interesting visual device – for you!

### 4 Video mailers

Instead of producing a printed mail piece, why not produce a short video programme about your product or service? You can use the cassette inlay to hold a response device.

### 5 The no-name mailer

Leave out the product name from the envelope. This works well when your product is financially sensitive or it has already been mass-mailed several times. (I once had to do this in the case of a credit card company that had already mailed to some 11 million households.)

### 6 The Jack-in-the-box mailer

Here the reader breaks open a seal – usually at the edge of the envelope. This reveals the leading edge of a piece of paper. The reader pulls the leading edge which unfolds a concertina-type mailer in which each sheet is attached to another.

### 7 The door-drop mailer

Rather than sending a direct mail piece via the post, you circulate it via a letterbox distribution company, door-to-door. The benefit of this approach is that you can be precise about which households receive your mailing piece, and you have greater control over timing its arrival.

### 8 The bang-tail envelope mailing

In this case, you include a special envelope which features a perforated 'tail' of paper, near the sealing flap, that can be used as an order form.

### 9 Bill stuffer

You include a leaflet or separate letter along with your invoices or statements. This is a very cost-effective way of making ordinary regular bills more beneficial. If your budget doesn't stretch to a separate leaflet, you can still use available existing space on the invoice or statement to highlight a creative message.

> **Total now due** £220
> **HAVE YOU APPLIED FOR YOUR PLUS CARD YET?**
> **IT COULD SAVE £££S ON YOUR SHOPPING**
> **AT SCOTDALE NORTHSIDE -**
> **FOR FURTHER DETAILS CONTACT**
> **THE PLUS CARD HOTLINE ON 0800 12345**

## 10 Birthday mailing

Write to someone on the occasion of a birthday, or an anniversary of first using or enquiring about your product or service. This is regularly employed by insurance companies who use the anniversary of an insurance policy – such as motor insurance – to remind the policyholder of the company's great deals.

> **12** MONTHS' ADDITIONAL PEACE OF MIND
> AT LAST YEAR'S PRICES.
> HURRY – YOU MUST RENEW YOUR POLICY
> WITHIN THE NEXT **11** DAYS.

## 11 Bounce-back mailing

Congratulations! You have successfully sold your product using direct mail. Now include a second special offer which is sent along with the product itself.

> NOW YOU'VE BOUGHT A PENPOD, USE THIS COUPON
> TO *WRITE OFF* 50% ON A PENPOD GIFT SET.

## 12 Member-get-member mailing

Also known as MGM, or 'friend-get-a-friend' or 'introduce-a-friend'. It is one of the most effective ways of enhancing your customer database. The technique often relies on a small incentive-led leaflet that details an additional free gift to the recipient just for 'recommending a friend'. This can be further strengthened by offering to provide an extra free gift if the 'friend' signs up for a product or service.

> **THIS GUIDE TO WINES IS YOURS FREE**
> JUST FOR RECOMMENDING A FRIEND.

> THIS CRATE OF SIX SPECIALLY SELECTED WINES IS YOUR **FREE**
> ONCE YOUR FRIEND STARTS TO ENJOY THE BENEFITS OF OUR CLUB.

Even if you don't have the budget to make a special incentive offer for an MGM, it is still worth your while to include a space for a recommendation within a reply device.

## 13 Pop-ups

Pop-ups can include anything from a pop-up-letter to a pop-up-coupon that places the order form directly into the recipient's hand.

## 14 Audio mailing

Audio mailings usually feature either pre-taped messages or pre-recorded compact discs. (Audio mailings are growing in popularity with car manufacturers.) During the 1960s and early '70s, companies selling record collections featured pre-recorded floppy 45 rpm records. Today, the sound medium is still an extremely effective way to convey atmosphere via the mail. One recent audio 'fad' has been the use of pre-recorded microchips. When the recipient of the mailing piece opens the envelope, a hidden microchip connected to a tiny speaker inside the envelope is activated and a voice can be heard literally from inside the envelope!

Whatever kind of audio technology you use, take complete advantage of music, sound effects and a compelling story. As with video mailings, be sure to use the inlay of either the cassette box or CD-holder to include elements such as order forms or coupons.

### 15 Embossed membership cards

This technique of including a plastic 'credit card' membership card – complete with the recipient's name embossed on it – was particularly popular during the mid-1980s. It can still be effective as a way to encourage custom and enhance personalisation.

Here's your PERSONAL Scotdale Northside *plus*CARD

5% DISCOUNT ON EVERY £50 SPENT
AT OUR WEST END BRANCH

**Please keep it safe, Ms Purkis. The more you use it, the bigger your discounts**

### 16 Pre-mailer mailer

Also known as a 'pre-announcement mailer'. This technique provides advance notification of a major mailing campaign. It works well when you want to announce something like a major prize draw.

WATCH YOUR POST. BY THIS TIME NEXT WEEK
YOU COULD BE OUR NEXT MILLIONAIRE!

As with birthday mailings, pre-mailers can be strengthened by including personalised details unique to the recipient.

> WE'VE SENT THIS NOTICE TO ONLY **23** PEOPLE IN QUEENSTOWN.
> YOU ARE ONE OF ONLY **4** PEOPLE IN YOUR ROAD
> WHO WILL RECEIVE IT. BY THIS TIME NEXT WEEK
> YOU COULD BE OUR NEXT MILLIONAIRE!

## 17  Keep-up-with-the-Jones's mailers

This is an example of database management working closely with copywriters. Assuming your product or service is mass market, check the geographic area that you intend to mail. Then produce a list of all nearby residents who have previously purchased a specific product or service. This neighbours list is called a 'cluster list'. Then...

> RIGHT NOW, YOUR NEIGHBOURS ARE MAKING
> GREAT SHOPPING SAVINGS WITH A PLUS CARD.
> WHY NOT JOIN THEM?

## 18  Two-halves-are-better-than-one mailers

| | |
|---|---|
| Dear Mrs Jones,<br><br>Last August you kindly purchased a mobile phone from us.<br><br>As a valued customer, you can now take advantage of a hands-free car adapter kit at 75% off the manufacturer's recommended retail price.<br><br>All you have to do is complete and send the second half of this letter off to us today. | Dear Mrs Jones,<br><br>Have you ever been at the wheel when 'ring' 'ring', someone calls on your mobile phone?<br><br>Boy, it's frustrating! Well now you can pick up that call without picking up the phone. Our hands-free car adapter kit is all you need. Simply complete the following and return it to us today. You'll |

| | |
|---|---|
| We look forward to hearing from you. | even save 75% off the usual price. |
| | Your name .................... |
| Yours sincerely, | Your mobile number .......... |
| | Your credit card number ..... |
| | Signature .................... |
| | Thank you |
| | Yours sincerely, |

## 19 Cheque book mailers

Cheque book mailers feature a cheque book format with each dummy 'cheque' being a valuable voucher that can be redeemed for an incentive, such as an additional entry into a prize draw or against the purchase of goods. The 'cheque stub' section of the book often incorporates letter text copy. Each page of text refers to that section's personalised 'cheque'.

## 20 Sniff-and-buy mailers

Scent strips are a cost-effective way of demonstrating, via the post, products such as perfumes. Handled creatively, they can spice up a mailing, such as a personalised letter, by incorporating scent strips alongside the copy. The overall sensation (or scentsation!) is a letter that you can read and smell as you go along.

YOU CAN SMELL THE SUMMER MEADOWS
IN A SCOTDALE NORTHSIDE AIR FRESHENER.

## 21 Go green

Direct mail advertisers who wish to convey an environmentally responsible approach to mailings may print their entire mailer on recycled paper. This is a popular option for organisations such as charities or political parties. The 'down side' is that recycled paper has a detrimental effect on print quality. The 'up side' is that this effect can demonstrate that an organisation (such as a charity) isn't wasting its budgets on stunningly beautiful advertising – instead it is investing in helping needy causes. (Ironically, recycled paper can be more expensive to buy than regular paper!)

## 22 Post and phone

This technique is another way to 'tease' the recipient's curiosity. You send a simple mailing containing nothing more than a postcard. On it you feature an intriguing headline which directs the recipient to make a phone call – when all will be revealed. Depending on your type of organisation and length of telephone message, this technique can be made even more cost effective if the phone number is self-financing with a premium rate telephone number.

## 23 The overseas letter

Curiosity can be further enhanced if you mail your piece from an overseas address. In certain circumstances, it can also save on postal costs.

## 24 Electronic mailers

Technology is one of direct marketing's greatest allies. Use it. Virtually every company in the country has a fax machine. Used sparingly – even with permission – you can take advantage of this to add immediacy and impact to your offer. From a copy viewpoint, try to keep your message on one page. Use large and bold typefaces and always provide details of how you can be contacted.

Another electronic mailer that uses technology is the e-mailer. Legislation permitting, this helps you take advantage of computer-networked mail. Subscribers to e-mail are usually listed in specialist directories. The advantage of e-mail is that it demonstrates that your company is ahead of the times: the disadvantage of e-mail is that unless the subscriber is hooked up to his or her e-mail service, and of course has the computer switched on, you can never be certain that a message gets read.

From a formatting point of view, you can send entire 'files' of text and graphics via e-mail, so just about anything you can print on paper can be published via e-mail. However, a word of warning about using e-mail: never send unsolicited mailers. The INTERNET community (to which a recipient needs to belong in order to receive an e-mail) is tightly knit. Word will spread that unsolicited information is being sent and what may have been an interesting use of direct mail could end up as hi-tech junk mail – renamed for the new super highway era as mail bombs. (See also Chapter 15 and page 278.)

## 25 Questionnaire mailers

This method exemplifies the essence of using direct mail to establish a good dialogue between a company and prospective customers. Questionnaires help to test a market or build a new database. They can show existing customers that you care about their opinion. They give you an ideal opportunity to contact customers and to strengthen the dialogue.

As with reply devices, you should write questionnaires with simplicity in mind. Questions should be clear, copy should be precise, terminology should be kept to a minimum, with each question requiring either one direct answer or one predetermined set of multiple choice answers.

There are nine copy tips for questionnaires:

1 Explain why you are sending the questionnaire. Use a covering letter to explain why you are asking for a response to the questionnaire. Always reassure your respondent that answers are confidential. If you intend to use the answers for other companies, give the respondent the opportunity to decline the option to share data with other organisations. Consider the merits of rewarding answers with a free gift;

2 Complete a sample question to show how to answer the rest of the questionnaire;

3 Don't put the horse before the cart. In other words, track your questions so that they first refer to a concept and gradually build up to a specific product or service that caters for a need;

4 Try, whenever possible, to avoid open-ended questions, such as, 'Why do you think...'; 'Explain your views...';

5 Include a 'Don't know' option. If you don't and the respondent really doesn't have an opinion on a specific question, he or she may think that the question is too difficult and so give up;

6 There are no 'right' answers. Always tell your respondent that the questionnaire is not an intelligence test. The only thing being tested is your product or service;

7 Don't cram too many possible answers into one question. Instead

of, 'Typically, how many own-labels products do you buy at Scotdale Northside?' ask about each of the product categories, one at a time  and then...

> **IN A WEEK DO YOU BUY**
> ONE ☐ TWO ☐ THREE ☐ CANS OF SCOTDALE NORTHSIDE VEGETABLES?
> **WHICH CAN OF VEGETABLES DO YOU BUY?**
> MUSHROOMS ☐ SWEETCORN ☐ CARROTS ☐

8 Intimate or personal questions should, if possible, be avoided. But if you have to be intimate, do so tactfully. Instead of 'How much do you earn?' Try...

> **IS YOUR INCOME BETWEEN**
> **£15,000–£20,000?** ☐
> **£21,000–£25,000?** ☐
> **OVER £26,000?**       ☐

If you cannot avoid direct intimate questions, explain why you need to ask them and clarify your precise interpretation. Instead of, 'Have you ever had an extra-marital affair?' Ask:

> **IN ORDER TO ESTABLISH HOW OUR SERVICE CAN BEST PROVIDE**
> **CONFIDENTIAL COUNSELLING TO COUPLES,**
> **PLEASE ANSWER THE FOLLOWING:**
>
> **IN THE LAST YEAR, HAVE YOU HAD MORE THAN ONE SEXUAL PARTNER?**
> YES ☐
> NO ☐
> **IF YES, HOW MANY?**
> **1–2** ☐   **3–4** ☐   MORE THAN **5** ☐

9 Always include a prepaid postage device – sealed and overprinted with the word CONFIDENTIAL.

## 26 Prize draw mailings

Prize draw mailings add excitement and energy to a product or service offer. Your prize draw can be a:

- Charity-based lottery;
- 'No skill or purchase required' selection of a predetermined number of tickets in a draw;
- Competition judged on a fair degree of physical or mental skill or judgement. In the United States this is a 'contest'. Some States will require a purchase or fee to be paid;
- 'No purchase needed, no payment required', no great skill or judgement game.

So, Scotdale Northside could:

- Ask customers to make a purchase and enter a *competition* to identify the country of origin of canned fruit and to complete a *tie-breaker* (in accordance with the UK code of sales promotion);
- Ask any person to enter a 100th anniversary *free prize draw* by completing a coupon to be returned by post (no purchase needed);
- Sell a *lottery* ticket for £1 with part of the proceeds going to charities and a top prize of £10,000 worth of shopping (as long as the company was registered as part of a voluntary body giving proceeds to charity and followed restrictions imposed by the Lotteries and Amusement Act);
- Ask anyone to play the *Shopping Game* and win a holiday (as long as the game is based on the rules for a draw and incorporated in the Gaming Act restrictions).

In copy terms, prize draws should lead with the big prize.

WE'LL PAY YOUR SHOPPING BILLS FOR LIFE.

Are there any runner-up prizes? If so, list them. The more prizes, the more chances to win! What's the total amount of prize money or prize value?

ALL IN ALL, WE'RE GIVING AWAY AN INCREDIBLE
£5,000,000 WORTH OF PRIZES!!!

The bigger the figures both in context and appearance on the page, the better. You could also feature the big numbers on valuable-looking prize draw certificates. One art director who I used to work with collected old bonds. He adapted the borders on each bond specifically to give an impression of value on prize draw certificates (see Figure 9.2).

**Figure 9.2** Sample prize draw certificate

If there are any previous winners, with their permission, give their names. (People like to see real people winning prizes.) Always discuss how easy it is to enter and win. Incorporate 'dream copy' into your text:

> Just think, this time next month you could be relaxing by the pool of the five-star Holiday Hut hotel in Hawaii. Fancy a drink? Your bar steward will be delighted to serve you anything from a tropical Pina Colada to a long, cool and refreshing Tequila Sunrise.
>
> In the evening you can step out in style. We'll lay on a chauffeur-driven limousine that will whisk you and your partner away to the sensational Tangles nightclub...

Or...

What would you do if you won £1,000,000? Buy a
mansion in the country? Ten Rolls Royces?
Your own light aircraft? Why not start up that
business you've always wanted to run? Take a
year-long cruise around the world...

**Always list your rules simply and clearly.**

1. Entrants must be residents of the UK and over
   the age of 18, but not employees, neither
   related to an employee nor to anyone connected
   with the draw.
2. All entries to be received by [date]. The draw
   for a Rolls Royce Silver Shadow car will be
   made on [date].
3. Only one entry per person is allowed.
4. Entry to the draw is free. No purchase
   required. Proof of posting will not be
   accepted as proof of delivery. Responsibility
   cannot be accepted for lost or mislaid entries.
   Damaged or defaced entries will be
   disqualified. No correspondence will be
   entered into.
5. The winner will be notified by post. The name
   and area of the prize draw winner will be
   available after [date] to anyone sending a
   stamped self-addressed envelope to [address].
6. No cash alternative will be offered.
7. The draw will be made by an independent body.
8. Entry to the prize draw is deemed to imply
   acceptance of these rules.

# A word about catalogues

Shopping by post often features a catalogue of goods and services. The suggestion of detailing everything about a product is particularly relevant for catalogue writing. Your style has to be direct. Captions relating to goods have to be benefits led.

Example fashion catalogue:

(Picture of a blouse – close-up of buttons)

> **PRETTY COLOUR CO-ORDINATED BUTTONS**
> **THAT ADD AN EXTRA TOUCH OF ELEGANCE.**

As with certain packaging copy explain how things look and feel, how they will make the user look and feel or cook or read or write, better than ever before:

> **YOU CAN BE WARM YET LOOK 'COOL'.**
> **THESE BOLD CABLE-KNIT CREW-NECK SWEATERS ARE DURABLE**
> **ENOUGH FOR EVEN THE TOUGHEST NORTH SEA CONDITIONS.**
> **YET THEY FEEL WONDERFULLY SOFT ON YOUR SKIN.**

Copy needs to compliment the visual layout and style of the catalogue. It must be enthusiastic and personal, as if you were the shopper's companion. As such, instead of literally being in a shop, pointing to a special detail of something you have spotted, you include steps of captions throughout the catalogue's pages. '*Look at this...*' '*Notice that...*' Apart from highlighting aspects, it helps to break up the general look of the page.

If you offer a credit facility, always include a small panel after each product description that shows how little needs to be spent over how long in order to buy the product (in accordance with the UK Consumer Credit Act).

Pages need to be accessible. Try colour coding to differentiate item types. You can also consider indexing including using section dividers. Why not incorporate extra details in panels about the history of goods and the dimensions.

```
┌─────────────────────────────────────────────────────┐
│            100% PURE TRIPLE-WEIGHT CASHMERE           │
│ YOUR CHOICE                                           │
│ OF COLOURS      MUSHROOM•  MID GREY•  TARTAN GREEN•    │
│ AVAILABLE SIZES S.M.L.XL.                              │
│ Our direct from Scotland price:                       │
│                 ONLY £xxx (UK & EEC)                   │
│                 ONLY £xxx (OVERSEAS TAX FREE)          │
│ JUST QUOTE      CODE XXXX                              │
└─────────────────────────────────────────────────────┘
```

You can even add interest by including background titbits about, for example, where a silk dress comes from. Or the manufacturing process behind an item:

THIS PEN HAS UNDERGONE **1000** PRODUCTION PROCESSES
BEFORE RECEIVING OUR WRITTEN APPROVAL.

Another method is to incorporate a testimonial from a happy user, or a guarantee panel.

Many catalogues also feature an introduction piece or letter. For this, follow the general rules of writing a direct response letter, with the copy acting as an all-embracing guide that explains:

- What makes this catalogue so special;
- The effort that went into its production;
- The range within;
- The easy ways to order;
- Any credit facilities;
- Reiterate the easy ways to order (shaded boxes or panels highlighting order Hotlines, perhaps featuring a telephone sales person are also a good idea to incorporate throughout the catalogue).

---

The first mail order business was incorporated on 15 September, 1871, as the Army and Navy Co-operative. The society published its first catalogue in February 1872. The catalogue contained 112 pages and featured goodies such as Ladies Merino Drawers at 5s 9d a pair.

---

## *Direct mail quick tips*

- Direct mail builds customer relationships.
- Direct mail is a personal business.
- Good copy with bad targeting is wasted copy.
- Mailings need to inform.
- Mailings need to involve.
- Envelopes should reflect a creative and copy tone of voice.
- When appropriate use the words 'free' and 'you' in copy.
- Entice recipients to open an envelope NOW.
- Letters should be easy on the eye and simple to understand.
- Letters should feature multiple entry points.
- Letters should be personalised.
- Letters should be benefit led.
- Use the three Ws.
- Explain why someone should reply.
- Make replying easy and fun.
- Offer guarantees.
- Use PSs.
- Feature only relevant gadgets.
- Consider different creative formats.
- Use leaflets and brochures to tell a fuller story.
- Use questionnaires to discover more about a prospect and enhance customer service.
- Use prize draws to add energy to a mailing.
- PPS – How about a PPS?

## *Over to you*

1 Write copy for three different types of zipper envelope.
2 Write a lead-in paragraph for a sales letter selling this book.
3 Write a lift letter from Hodder and Stoughton urging people to buy this book.
4 Look at any example of direct mail and highlight the three Ws in the text.
5 Look in your wardrobe. Write a 20-word direct mail catalogue description of an article of clothing.
6 List six different ways to communicate 'FREE'.

# 10

# DIRECT MAIL
# AND CHARITY

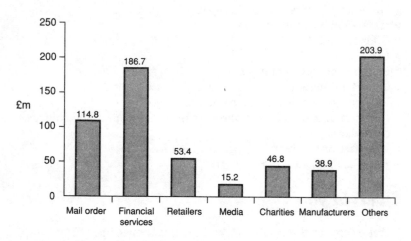

**Figure 10.1** Breakdown of direct marketing expenditure by industry sector (value), 1994

Source: Royal Mail, Industry Source, Data Monitor

One of the most emotive uses of direct mail is the charity mailing. Although most charities are viewed as a good cause, there are certain creative criteria which have been shown to be intrinsically motivating. These are either: goal orientated – towards a specific tangible cause (e.g. human rights in the former Yugoslavia) or by providing an essential service (e.g. blood transfusion) – or for the helpless – associated with children, animals, the sick or handicapped.

# Donors

There are two kinds of donor – the committed donor and the occasional donor. The committed donor gives frequently or large amounts. He or she makes a conscious decision which charity/charities to give to. Committed donors are concerned about social problems. They may do voluntary work or know a disabled person. They may have a religious commitment. Being realists they have a less shocking attitude to disability, based on knowledge. Their straightforward attitude towards giving help is not usually complicated by guilt feelings.

The occasional donor gives less often, but gives when asked directly. He or she is concerned about social problems, but passively, and may do voluntary work or know a disabled person. Occasional donors tend to have an ambivalent attitude to charities/disability, based on ignorance or guilt feelings – 'Should I be doing more?' They can be sensitive, to the point of resentment, to 'high-pressure' tactics.

An occasional donor may become a frequent giver because of a change of lifestyle (often by having children), close contact with illness or disability, or by maturing – becoming less self-orientated and more secure about his or her role in society. (See also VALS on pages 58–9.)

## What motivates people to give?

There are two basic motivations to stimulate donation: the direct and the indirect behavioural trigger. The direct behavioural trigger involves pushing a collecting box under someone's nose. This tends to cause an 'involuntary' donation, since it is often harder *not* to give. The indirect behavioural trigger relies on rational and emotional evaluation of the cause. A sick child in an advertisement will cause the person to appraise the cause rationally before he or she is moved to contribute. Both triggers are important to a charity that wants to be more effective. The level of direct fundraising activity is as important as the indirect promotion of the charity's image and appeal.

Committed charity givers are more likely to respond to a 'worthy' cause, regardless of their own personal preference. In other words, they are willing to give to others in need. Occasional givers are more likely to be motivated by a more personally relevant cause. In other words, they want to know what's in it for them (e.g. safe sex information regarding AIDS).

# —— Types of creative message ——

More intense competition in the charity market means that professional marketing of 'the worthy or good cause' is becoming increasingly vital for survival. Charities adopt professional creative standards already used in the marketing of consumer goods. However, charity advertising, including direct mail, remains a sensitive area. Your copy should, therefore, be sensitive to recognise and respect their feelings. It is a waste of time to write copy that overdramatises to such a point that the reader is subjected to intolerable emotional pressure. Having said this, your copy should be realistic and subjects may not always be pleasant. Sympathetic realism is permissible, emotional blackmail is not.

In addition, flamboyant television or press advertising which clearly costs a lot of money may be perceived as a wasteful use of funds. Here, direct mail may play a particularly powerful role through use of methods such as recycled paper and two-colour printed simple leaflets. It is proven that if one charity helps another through sharing the names of their supporters, it can save money in buying lists and improve responses.

Types of charity advertising can be broadly categorised as:

- Shock/horror – ranges from starving children to frightening statistics. The first creative port of call for copywriters is often the horror story. This is not necessarily the best route to take. Overtly shocking visuals may stimulate a high degree of negative reaction from even the committed giver;
- Case histories – if a charity has an emotive story to tell about how someone has benefited from their help, a case history can be an involving and an interesting way to communicate its activities. To do this it needs to provide an emotive aspect of the case histories (children are potentially good for this) and show how previous donations have helped transform a particular person's life.

> **£20** WILL GIVE THIS GIRL THE GIFT OF A BETTER LIFE.

## Use of personalities

Endorsement of a cause by a popular and respected personality not only increases the awareness of the charity but also can add to the credibility of the cause. Obviously, the choice of personality is an important consideration since the perceived image of him or her will be seen as representative of the charity itself.

## Legacy direct mail

This kind of direct mail often arises from the results of small-space advertisements, usually placed near the 'wills' and 'deaths' columns in daily newspapers by those charities connected with the fight against terminal diseases, and with old age.

> **5,000** CHILDREN KILLED EACH YEAR BY MALARIA
>
> NO FLOWERS PLEASE.
>
> BUT YOU CAN MAKE A LEGACY DONATION
>
> TO MALARIA AID
>
> PLEASE WRITE TO [ADDRESS]

## Begging

Neither an aggressive nor a feeble begging request for money is going to motivate someone to make a donation. This is especially true for the major charities which must communicate an authoritative image to retain their level of credibility. While it is important to show how reliant you are on donations, the tone in which you do so is crucial.

## Dial 999 now!

With so many worthy causes and so much work to be done, day-to-day needs, however urgent, can overwhelm the potential donor. One creative way to overcome this is the 'Action 999' approach. This is when you turn an ongoing crisis into an emergency. This can be achieved by concentrating on one aspect of a specific need. For example, the overall cause may be for a remote country but your Action 999 approach is shelter in that country.

> **£10** WILL SHELTER THIS CHILD FROM HURRICANES,
>
> FREEZING RAIN AND FROST BITE.
>
> TAKE ACTION, PLEASE GIVE TO
>
> THE EMERGENCY SIBERIAN APPEAL TODAY.

Another way to use the Action 999 approach is to time your appeal to coincide with a traditional 'giving' season. Christmas is the firm favourite. However, you could also chose Diwali, Rosh Hashanah, Chinese New Year, Easter, and so on.

## We can't do anything without you

This type of creative message explains exactly what the charity does and how it spends its money.

> HERE'S WHERE *YOUR* DONATION GOES.

Always ask for a specific sum of money.

> **I WOULD LIKE TO HELP.**
>
> (PLEASE TICK THE RELEVANT DONATION BOX.)
>
> ☐ **£25** WILL FEED A FAMILY OF FIVE FOR 2 WEEKS.
>
> ☐ **£15** WILL CLOTHE A REFUGEE FOR THE WINTER.
>
> ☐ **£10** WILL IMMUNISE THREE CHILDREN AGAINST TYPHOID.
>
> ☐ I WOULD LIKE TO DONATE (          )
>
> *THANKS FOR YOUR GENEROSITY.*

(Notice how the largest sum was shown first and that none of the sums are excessive. Also note the option for the donor to give a sum of his or her own.)

Whenever possible, veer your copy towards helping people, not alleviating conditions. By all means use visual supports to show the scope of a problem, but centre both your copy and visual on individuals' cases within an overall problem.

For example:

> **LUCY IS FIFTEEN YEARS OLD AND HOMELESS.**
>
> **£10** COULD PREVENT HER FROM MEETING MEN
>
> WHO ARE ALL TOO WILLING TO PART WITH **£10**.

Never word a creative request so that the problem sounds so vast that any donation would appear to be a drop in a bottomless ocean, for example 'Each year it costs £12 million to keep children off the streets. Can you help?'

# 11

# MOVING PICTURES

I left writing about copy for television until the latter part of this book. Too many would-be copywriters believe that the ultimate goal for every great creative copywriter is television. As I hope you have seen by now, the craft of copywriting is multifaceted with opportunities to excel in many specialist areas.

Since 1930, when Bill Hay acted as compere in the world's first TV commercial, television has played a major role in communicating a sales message. At the beginning of the twenty-first century, this role will become increasingly more important. Satellite television networks are already making the planet a smaller place. Irrespective of political borders, commercial broadcasting enables sales messages to be transmitted across international borders direct to the consumer.

The rapid rate of television penetration is amazing. From a creative copy view, there are two sides to growth. Originally, television copy was directed to vast mass markets. So copy detail specifics were kept to a minimum. Television still needs to be minimalist by concentrating on a single message. However, the mass-market approach is not always the right way to tackle writing television commercials because wider distribution of television signals creates greater demands for television sets (see Figure 11.1). More viewers want more channel options. More channels means more choice. More choice gives rise to more television sets. (One person may watch a programme on one side, while another person in the same household watches another channel.)

**Figure 11.1** Television ownership and reception capabilities

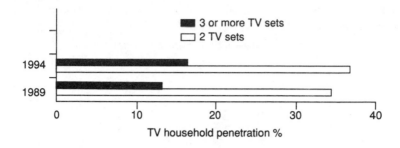

Source: BARB/ITC survey, March 1989 – June 1994

Greater choice gives rise to higher levels of specialisation. Specialisation requires more defined targeting. Defined targeting means narrower markets. Narrow markets call for more specific copy. 'Tighter' copy speaks to smaller groups. Smaller, defined groups are more likely to be interested in a specific proposition.

So, while the growth of television penetration and channel proliferation is 'breaking up' the old mass-market benefits of television advertising, the resulting choice of specific interest channels, such as shopping channels, children's channels, educational channels and even sex channels, means that copy can be more targeted to discrete interest groups.

The down side of all this is that from a viewer's perspective, vast choice may lead to confusion. Most definitely, it leads to viewers becoming instant arbitrators of which programme to watch. Quick judgements have to be based on what the viewer initially sees as he or she 'zaps' channels (or to use an INTERNET expression, 'surfs') with a remote control. This results in television designed with preference given to the visual content rather than word content. Copy has to be trimmed down to the most basic information: viewers' attention spans are quite shallow. This is demonstrated by various pieces of research carried out in the late 1970s in which it was proven that a fairly elaborate picture takes 1.5 to 2 seconds to process. (The time your brain takes to process the words of this sentence.) The problem of short attention span is further illustrated by data from US-based Newspaper Advertising Bureau (see Figure 11.2). As viewers become more and more desensitised to the power of television advertising, the task for copywriters to produce highly memorable commercials becomes increasingly difficult.

**Figure 11.2** Correct recall of last brand of television commercial seen

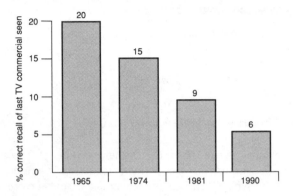

Source: Newspaper Advertising Bureau Inc. (1965–90, New York)

## —— Attracting viewers' attention ——

Before you can write a television commercial, you have to consider the actual act of watching television – what it involves and how it affects the viewer. Our minds constantly process various stimuli. When that ongoing process is interrupted, the brain starts to concentrate on the source of the interruption. In the case of television commercials, when a sight or sound draws attention to itself, the pupil of the eye dilates. This, in turn, causes the lens to focus on the television screen. So a bridge is established between the viewer and the television commercial.

This process of diverting the mind to one specific area of attention takes less than a second to establish itself. During that time, a decision has to be made about whether or not to continue to allow the 'bridge' to stand and so enable more detail from the source of distraction (i.e. the television commercial) to be processed or ignore the stimulus and go on to something more interesting instead.

With so many other possible distractions that demand attention from the viewer (such as an 'itchy' hand or the feel of a warm cup of coffee that demands drinking), this process is virtually impossible to control. However, by understanding which stimuli are likely to arrest attention in the first place, it is possible to influence the viewer's propensity to becoming distracted by a television commercial.

The good news for a copywriter is that providing the commercial is broadcast during a programme that is already of significant interest to the viewer, the chances are improved that he or she will be less likely to be distracted away from the screen during a television break. Likewise, the sooner the commercial falls within the start of the break, the higher the probability that the viewer won't be distracted by something else.

Possible routes to attract attention include:

**Material meanings**

| | |
|---|---|
| *Colours* | Vivid colours alert: pastel colours pacify |
| *Sounds* | Overtly loud or unusually muffled stimulate interest |
| *Movement* | A moving object is often more 'moving' than a stationary one |
| *Size* | Unusual sizes and shapes attract interest |
| *Light* | Contrast stimulates |

**Social interpretations**

| | |
|---|---|
| *Eyes* | Express feelings and depth (very good for close-up shots) |
| *Facial Expressions* | Provide further details of such emotions |
| *Hands* | Accentuate key points |
| *Posture* | Helps sets the mood – casual, attentive, professional, laid back |
| *Sexual undertones* | Incredibly strong attention distracters |
| *Children* | 'Bring out' natural paternal or maternal protective instincts (this also applies to animals or pets) |

## The 'trigger'

Once you have attracted the viewers' attention and so constructed a 'bridge', you can begin to think about ways to make those images work with copy that 'triggers' the right types of emotions associated with a product or service. To do this you must consider the way in which you present the basic attention stimuli, for example:

- *movement*                    animated
- *size*                        huge shopping trolley
- *sound*                       music
- *incongruent, novel or surprising ...*
- *hands*                       expressive
- *face*                        animated
- *posture*                     lively

The television image could be of a tin of Scotdale Northside baked beans pacing up and down in a shopping trolley singing:

(To the tune of 'Please Release Me')

> 'PLEASE RELEASE ME LET ME GO.
> YOUR KIDS WILL LOVE THE WAY I TASTE
> AT A MERE 20 PENCE A TIN.
> VALUE MY FREEDOM,
> OR I'LL BE A HAS BEAN.'

(The commercial ends up with a mother removing the tin of baked beans from the shopping trolley and handing it over to an eager child.)

This cheerful approach to selling baked beans sets off a wider and deeper range of psychological 'triggers'. In this case, those 'triggers' could include:

- fun
- cheap
- cute
- children

The viewer then processes this information and draws a conclusion. The product is fun to eat, cheap to buy and will keep the kids happy.

Each time you use a certain approach within your creative interpretation of a television commercial, as with all forms of advertising which help reinforce a brand name, show the company logo either throughout the commercial (on the tin of baked beans) or/also at the close of the commercial. In this way the viewer is stimulated to associate the two images.

# —— Practical creative approaches ——

Let's consider some popular creative television genres. Unlike press advertising or direct mail, television – and to a lesser extent its cousin, radio – are both centres of entertainment. Unless totally dedicated to news and education channels, the majority of viewers spend most of their time watching television entertainment. Therefore, your television commercial has to entertain as well as inform. By doing so, a commercial acts as a catalyst for creative concepts to be embraced rather than endured.

## 'How to...' commercials

If television reflects life, then the sales style or 'sales spiel' of a market trader reflects great 'how to...' television commercial copy techniques. The trader shows you:

- what is for sale
- what is does
- how it compares
- how durable it is
- how cheap it is
- why it has to be sold NOW
- why you'd be crazy not buy it

The sales spiel is confident. The trader will use every sales gimmick from throwing an unbreakable china plate on to the ground to chopping a variety of vegetables with one simple cutting device. The customer is repeatedly shown the virtues of the product. One benefit rapidly follows another. It all culminates in an orgy of customer demands to buy that product NOW!

Likewise step by step, the 'how to...' commercial explains how something can be done quicker, slower, easier, softer, cleaner, cheaper, and so on. Nothing is left to speculation. Everything is assured. In the United States it is commonplace to put market traders in a studio, give them television air time and get them to sell. The problem with this approach is that a good sales pitch needs time to 'warm up' an audience until they are driven into a heated frenzy to buy, buy, BUY! (Which is one reason why sponsored TV programmes are so popular in the United States.)

One method of stirring up interest, demonstrating a product attribute, and stimulating sales in a limited time is to use an unusual, even far-fetched demonstration. The following example shows how this technique could be used for PenPod.

| VISUAL | AUDIO |
|---|---|
| Man sits in a demolition truck. He is about to 'swing' the demolition bolder against the wall of an old building. | *Male aged 35 plus, Voice Over (VO) very confident.* 'PenPod is the strongest, most reliable pen you can buy. |
| Close-up (C/U) | But don't take my word for it.' |
| PenPod adhered to a brick wall. It is stuck on to the 'bulls-eye' of a painted target. | |
| Bolder swings and hits the pen at full impact. The wall collapses. | *Sound Effect (SFX)* *Crash* |
| Man walks through the rubble and uncovers the PenPod. It is in perfect shape. He dusts it down, opens it and begins to write on a piece of paper. | 'Well that's all write then.' |
| PenPod LOGO superimposed on the screen. | 'You'd be lost for words without it.' |

The secret of writing a successful demonstration commercial is really to put your product 'through the mill': defy speculation.

BEFORE WASHING THIS T-SHIRT IN SCOTDALE NORTHSIDE
BRILLIANCE POWDER IT LOOKED LIKE THIS. ('GRIMY')
NOW IT LOOKS LIKE THIS! ('SHINY')
MRS JONES THOUGHT THAT NOTHING COULD BEAT HER
WASHING POWDER. NOW SHE HAS TO THINK AGAIN.

Be proud to show off every detail, from a working engine – seen from inside the engine – to a plank of wood that has been treated with fire-resistant paint being lowered and successfully retrieved (in one piece) from the mouth of a volcano.

## *Get in the driving seat*

Car commercials often embrace one or more of the following aspects:

- Show the car in action;
- Show someone using the car in action;
- Show interior and exterior of the car. (Exterior footage should feature the body highlights, lines and curves of the vehicle);
- Show the type of person who drives the car;
- Show the type of person who typically drives the car, driving the car;
- Concentrate on specific mechanical and technical enhancements (e.g. safety);
- Don't show anything, but ask the viewers to 'test drive' the car at a dealership for themselves.

It is popular to show the car in action in a suitably dramatic landscape. Such commercials rely more on art direction than copywriting. Here, lighting, music and scenery takes centre stage. The down side of this kind of commercial is that you can spend vast sums of money just searching ('reckying') for a suitable location before you even get to film anything. Also, as you'll want to invest in capturing the glamour, 16 mm or even 35 mm film is often chosen in preference to video: unless the format is Digi-Beta, D1 or D5, video may not capture colour tones as vibrantly as film.

Special effects, ranging from clever use of lighting to computer-aided visual procedures, are all fine and good. Finishing touches such as film format, sound, set design, lighting, make-up wardrobe and location all come under the term 'production values'. The more time and effort taken over each production value, the more expensive will be the final presentation of the commercial.

Most special effects are inspired by music videos and cinema production effects. (Advertising usually follows trends, not sets them – see page 88.) However, no effect can ever replace a strong, single-minded message. Anything else may distract from the simple, Big Idea and is icing on the cake. (Mind you, who can resist a nice bit of fondant icing?!)

## Slice of life

Television broadcasters have always recognised the power of 'soaps'. According to British Telecom research, during the mid-1990s over 40 million UK viewers per week regularly tuned-in to TV soaps. Why? Because viewers identify with soap characters. Drama based on real-life situations and real families makes addictive viewing. As you have seen, television commercials take a sales message directly to the heart of a family home. They provide a great opportunity to introduce the viewer's family to the product's fictitious family.

This 'slice of life' technique helps establish a product or service as being something that is accessible to 'ordinary everyday people'. More importantly, through showing the product being used by everyday 'real' people – people like the viewers – it gives the product additional 'street credibility'.

Slice-of-life commercials help reinforce lifestyle values of a product or service. This can be effective when your product or service is one of many in its field. For example, BBC's television breakfast programme research found that during the mid-1990s there were over 3600 superstores in the United Kingdom. Slice-of-life television commercials were able to attach a certain lifestyle value to each chain of superstores. Such commercials featured the buying experience (for example, the wider shopping aisles, facilities for children, an in-store restaurant...) and the broader purchasing rewards (for example, convenience shopping helping to make a busy parent's life easier), and the practical value of fresh food that is easy to prepare, as well as the traditional low prices and high service values.

Slice-of-life commercials can feature any person in a family: the kids; the kids and mum; mum and dad; mum, dad, and the kids; grandparents; grandparents and any of the above. In addition, they can feature friends of the family, and would-be-lovers.

During the 1990s in Vancouver, Canada, a group called Adbusters campaigned against immoral family values created by advertising commercials. They called such advertising 'mental pollution' and adopted slogans such as *'American excess: leave home without it'*.

Being everyday people, your dialogue should be written in a casual tone. Think of your copy as a transcript of a piece of dialogue taken from eaves dropping on people: at work; at the bus stop; at the dinner table; shopping; watching TV, and so on.

Subjects need to be based on everyday occurrences or possible (given acceptable creative licence) everyday occurrences. Budget permitting, the best slice-of-life commercial campaigns have an on-going theme that spins out across several TV commercials. For example: Will the girl ever get the boy? Will the kids ever appreciate their parents? Will he ever know it is her? Will she ever get a promotion?

In order to write a successful slice-of-life commercial, it is important that the slice of life revolves around the product – not vice versa. So, for example, if you were to produce a slice-of-life commercial for a PenPod, the pen would act as an anchor point for the action.

**First commercial**

Character B passes by a window of a shop selling a Penpod and daydreams about Character A who is on business 1000 miles away.

Character A wants to write a letter to Character B. Looks for a pen but can't find one.

Beautiful Character C enters the scenario and offers to lend Character A her PenPod.

End of first commercial.

*Who is Character C?*

End title reads:

**GET THE MESSAGE WITH PENPOD**

**Second commercial**

Character B receives the letter from Character A and writes back a love letter to Character A.
Meanwhile, Character C (who is at home) is seen writing with her PenPod, signing a letter and then posting it.
Character A receives a letter, opens it and smiles.
Character B in her location, smiles. Character C in her location smiles.
*(Who wrote what to whom?)*
End title reads:
GET THE MESSAGE WITH PENPOD

And so on...

## *Intimate moments – handling sex on TV*

You may have noticed that I included 'would-be lovers' in the slice-of-life category of television commercials. Television can sometimes be considered as the eaves-dropper's magnifying glass on the world. It demonstrates – often graphically – what can be achieved, given the right tools in everything from business to love to sex. (During the summer of 1995, the US Senate passed a Telecommunications Bill requiring broadcasters to rate television programmes, and manufacturers to fit television sets with 'V' chips (V = violence). In this way, parents could block programmes that they found objectionable.)

Sex, being taboo, is sometimes seen as seductively alluring yet tantalisingly forbidden. That's why so many products that may be considered lavish, potentially bad for your figure, indulgent, and so on, make great intimate-moment television commercials. Ideal product candidates include: ice-cream; chocolates; bodycare products like foam baths; keep-fit equipment and health programmes.

Sexual undertones can be really subtle yet powerfully effective. One common creative 'trick' is to endow a phallus symbol to an inanimate object. For example:

A woman snuggles up against a rolled-up towel and discusses how soft it feels against her skin.

A ruby-red-lipped model takes a long and sensuous 'crunch' into a ripe apple.

A man caresses a female-shaped bottle of aftershave.

A woman drinks from a stream of clear, frothy water cascading out of a long-necked bottle.

Another type of intimate-moment television commercials is the 'secret sex' approach. This can include an intimate confession about: cleavage-enhancing bras; sports and leisure activity supportive underwear; leg-caressing tights; passion-arousing perfume; discreet sanitary towels that help you get on with your life.

## *The big star on the small screen*

*I'm still as big a star as ever. It's only the screen that got smaller*
(Gloria Swanson)

If you are going to hire a celebrity to endorse a product or service on television first ask yourself who is going to be the real star of the production, the celebrity or the product?

If, on the screen, that star dominates the product, your creative message won't wash, so don't use the celebrity. Many cases have been known where a television commercial makes the star an even bigger celebrity. That's acceptable. However, the product gets forgotten somewhere along the line. Worse still, the star's new image means that several commercials down the road, the star's agent will demand more money. (A good case for settling fees for all star appearances in writing before embarking on a long-term campaign.)

As with testimonials used in press advertising (see 'Question head-lines', page 74) it is important to understand the style of dialogue used by a specific celebrity. Write as the person would speak. If the star is really talented you may be asked to suggest an outline script and allow the celebrity to add the finishing touches. (Assuming you or your client is prepared to take the risk.)

A popular strategic creative option is to use television stars rather than big-screen stars. First, they usually cost less and, second they are more familiar 'visitors' to the viewer's home and therefore, more credible. Such stars may include soap-opera characters. Stars needn't come from the show-business galaxy of glitz and glitter. Industry-specific 'stars' add extra credibility, for example: a policeman endorsing a safety belt; an industrialist endorsing a computer; a cook endorsing a food product; an author endorsing a pen.

If you really want to add public credibility to a product or service, you could always get 'ordinary people' to endorse it. This approach makes a product appear practical but not as aspirational as a star endorsement. One way around this is to feature 'ordinary people' using the product and 'stars' introducing the product to the 'ordinary people'.

Other creative techniques to try include:

- On-the-street interviews/door-step interviews (in which the star interviews people outside their homes about a specific product or service);
- Extreme close-ups of people discussing the product (known as 'talking heads');
- Ordinary people acting like stars – because of the glamour associated with the product in question (e.g. one taste of Scotdale Northside ice-cream makes an ordinary woman enter a fantasy world where she takes on the appearance of a well-known 'sexy' actress or singer);
- Company directors demonstrating their own product and confidence in that product (see 'Appearing in your own advertising', page 86).

## That's all folks – animation

Animated characters are cute. The question you must ask yourself before enlisting the help of an animator is, 'Just how cute' is the image that you wish to convey?' Cartoon characters can make:

- a weighty subject lighter
- another 'me too' item lively
- a toy more desirable
- a boring subject interesting
- a brand name person-friendly by becoming the spokesperson for the brand (e.g. 'Peter PenPod' could be a talking, walking PenPod

who introduces and demonstrates the product, or 'The Fruities' could be a pop band made up of Scotdale Northside fruit yogurt characters).

Beware of writing an entertaining commercial that just *happens* to sponsor a product rather than an entertaining sales commercial.

Animated commercials should be uncomplicated. The best animated characters have 'human' expressions. Indeed, the more 'human' the qualities, the more charming the character appears.

Take as much care over choosing suitable soundtracks as you do in choosing an animator. Music soundtracks feature the great classics or can be parodies of existing pieces of music. The band The Beatles forbad advertisers to use their lyrics, even if the band did not endorse anything. In 1987 Yoko Ono was prevented from allowing *Revolution* to be used in a sportswear advertisement.

Example of an animated ad, sung to Elvis Presley's 'Hound Dog':

(ANIMATED DOG, DRESSED IN 1950s' SUIT, SINGING TO A CAN OF DOG FOOD)

> You ain't nothing to a hound dog,
> Your meat is just brine.
> You ain't nothing to a hound dog,
> You taste like cheap wine.
> Just give me back my Scotdale
> And I'll be doing fine.

(SPOKEN TO CAMERA – IN ELVIS' VOICE)

> 'You may step on my suedes, but never mess
> with my meal, man!'

I once adapted the original Adams Family cartoon theme tune to promote the animated cartoon series of *The Adams Family*:

Title:   Lurch sings                    Duration:  30 seconds

Notes:  Lurch sings the whole commercial to the Adams Family theme
       tune. Each scene enters screen from top, left, bottom, right,
       and so on, in sequence.

| Video | Audio |
|---|---|
| (Cartoon Channel logo) | They're |
| (Animated explosion reveals action) | |
| Bear looks shocked and jumps out of picture | cooky |
| (2 seconds) | *(SFX – bear in shock)* |
| American presidential statues have a shock | and they're spooky |
| (3 seconds) | *(SFX – crumbling rocks)* |
| All the family dancing | You'll find them on the telly |
| (9 seconds) | So tune in, be there early |
| ID of all the family | for the Adams Family. |
| (2 seconds) | |
| Boy makes boggle eyes | It's on the Cartoon Channel |
| (2 seconds) | |
| | *(SFX 'boing, boing')* |
| Uncle Fester eats a chain | Uncle Fester |
| (1 second) | |
| | *(SFX 'crunch')* |
| Lurch thumping his chest like Tarzan | and me Lurch |
| (2 seconds) | |
| Mr and Mrs Adams and Uncle Fester get groovy with electricity | We'll welcome you to join us |
| (4 seconds) | *(SFX – electricity buzz)* |
| | On the Adams Family. |

| | |
|---|---|
| Rain cloud appears and<br>fills moat around the car<br>(3 seconds) | If you think my voice is weird<br><br>*(SFX – thunder clap)*<br><br>Like a soprano with a beard |
| Grandma cooking up a brew<br>(4 seconds) | It's nothing as bizarre<br>*(SFX – bubbling stew)* |
| Cartoon Channel credits<br>fall from top of screen | As the Adams Family.<br>*(Spoken to himself)*<br>With my musical talent, maybe<br>I should get an Agent.) |

When you write copy for a cartoon character, watch the clock. (Notice how the script for *The Adams Family* showed how long it took for each piece of action to be 'acted out'.) In the case of a 30-second commercial, reduce your word count from 60–70 (for live-action commercials) to 40–50 for cartoon commercials, unless it is sung. This allows the cartoon to animate into life without being shackled by too many words. As with all television and radio commercials, act out your animated sequence to see if it fits within your allocated time slot.

Not all animated commercials feature cartoons. You can consider animation as part of a live commercial to demonstrate the mechanics of a product, enliven a company logo or add emphasis to a sales message. For example:

**A** PERSON POURS SOME **S**COTDALE **N**ORTHSIDE DETERGENT DOWN A KITCHEN SINK AND THE PLUG HOLE ANIMATES INTO A SMILE.

Animation can also be used as a special effect. For example, you could stretch a person's face in awkward directions using part live action and part animation. You could use stop-frame animation to transform an ordinary scene into a Keystone Cop style 'flickered' image. You could fly people on a magic carpet or even have them dance with an animated product.... The possibilities are endless.

One final advantage about animated commercials, especially those which feature cartoon characters, is the fact that sadly a large number of people have reading difficulties due to a number of factors ranging from social, psychological or educational to simply being new to the country. As with newspaper cartoon strips, animated cartoons help to get a message across simply and in an entertaining way.

## The last laugh

Humourous copy in television commercials can help give a fading brand a bit of shine. (Where possible, you should not apply overt humour to new brands as there is a danger that the humour will distract from the sales benefits.) Viewers like to laugh. So if you can make them laugh, hopefully they will pay greater attention to your message. Of course, if your humourous message is too hilarious, its overall effectiveness will be impaired as the viewer will spend too much time laughing at the gag rather than thinking about the product or service! On the other hand, a great joke can distract the viewer's attention from any arguments involved with making a purchase, such as cost.

With so many possible directions it is not surprising that this type of commercial is one of the hardest to write. Even if you do get the gag right, there is only a finite number of times that you can broadcast the same joke.

One of the main difficulties with managing humour for a television commercial or even cinema commercial is that a good joke needs time to make an impact. Most television commercials are 30 seconds in length. Seven of those seconds are taken up with establishing a scene and the end-of-sequence logo branding. A gag with bite calls for:

- a well-structured plot
- an easily accessible set-up
- an interesting character
- a precision-timed delivery
- an unexpected punchline

All in 30 seconds!

Assuming you are convinced that a humourous commercial is the best way to sell a product or service, you still have to consider upon what to base the humour. One of the best ways to look for something funny is to look at yourself. This is very hard as you have to observe your own frailties and shortcomings, then list them, honestly – warts and all.

Use the same technique on friends and family. Hopefully, eventually you will start to see an emerging pattern of similarities. Use the most poignant of those similarities to add dimension to a central character. Creating empathy with a character takes time. There are two ways to address this:

1 Borrow a character from a comedian, comic strip or amusing piece of animation;
2 Build a long-term campaign revolving around the central character.

Give the character a task against which, try as he or she might, it seems that the entire world is ganged-up to foil. However, the problem is solved thanks to a particular product or service. This helps create sympathy with the character who is trying so hard to do something.

| VIDEO | AUDIO |
|---|---|
| Scotdale Northside shop assistant 'builds' a traditional pyramid of tins of Scotdale Northside baked beans, as an end-of-aisle sales promotion device. She places the last tin on top of the pyramid. The pyramid collapses. She replaces the tin. The pyramid collapses. She replaces the tin. | *(Male Voice Over – MVO)* 'No-one' |
| The pyramid collapses. She replaces the tin. The pyramid collapses. Graphic – animated ink stamp thuds on to screen. It reads: | 'But no-one can stop our prices from falling. Scotdale Northside price savers. Good food has never been at better value.' |

> Scotdale Northside
> Baked beans
> just 10p a tin.

You could consider making your character talk to inanimate objects or treat awkward objects (such as something incredibly large like a grand piano, or tiny like a microchip, or absurd like a false leg) as if they were alive. You could place your character and product or service in unfamiliar surroundings: a different country, different time, different place, different planet. You could mingle new technology with traditional ideas. You could use 'upside-down' logic – *Instead of hitting a nail into the wall, hit the wall into the nail*. You could draw illogical conclusions from logical summations, and so on.

Consider introducing your character with peculiar afflictions, like a nervous twitch or a compulsion to 'squawk like a parrot' – the stranger the better. Consider exposing an unspoken social neurosis or depression. (However, keep in mind that your viewer may suffer from such an illness.)

Don't just settle for small problems – give your character vast problems. Exaggerate the predicament: exaggerate a solution by finding the answer using the most convoluted of routes. If things have to go wrong, make then go disastrously wrong – allowing the product or service to act as the catalyst that saves the day.

Above all, remember that its okay to see the funny side of life as long as that image does not insult the integrity of a product or service nor the viewer's instinctive perception of what is politically, socially and morally acceptable.

| VIDEO | AUDIO |
|---|---|
| Sombre, moodily lit room. In the centre is a psychiatrist. She is talking to a patient (whom we can't see). The doctor sits on the edge of her large leather chair, | *(Psychiatrist speaks)* It's down to you. |

| | |
|---|---|
| looking concerned – obviously very involved with her patient's case. | |
| Close-up of the psychiatrist trying to reason with the patient. | Things appear dark now. It needn't always be that way. |
| The psychiatrist stands up and walks to the other side of the room. | You *really* have to want to change. |
| | *(Light bulb speaks)* |
| Close-up of the patient who turns out to be an animated branded light bulb. | OK already. Point me to the fitting and screw me in. |
| Titles appear on the screen – logo is a light bulb that a hand 'switches on' as the switch clicks so the words 'Have you seen the light?' appear. | *(Male Voice Over)* Brillo Lights Have you seen the light? |

## TV you read

Once you have captured a viewer's interest, you need to retain it. One way of driving a message home is to turn a television commercial into a graphic bulletin board. Instead of relying purely on a powerful image accompanied by memorable music and convincing dialogue, why not go all the way and add graphically designed titles that reinforce key benefits?

So a PenPod TV commercial could show a beautiful actress in a romantic setting, writing with a PenPod. At the same time the dialogue (or voice over) could be saying:

THE STYLISH WAY TO WRITE – RIGHT FROM THE HEART.

and the superimposed titles could animate out of the apparent love letter, varying in shape and length, reading:

# Write

...*from the heart.*

Through forcing the viewer to read text rather than just hear and watch images you are able to reinforce a key statement.

## *TV jingles*

Contrary to popular belief, jingles are not meant to 'sing out' the end of a commercial. If that was their sole purpose, they would be self-defeating. Every jingle, no matter how melodious, would serve only as a sign to the viewer that it is time to lose interest in the commercial. All jingles, including radio jingles, provides instant recognition of a brand. It is a musical *aide mémoire* which combines the evocative pull of a musical score with the selling clout of a persuasive piece of copy. The craft of jingle composition may sound quite easy and even trivial. However, catchy jingles like catchy headlines are not that easy to write. A jingle has to reinforce a product or brand name.

PENPOD, PENPOD

It has to inform, add personality as well as amuse.

I'VE NEVER HAD A PENFRIEND LIKE A PENPOD.

It has to make sense while rhyming.

> **IT'S THE ONLY ONE I'LL EVER NEED – A WRITTEN GUARANTEE**

It has to summarise everything in one simple statement.

> **GET THE MESSAGE ACROSS, PICK UP A PENPOD.**

A popular product category to use jingles is the toy industry. Jingles can have an important role in children's play time. Each time a game is played, the child could think of the jingle associated with the toy character involved in the game. Even everyday tasks can be turned into play. Every time 'mum' or 'dad pours out the breakfast cereal, so the child could recall a character on a television commercial who uses the jingle, especially if there is a free model of the character inside the box.

Finally, a jingle should be enduring. In the United Kingdom, the 'ovalteenies' jingle was still going strong in the late 1980s – some 50 years after first being broadcast. The oldest reputed US jingle, for a cereal called 'Wheeties', still in use in the 1990s was first broadcast in the 1920s.

## *Get the picture? – Story boards and animatics*

Standard 35 mm or 16 mm film runs through a projector at 1440 frames per minute. A story board, which is a series of illustrated 'frames', helps capture the essence of the action shown in a piece of film. It is a vital tool to assist commercial directors with creative aspects such as lighting, mood, camera angle and general character positioning. It can show you or your client how the commercial will appear on the screen. However, there is a problem with story boards. There are many excellent artists who can show copywriters and art directors portfolios of different styles. Yet unlike film, a story board can capture only the basic creative essence of a commercial, including shot continuity and the general flow of action. In order to represent the entire (30 seconds) production accurately, it would have to feature 720 separately illustrated frames! Another version of a story board is called an 'animatic.' This is a crude animation of the commercial, sometimes used for research purposes.

Ask yourself, 'Do I really need an expensive animatic or story board? If so, at what stage of the creative process?' I recommend that you save your story board until you have settled for a typed television script. If you have to sell the commercial further, act it out. Read the script aloud, get colleagues to read parts. Titillate your audience. If you are selling the idea to a client, give the client credit that he or she has an imagination – your job is to stimulate it.

Writing television commercials requires you to 'play' the commercial in your mind before committing it to paper. If you can capture what you see in your mind on paper, then you should be able to develop what's on the paper through discussion.

Once you have arrived at an agreed script, then think about story boards, especially if you are going to subcontract the actual production to a producer and director. Rather than dictate what you want, which restricts creativity, a story board helps provide you with peace of mind. What you originally played in your mind can be better understood by the person who has to put the image on the final version.

## *Writing a script*

As for script layout, please refer to the scripts that I have included in this chapter. Don't worry too much about technical jargon. If you like to use 'buzz words' the following list should be enough to ensure that in terms of mechanics, your final 'picture' is seen and understood by everyone. If you want to describe a more complicated camera angle or technical aspect, do so in words, but never forget a director should be accredited with the imagination to take your words and turn them into a moving experience.

### Buzz words

**ad lib**   spontaneous dialogue – not scripted (ideal for on-the-street interviews)

**animate**   to arrange an inanimate object or graphic in a way that, when seen as part of a finished film, gives the impression of movement

**CU**  close-up
**cut**  change camera angle or scene
**dissolve**  fade out of one picture or scene into another
**eyeline**  the position of a subject's eyes on the screen
**fade in**  brighten the illumination of a scene (usually at the start of the scene)
**fade out**  darken the illumination on scene (usually at the end of a scene)
**freeze**  stop the action by 'freezing' it in time
**FVO**  Female Voice Over
**lead-in**  initial words spoken by the VO at the start of the action
**MCU**  Medium Close-Up shot – the person is seen from the chest upwards
**MS**  Medium Shot in which a person on screen is seen from just below the waist upwards
**MVO**  Male Voice Over
**SFX**  Sound Effects
**super**  superimpose one action or scene on top of another
**track shot**  horizontal camera movement which zooms in or follows something
**VO**  Voice Over
**wipe**  change of scene from 'A' to 'B' using a graphic device (e.g. scene 'B' 'wipes' diagonally across scene 'A')
**zoom in/out**  increase/decrease magnification of a subject

If you are going to hand over your script to a director eventually, then you have two possible ways to write it:

1 If you are totally confident in a director's abilities, just write the dialogue and describe the action;

2 If you want to have greater control over the actual interpretation, also include the camera angles.

*Pros*
1 The director has the chance to enhance a production by giving the commercial an 'angle' that you may not have considered;
2 You know what you put down on paper will end up in 'the can'.

*Cons*
1 Are you seriously going to leave your 'baby' in another person's hands?
2 How would you like to have *your* creativity shackled and, more importantly, how do you think that will affect the final results?

# —— Direct response television ——

One of the most exciting growth areas of television copywriting has been in direct response. Direct-response television commercials, like all direct-response advertising, is cost quantifiable (how many people replied).

During the mid-1990s, at least a quarter of television commercials shown in the United Kingdom featured some sort of response mechanism (see Figure 11.3). In the United States, depending upon the time of day, up to 85 per cent of all television commercials featured some kind of response mechanism. The American magazine *Teledirect* suggests that the best time to air a DRTV commercial in the United States is after 10.00 p.m. According to research carried out by British Telecom and Channel Four, the best time for DRTV commercials in the United Kingdom is 12.00 a.m. to 2.00 p.m.

**Figure 11.3** UK television carrying a response device

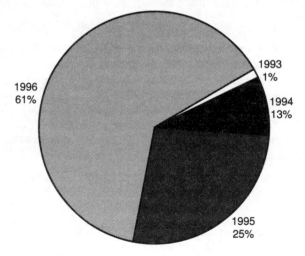

Source: Mediacom Direct

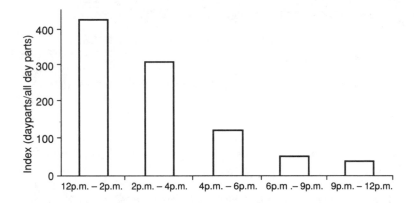

In the United Kingdom, original Direct Response TV (DRTV commercials lasted about two minutes. The copy style was usually led by demonstration techniques with a great deal of emphasis given to the response details. However, broader-stream advertisers who preferred the repeated 'short sharp' 30-second commercials persuaded the TV networks to put a stop to the mini-epics, as all the best 'prime time' commercial spots were being lost.

Financial organisations are leaders in DRTV. Commercials can be for anything from life assurance to savings plans, car insurance and home insurance. The copy style of such commercials still tends to rely on the *here's what it does and here's how you respond* approach. Continuous graphics showing telephone numbers are vital to reinforce the response mechanism. You will recall the technique discussed on page 65 where you learnt about the importance of repeating the product name several times during an advertisement. In DRTV, the same applies to the response device. 'Weave' the telephone number into the presenter's dialogue. By all means use clever techniques like animated talking telephones or music to give the response device even greater impact. As long as the technique doesn't distract from a clearly understood explanation of why the product or service is beneficial and how to get in touch. For example:

MAKE A NOTE OF THIS NUMBER **0800 123 456**.
(Graphic shows the number.)

IT CONNECTS YOU TO THE CHEAPEST, YET BEST-COVER POLICY
MONEY CAN BUT.

BOB IS 21

HIS REGULAR MOTOR INSURANCE COMPANY QUOTED HIM OVER
**£1000** FOR HIS POLICY.

JUST ONE CALL TO CUT PRICE INSURANCE ON **0800 123 456**
COULD HAVE SAVED HIM **£500**.

THAT'S RIGHT. JUST ONE CALL TO **0800 123 456** COULD HAVE
CUT HIS PREMIUM IN HALF!

The creative challenge in writing a DRTV commercial is to 'wake up' the viewer to take some kind of action. A busy, all-singing and dancing commercial may lose its single thought direction. Also if every DRTV commercial featured a presenter shouting or even singing a telephone number, the viewer would switch off the 'noise'. A good DRTV commercial has to:

- demonstrate
- stimulate
- activate

This is achieved by combining a convincing message in a credible not overtly pressurised setting. Target a specific audience and urge them to call a response number.

On 30 September 1995 at 9 p.m. (GMT) the home shopping channel QVC became the first such channel to broadcast live simultaneously in the United States and the United Kingdom. It featured American comedian Joan Rivers selling her classic collection of jewellery.

DRTV also works particularly well for charities. According to the Target Group Index (TGI) during 1994, in a survey of response of television promotions and appeals over a 12-month period, charity was the second most popular sector for receiving a response – 8.7 per cent response.

From a copy targeting appeal, it is interesting to note that in a study undertaken during 1994–5, the British Henley Centre, Media Futures, claimed that the best people to aim a charity DRTV commercial at were females, aged 16–24 in the AB socio-economic group. Like all charity advertising, in addition to giving a great deal of emphasis to the response device, the commercial should stimulate a human response to a human need by explaining how to help and show the donation contributing to make someone's life more fulfilling.

## Now here's the bill

There's no denying it: television can be costly. According to the Guinness Book of Records, the highest television advertising rate charged by a commercial broadcaster was $800 000 per 30 seconds for NBC network prime-time during the broadcast of Super Bowl XXV on 27 January 1991. Thankfully, not all television rates are even close to that figure. In June 1995 you were able to purchase 30 seconds in the London region from just £500. The down side was that the commercial would be aired at the dead of night. Yet, the price wasn't bad considering that in the same week, a black-and-white, quarter-page advertisement in a London circulation evening newspaper cost just under £3000.

Television commercial costs are based on rating, time, demographics and position. A rating is another way of saying 'percentage of chosen type of audience'. So if you want to attract (or 'reach') a proportion of housewives in South East England aged 35 and over in a socio-economic A1 grouping, you would want a rating of perhaps 90. (Please refer to the categorisation on page 58.)

Timing depends on the time of day that a commercial is shown. Daytime television or very late night/early morning television is generally cheaper than prime-time television when most viewers watch.

Then you have to consider the popularity of a programme and, more specifically, how popular a programme is for the type of person that you wish to reach. Finally, you have to consider the position within a commercial break that your commercial appears: first during the first break? last during the middle break? and so on.

Returning to the figures for June 1995, I discovered that if I wanted to purchase airtime on a London commercial television station during the broadcast of the final quarter of the Rugby World Cup final, if the home team England had not been defected by the mighty New Zealand All Blacks, I could have expected to pay around £75 000 to £100 000 for 30 seconds. However, if another advertiser offered to bid even more, they would have been given the 'spot'.

It is usually wise to purchase your television time through a television airtime media broker who has a large portfolio of clients. If you are a particularly effective negotiator as well as copywriter and have a highly marketable product to advertise, you could still get a very reasonable commercial rate. However, I would advise you against even attempting to negotiate. It is far shrewder to direct your creative skills to raising viewers' interest by entertaining and compelling informative copy rather than trying to negotiate a higher viewing 'rate' at a lower budget cost.

Before you worry about the cost of broadcasting your masterpiece, you have to consider the cost of producing it. Remember, never let razzmatazz get in the way of a simple, single-minded idea. A straightforward, one-scene, one camera angle and one actor may be just as powerful as an all-singing, all-dancing Hollywood-style production. (Why not substitute the dancers for a couple of pairs of hands, with little skirts tied around the fists and a face drawn on the back of each hand?)

If the creative treatment matches the style of product and the tastes of a market sector, anything goes. (Incidentally, the most expensive television commercials ever produced were reputed to be those made in 1988 by Pepsi Cola who paid Michael Jackson £7 million to appear in four commercials.)

Budget allowing, my suggestion is, recruit an independent producer who can negotiate on your behalf and 'marry' you with an appropriate commercial director – often easier said than done. (He or she will want to make the commercial one way, while you...)

# ——— The future of television ———

Digital television brings crisper images, sharper sound and, from a marketing point of view, even broader access. Digital communications will feature even greater use of direct response television. One swipe of a credit card in a slot at the top of the television is all it will take to pay for an advertised product or service. Even in the mid-1990s indications were strong that the start of new millennium held a promise for greater prevalence of pay-TV (you pay for what you watch).

Since the 1990s there has been continued growth of shopping channels – where you can shop from home using the telephone to pay via a credit card. Satellite television channels offer cost effective production and broadcast facilities for airing a commercial with a response device across country borders. As technology becomes more sophisticated it will become more accessible. A production featuring animated computer graphics could in the 1980s cost close to the equivalent of £80 000. In the 1990s, you could produce a similar – even better – commercial reflecting quality, such as used in the 1996 software launch of Ultra Mario Brothers 64, for less than half of the cost. In the future, it will be even cheaper. This is good news for independent copywriters with a limited budget for huge productions.

Some argue that the growth of shopping on television will eventually be felt by retailers on the High Street. Personally, I believe that shopping by television will be the best thing that could ever happen for the retail sector and, more relevant, the creative team who help retailers sell products and services. Shops may join forces to create their own multi-media retail approach. Television channels will be broadcast in the shops as well as at home. So the buyer/viewer can have the option of handling the goods as well as seeing them demonstrated on the screen. Brands will be reinforced strategically by programmes that appeal to specific audiences. During 1995, the first-ever television channel on British buses was introduced. It featured a three-hour video tape, including advertisements. The tape was shown en route.

The concept of entertainment sales channels will spread across television to the INTERNET and beyond. Even airlines will feature pay-as you-watch-as-you-fly television where you watch a television commercial for a duty-free product and purchase it with the swipe of credit card during your flight. Copywriting will be a premium commodity.

In the twenty-first century, depending on the demand for each channel, advertising rates will either be conversely high or low. The media as a whole will become more integrated – multimedia. Newspapers will be viewpapers. The television will be the eye on the universe where the world of entertainment and information merge into one gigantic galaxy of endless creative communication possibilities. The centre of the universe will be as near as your monitor.

In terms of copywriting, it is a question of 'watch this space'. Unless you close your eyes and open your mind to an even more vivid picture ...

## *TV commercial advertising quick tips*

- Commercials have to entertain as well as inform.
- Demonstration commercials work well with extreme examples.
- Special effects should enhance rather than distract from a single thought message.
- People like people 'slice-of-life' television.
- 'Sexy' commercials can make viewers turn guilt into desire.
- A celebrity may be a star in his or her own right, their appearance is that of a guest – the product or service plays the lead.
- Animation can be cute. It must be relevant.
- Cartoons 'speak' clearer if you make them say less.
- Never laugh at a product or service. Laugh with it.
- Television graphics of copy make messages more memorable.
- Television jingles should say 'buy me' rather than signify the end of a commercial.
- Story boards can capture only the essence of a commercial. Not the soul.
- DRTV sells off the screen as you would sell off the page; make sure you can handle the response.
- DRTV repeatedly informs the viewer how to respond.

## *Over to you*

1 The brand new Pastiche 200 series car has a sunroof that when open in the rain disperses rain water away from the car so that

driver and passengers always remain dry – whatever the weather. Write three television commercial treatments in script or story board formats which advertise this useful feature.

**2** Write a 20 second television commercial that encourages motorists to be extra nice to traffic wardens during a special 'Hug a warden' week.

**3** Write a 60-second dialogue between two housewives discussing a new kind of washing powder that helps to iron-out creases.
Now, keeping all the essential parts of the dialogue, cut the script down to:

**a)** 30 seconds

**b)** 20 seconds

**c)** 10 seconds

**4** Adapt a top-ten single lyric to sell a PenPod.

**5** Without changing any lyrics, choose two well-known songs that could be used to convey the right atmosphere and message for a PenPod TV commercial. In no more than 50 words each, describe the action of the two commercials.

**6** List six different ways to write:
CALL NOW ON 0800 123 123

**7** Video tape two television commercials, then rewrite the commercials, conveying the same messages without dialogue, just vision.

**8** List eight different way to write:
NOT AVAILABLE IN THE SHOPS

# 12
## LISTEN TO THIS!

Unquestionably, television broadens the mind. Radio, on the other hand, can really stretch the imagination. Another difference between television and radio is that you can listen to the radio just about anywhere, while television demands that you are visually as well audibly 'connected'.

## —— Creative advantages of radio ——

Because it is portable and intrusive, one of the creative advantages of using radio is that the medium is so accessible. People listen to radio everywhere. A 1994 survey by Radio Days found that more than 72 per cent of listeners listen in the kitchen, while over 27 per cent of listeners listen in the bathroom (rising to 43 per cent among 15–24 year olds). Radio Joint Audience Research Limited (RAJAR – jointly owned by the BBC and Association of Independent Radio Companies) found that 17 per cent of commercial radio listeners who listen in the car between 9 a.m. and 12 noon are part-time or non-working women. Radio Days also found that 25 per cent of female shoppers say that they are likely to be listening to the radio when planning what food to buy. RAJAR figures show that the under 24 age group have the largest share of total listening hours of commercial radio (see Figure 12.1).

So a good radio commercial is aimed at ordinary people doing ordinary things like eating – a good time to target a snack food – or shaving – a good time to target a shaving product.... your audience is in situ. As long as your copy is realistic, accessible and believable you can be certain that when your copy 'talks', your audience will hear.

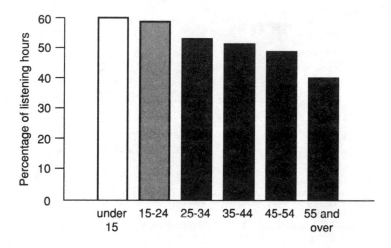

**Figure 12.1** Share of listening hours by age group
(Source: Wireless Wisdom: Radio Advertising Bureau RAJAR Q 294)
The RAB acts as the central marketing department for commercial radio as an advertising medium in the UK.

Academic research has shown that: '[Radio] as a secondary medium accompanying its users while they are engaged in primary activities, can infiltrate their view of the world in a way which is all the more powerful for being half-conscious.' (*Understanding Radio*, Andrew Crisell, 1986 Methuen.) According to Capital Radio, in the United Kingdom, one third of households have five or more radios in their homes. Commercial radio has 28.6 million listeners (61 per cent of the adult population) every day, according to independent broadcasters' statistics.

During 1995, research carried out by CIA Sensor asked: 'If you were marooned on a desert island which ONE of these things would you have with you?'

- A radio which works?
- A subscription to your favourite magazine?
- A subscription to your favourite national newspaper?
- A television which works?

The respondents' answers are summarised in Figure 12.2.

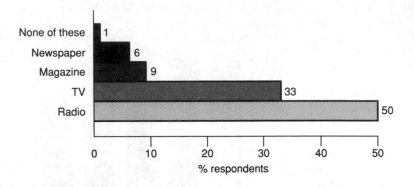

**Figure 12.2** 'If you were marooned on a desert island which ONE of these things would you have with you?'
Source: Telephone survey of 1000 adults conducted in 1994 by Audience Selection.

Radio can bring a listener closer to a product or service:

> *MVO (Male Voice Over)*
>
> The nib on this PenPod is so smooth that the ink (whooooah!) slides down and through it effortlessly.
>
> *(SFX – Sound Effects – MVO brushes himself down)*
>
> so giving a smoother, more professional finish to everything you write.

When writing a radio commercial don't 'write' for the listener. Use your copy to 'paint' evocative visual images, not just interesting sounds. There is absolutely nothing that the eye can see that the mind can't 'see' even clearer. You have a powerful arsenal of creative weaponry at your disposal to hammer home a picture. These weapons include: choice of Voice Overs – young, old, male, female, rich, poor, indifferent, professional, zany, serious, happy, sad... and so on; sound effects (SFX) – good SFX can add humour, drama and, above all, 'show' a minute yet essential detail that builds tension and delivers credence to your commercial.

Would you like to 'show' the listener a shopper choosing something from a Scotdale Northside store?

*FVO – Female Voice Over (Young mum type – thinking to herself)*

*SFX – Busy Scotdale Northside store*

Hmmm. Dave wanted something special for dinner tonight . . . Fisherman's Pie only £1.50. Not bad.

*SFX – Places pie in the trolley*

Hmm. Something to wash it down? Ah, this looks like the Job – Scotdale Northside's own-brand Muscatel, just £1.99 a bottle. That should do nicely.

As for deserts. . . *(giggles to herself)* Well, I don't think that even Scotdale Northside can take off what I have in mind this evening!

*MVO*

Scotdale Northside. Good food, terrific value.

Or, you can 'show' the listener the shopper at home.

*SFX – busy meal time at home – TV in background – general household pandemonium)*

*(Very young son)*

Mum! Mum! What's for dinner?

*(Husband)*

Hello luv.

*(Very young son)*

Mum! Mum! Sue won't let me play with the football.

*(Young teenage daughter)*

Hi Mum, any chance of getting this blouse done for the disco tonight?

*(MVO – middle-aged, warm, friendly)*

At Scotdale Northside we appreciate that busy mums lead busy lives.

*(Mum)*

The answer is, 'Wait and see', 'Good day at the office?' 'How many times are you going to wear that thing?'

*(MVO)*

So we've created the healthy meal-maker range.

Each tasty meal is nutritional, balanced with only the freshest of ingredients. Just pop a meal-maker in the microwave and within minutes you can serve up a little masterpiece.

*(Teenage son)*

Not bad.

*(Dad)*

Mmm . . .

*(Daughter)*

Maybe the diet should start tomorrow.

*(Dad)*

Watch it you two.

*(Friendly MVO)*

Meal-makers for Scotdale Northside. Perfect meals in minutes.

## Turn up the creative volume

Radio has often been considered a very poor and distant relation to television. Personally, I think that, while direct response is the most dynamic way to measure a creative campaign as well as the most sustainable way to nurture client relationships, radio is one of the most exciting forms of pure copywriting.

But does advertising on radio work? One piece of research carried out by Saatchi and Saatchi proves that it does. The agency invited more than 300 housewives to test a new ironing product. While they were ironing, the agency made sure that a radio was being played in the background, to make the atmosphere easy-going. In fact, the real purpose of the exercise wasn't to test the iron but the power of radio. The housewives were able to recall a specific radio commercial that was played during a music programme, right down to the name of the brand and details of what was said about it. Significantly, creative treatment played a major role in recall.

As I have explained, radio is intimate. Listeners are loyal and compared to many other media, targeting is incredibly sharp. Commercial radio stared in the United Kingdom in 1973. At first there were only three radio stations – Capital and LBC in London and Clyde in Scotland. Hardly a year, sometimes a month, goes by without another specialist radio station entering the airways. You can target anyone from a jazz enthusiast to a news hound. And the more stations there are, the greater the choice for the listener.

---

One of the earliest experiments in commercial radio was broadcast in 1925 when Selfridges sponsored a fashion talk from the Eiffel Tower in Paris. The London Broadcasting Company (LBC) transmitted the first radio commercial in the United Kingdom. It was a 60-second spot at 6:08 a.m. on 8 October 1973 for Bird's Eye Fish Fingers. The first radio commercial in the world lasted 10 minutes. It was transmitted in 1922 by New York station WEAF, and advertised apartment space.

---

As you have seen in the commercial for Scotdale Northside meal-makers, radio is about the only medium that allows you to describe a thought as well as an action. This makes it ideal for the kind of commercial that can give the impression of delving deep into a narrator's psyche. Here's another example for PenPod:

*(MVO – grumpy, slightly zany)*

What kind of a name is PenPod? Pen, pod. I can see it now. Hot summer's afternoon, big farm. Lots of strawberries. Lots of girls picking the fruit.

*SFX –summer day in the background)*

Girls. She's nice. 'Hello . . . (Hmm)

. . .How's it going? she asks. "Oh fine," I reply. 'Lovely day for it. Look I've picked hundreds and hundreds of ripe pens off the pod.' 'That looks tasty,' she replies.

Then one thing leads to another. I take her name. She asks for my number. . . . Ah yes. Pen Pod. Fruity if you ask me.

*(MVO 2)*

Get it off your mind. Get it down on paper with PenPod.

## Delivering the message

It's not good enough to ensure that your radio commercial is heard. Your audience has to listen to it. Radio is ideal for conveying otherwise complex information. Just tune into a 'talk radio' show – there is news, weather, traffic updates, guests talking about different subjects.... Like all messages, as long as your creativity is single-minded, radio will deliver direct to the consumer's mind. As with television, it is vital that you use your first few seconds of a commercial to attract the listener's attention. Address your target audience. Make your commercial lead into or out of a scheduled announcement.

For example, following a weather forecast:

> (SFX – hot summer's day)
>
> (FVO)
>
> *Weather like this is something to write home about. Here's your forecast from PenPod.*

During a Top Forty pop music chart show:

> (Male rapper)
>
> Yo! Listen up. You can get a pack of 12 Colas from Scotdale Northside at a price that's as cool as it is refreshing.
>
> (SFX – opens a can of Cola and drinks)
>
> Ah. (wipes his lips) Who said you can't be tops if you're not number one?

Always consider link sentences:

> WANT TO KNOW MORE? LISTEN TO THIS. . .
>
> BUT THAT'S NOT ALL . . .

A good radio commercial is like a good old-fashioned chit-chat between friends. One piece of news or gossip naturally follows another. As radio is so personal, people draw individual conclusions about what you say. They judge your message very subjectively, rather than allow others to 'interfere' with the one-on-one radio listening experience.

## *Attention grabbing devices*

Proven creative listener grabbing devices include music, SFX and scripts that are read quickly. It has been suggested that by electronically compressing a radio commercial recording, you can speed up the commercial by as much as 15 per cent without having a detrimental effect on its quality. That means you could literally squeeze 38 seconds worth of scripting into 30 seconds. In the United States, tests have shown that this creative technique delivers up to a 40 per cent improvements of aided recall over normally read commercials.

Another attention grabbing technique is to record the commercial at slightly higher volumes than normally required. This idea is also commonly used in television commercials.

Radio commercials are considerably cheaper to produce than television commercials. This means that longer-length commercials are more affordable. A normally spoken radio commercial allows for about 70 words in 30 seconds. One minute gives you about 150 words. However, depending on the 'mood' of the commercial, you could easily double those figures (for a quickly spoken, *'hurry, hurry, hurry...'* type of delivery or half that figure (for a slow, seductive commercial that makes the listener savour every single moment). I once heard that the only accurate way to time a commercial is to measure the script in syllables: up to five equals one second. Personally, I believe that the only way to time a radio commercial accurately is to buy a stop-watch!

Another radio attention grabber is the question teaser:

WHERE CAN YOU BUY OVER THREE HOURS OF SOUL MUSIC FOR JUST £19.99?

ARE YOU FED UP TO YOUR KNUCKLES WITH DETERGENTS THAT TREAT YOUR HANDS LIKE WIRE BRUSHES?

## Two varieties, one flavour

Commercial radio is usually broadcast on either the AM or FM frequency. Most people listen on FM stereo. However, many stations don't offer a choice. So your ideal target audience can listen only on AM (mono). Therefore, when producing a radio commercial by all means listen to the results in the studio on an impressive sound system but also insist on hearing how it will sound on a small radio. Developed by Seattle-based Progressive Networks, FM is also available via the INTERNET.

## Music

Please refer to the section in Chapter 11 dealing specifically with jingles (page 232). If you do chose to use music – and why not, most radio stations are built on music – make sure that you have permission to use a track. It's no good featuring the Beatles' song 'Paperback Writer' for a PenPod commercial if you can't obtain the music rights. You may decide to parody a track. Instead of 'paperback writer', you could consider the words 'PenPod writer'.

Whenever you write a musical lyric, make sure the words and sentences are short. Radio relies completely on sound. A simple sentence that can be understood first time is always preferable to a complicated, longer description.

Once you secure the rights for a piece of music, you have to budget for the airplay royalties. A great idea could end up costing a great deal. There are companies who will take publicly available music (known as public domain music) and edit it into useable ten or five-second segments (known as pre-recorded needle-drop music). You can also purchase existing music in commercial 'chunks' from specialised commercial music libraries.

There are two schools of thought about music parodies:

*Pros*
● Typically teenagers and some housewives listen to radio music so they will appreciate musical commercials;
● You can vary lyrics and even styles;
● You can vary singers;
● Music can evoke a time and mood.

*Cons*
- What is 'in' today is 'out' tomorrow;
- Music parodies are a poor excuse for an unoriginal creative idea;
- The royalty costs may have a deeper impact than the campaign;

## Involve your listeners

As with television, ensure that your creative idea is single minded. Don't let complicated production enhancements get in the way of an easy-to-grasp message. Ensure that your brand name is repeated throughout the commercial and, of course, tell listeners how to get hold of the product or service: either by phone, or in person.

If you want to discuss a special offer, as with direct mail, consider setting a time limit to the offer.

> BY THIS FRIDAY AT 5 P.M., WE'RE CLOSING THE OFFER FOR GOOD.

(Notice the 5 p.m. rather than simply, Friday. This adds even greater urgency and believability. As with television, its the small details that help build a bigger picture.)

You can also consider celebrity endorsements – especially radio presenters. This is quite prevalent in the United States where presenters discuss products or services during the course of a programme. To date such 'disguised' endorsements are not allowed in the United Kingdom. However, you can still use the presenter during an obvious commercial break. As with all forms of dialogue copy, make sure that your copy sounds 'real' and as the presenter would normally speak.

One way around the UK radio regulations is to make your commercial part of a broader promotional package. This could be as part of a scheduled programme competition to win a major prize. Such competitions are always in demand by breakfast DJs who are looking for new ways to stimulate their early-morning listeners' 'get up and go' without encouraging then to 'stand-up and leave'.

One of radio's greatest strengths is that it encourages listeners to participate in activities – 'Listen to this, then ring this number.' So any promotion featuring interactive ideas, like a vote-line or quiz, music dedication, and so on, is going to increase interest and response. Of local radio listeners 27 per cent have physically interacted with the station in some way – phoned in, had a dedication read out, entered a competition, attended a road show... (Radio Days, 1994.)

Scotdale Northside could run such a promotion. For example, the breakfast DJ could give away £100 worth of shopping vouchers every day for a week, as part of the Scotdale Northside centenary celebrations. This could be reinforced with a Scotdale Northside commercial.

# Radio production

Some of the greatest fun you can have as a copywriter is at a radio commercial production suite. Unlike with television it is usual for copywriters to direct as well as write an entire production. Just as in television, you give the director the credit that he or she has the imagination to enhance your commercial, so in radio you should credit the actors and sound engineers with the ability and talent to take an idea and make it sound even sweeter to the ear.

I am always impressed with the versatility of radio Voice Overs. One good actor can deliver in excess of seven distinctive voices – so saving you time and money employing lots of actors for one script. Once, I asked an actor to deliver a line 12 different ways. He obliged – brilliantly performing the line, 'What, are you joking? I've *really* won a hundred thousand pounds!' in a variety of accents. (Try the line yourself!)

Make sure you have enough scripts for everyone. Tell the actors everything about the product. Who's going to buy it. Why they would want to buy it. What you had in mind when you wrote the commercial. A good actor needs a sound brief to make words work. Give it, even down to helping them give emphasis to key words in the script: 'What, are you joking? *I've* really won a hundred thousand pounds!'; 'What, are you joking? I've really *won* a hundred thousand pounds!'

It is well accepted that radio commercials can be produced quickly. This is useful if you want to make an important 'overnight' announcement or capitalise on a latest news story. However, whenever possible, plan your commercial with enough time to get the best Voice Overs and research the most relevant creative enhancements such as music, jingles, sound effects, and so on.

If a commercial lasts 30 seconds, you should allow for a minimum of two hours in a studio: half an hour for recording and the rest for production. Ideally, book three hours. If the commercial is complicated or requires more than three actors, you may need to increase this time to even longer.

## *Radio commercials quick tips*

- Write a 'mind picture', not a sound track.
- Concentrate on a single thought.
- Target your audience.
- Allow your copy to 'talk' one to one.
- Consider capitalising on a radio spot (e.g. the weather, a type of programme, and so on).
- Consider writing two radio commercials for one commercial break – one that leads into the break and one that leads out.
- Consider making your advertisement part of a broader promotion such as an on-air competition.
- SFX build interest and reinforces believability.
- Don't overwrite a commercial. If you have to describe a detail, let SFX provide it.
- Radio is cost-effective to produce. Consider producing two versions of a commercial – this avoids people getting bored with hearing the same commercial and can be used as a form of creative testing.
- If you need longer than 30 seconds to convey a message, use longer (and vice versa).
- Choose your VO to reflect your product and its audience.
- Involve your audience.
- Repeat the product name throughout the commercial.
- Radio is intimate – speak directly to your listener, in the bath, in the garden, in the car, at work...
- Write as people speak.
- Capitalise on the trust and faith which people attach to radio.
- Use music prudently and watch costs.
- Voice Over actors can be incredibly versatile.
- Don't be fooled into allowing insufficient time for high production values.
- Pre-plan all jingles and music.
- Unlike TV, listeners 'zone in' to radio programmes rather than 'zap' past commercials.

- As working patterns change and more people work at home and are kept company by the radio, so the medium will become ever more important. Think about that when planning for target markets.
- Radio is like direct mail that you 'post' a message in someone's ear and it gets delivered to their mind. Target your copy and you'll be on the right wavelength.

## *Over to you*

1 Write a 30-second radio commercial advertising the power of radio.
2 Adapt a well-known lyric from the Top 30 to sell a packet of Scotdale Northside washing-up liquid.
3 Look around your room and match six products to six possible locations where people could listen to the radio.
4 Write a five-second sponsored introduction from Scotdale Northside restaurant Directions to a programme about food.
5 Write the titles of three popular songs that could be used to promote this book.
6 Write a 30-second commercial aimed at business people, for this book.

# 13

# POSTERS

Keep the message simple. That's probably the best advice you can have for outdoor poster sites. Unless a poster appears in an area where people are virtually forced to stare at it (e.g. a railway station platform), there is precious little time to get a message across. Instead, you should be thinking about producing a fast-to-read, easy-to-grasp, piece of creativity that relies on blanket-wide exposure rather than intimate targeting. That can be harder than you think. Brevity can lead to banality. Writing four words, instead of a long sentence that says the same thing is incredibly difficult. Winston Churchill said that he would spend ten times longer on writing a few well-chosen words than preparing a lengthy speech.

Typically, posters are seen primarily by drivers in traffic. As roads become more and more congested, so the poster audience becomes greater and, being stuck in traffic, people have longer to read advertising messages. Which leads to another benefit of posters: apart from informing, posters can turn a drab tarmac environment into a colourful and entertaining landscape.

Poster copy, including that for smaller instore posters which are usually A2 size, needs to be blatantly obvious. There's no point in writing something lengthy (unless in situations, like railway stations and bus stops, where the reader has nothing else to do than read your message.) In the case of outdoor posters, one good reason for this is that, due to their physical size and positioning most posters are designed to be read from distances in excess of 18 m. If a motorist is approaching a poster 75 m away while driving at 40 mph, he or she will have less than 4 seconds to 'take-in' its message safely.

Graphics can be lavish as long as they are not overcomplicated. Also there is a safety argument for not over distracting a driver's attention. For example, a poster featuring a naked woman hitching a ride with the headline 'Don't watch me, watch the road!' may indeed be an interesting way to promote driving safety, but may have the reverse effect of what it is trying to communicate!

## ───── Three signs to watch for ─────

A poster, if it is to be effective, should have:

1 an intriguing headline
2 a dynamic, complimentary graphic
3 strong company branding using logos

Poster copy is too short to sell a detailed commercial message. As roadside commercial signs, posters can remind people about a larger campaign on television, in the press or on radio (unless the product in question is banned from other media – as is the case in the United Kingdom for most tobacco advertising). Often poster copy needs to be a shortened adaptation of a television, radio or press advertisement, creatively different yet part of a single-minded campaign. Posters can also be used as a sole medium to convey a message direct to the buying centre of a community.

Unlike television, radio or the press, posters do not rely on editorial content. No-one can 'zap' out posters with a television control. No-one can skip pages. No-one can turn a poster off. No editorial background means that posters are only as effective as their creative message and location. Ever since the first poster appeared in 1866, the medium has been an integral part of the environment. People often take posters for granted, so creativity has to work hard to get noticed. However, because posters are part of the everyday environment, when messages are read and appreciated, the advertised product or service takes in the kudos of something that is also part of everyday life and so an essential community commodity.

**Good posters make people think.**

(Burnt poster site – half of the board is actually burnt away)

Headline:

**FIRE KILLS.**

Good posters often make people laugh.

**POSTERS ARE *SEXY***
(THIS ONE'S TOPLESS)

Good posters get to the point.

**£120 TO GO IN *SEINE***
(LONDON TO PARIS AT CRAZY PRICES)

Good posters are unsubtle.

(Picture of car suspended in the air over a road)

**£10,500**
(ON THE ROAD PRICE)

Good posters make a dull journey stimulating.

(Poster one – picture of housewife carrying lots of shopping in a superstore, looking directly at the 'camera' in shock)

**THIS IS A HOLD UP.**

(Poster two, 50 m down the road – same housewife smiling as she is sped through the 'wide and quick shopping aisle' in Scotdale Northside.)

## THIS ISN'T.

**Good posters offer a different interpretation of the subject.**

(Poster showing two pictures: a computer and a PenPod)

Headline:

## ONE OF THESE WORD PROCESSORS WILL NEVER LET YOU DOWN.

A 'living' poster, part of the 1995/6 AIDS awareness campaign, featured a live person sitting in front of copy requesting not to be ignored because he was HIV positive.

# Targeting your message with posters

Posters are not *purely* for the mass markets. They can be targeted in key locations. For example, if you want to attract business people you could consider placing a poster along a main business traffic route.

(A super-sized poster for Scotdale Northside glue – three cars actually stuck to the poster)

Headline:

## STUCK IN TRAFFIC?

You can also target by area.

(Poster featuring a picture of a new Scotdale Northside superstore – covered by gigantic curtain)

> **OPENING SOON**
> **QUEENSTOWN'S BIGGEST**
> **EVER SUPERSTORE**

### *Next stop, start buying – transit posters*

Travel cards on buses and trains allow you to write longer and more detailed copy. It doesn't matter if the passenger doesn't read all the message the first time. Like all poster advertising, the medium relies on sustained and broad coverage rather than a one-off impact. Some of the best transport advertisements take full advantage of the actual environment in which they appear. Copy can discuss commuting to work by bus or train. The poster can be designed to utilise the shape of, for example, a British double-decker bus. Use taxi panels, coach or bus front, back and side poster messages to talk directly to drivers.

(Poster on the back of a bus, read by motorists)

Headline:

> **FOR THE LATEST TRAFFIC NEWS TUNE IN TO TRAFFIC FM.**

> **FOLLOW ME TO THE NEWEST SCOTDALE NORTHSIDE SUPERSTORE.**

Posters are fun to write and create.

You can smash holes through them.

You can suspend things from them. You can make them move. Some poster contractors offer revolving poster faces that feature slats like blinds which revolve one after another to display different advertisements. The blinds can be controlled to revolve one direction or another in a timed sequence. So, PenPod could feature a series of revolving blinds to give the impression of a handwritten line of ink that grows longer and longer, developing into the headline copy:

You can use posters on buses, taxis, trams, motorbikes, vans, cars, lorries and coaches to literally spread the message all around town.

# Posters quick tips

- Keep copy short.
- Utilise shapes and surroundings.
- Think nationally, write locally.
- Let visuals do half 'the talking'.
- Take longer to keep copy shorter.
- Amuse, attract and arrest.

# Over to you

1 Write an in-store poster for a high-street printer promoting 25 per cent off printing charges.
2 Write a transit poster promoting pogo sticks as an alternative transport to cars.
3 In which year did the first poster appear?
4 How would you design a poster for the blind?

# 14

# TRADE AND 'YELLOW PAGE' DIRECTORIES

One of the most popular mediums for small businesses to advertise is in *Yellow Pages*. By the mid-1990s there were around 74 editions in the United Kingdom. (In the United States there were almost 6000 editions).

Yellow pages are ideal creative platforms for businesses targeted at consumers at home. Their success has spawned specialist business-targeted directories which feature similar page layouts. The key thing to remember when writing copy for *Yellow Pages* is IMPACT.

Yellow Pages is printed on porous paper so photographic images showing fine details (unless printed on other paper material that is bound into the publication) are not sensible options. Instead, use big, bold graphics and typefaces. Always feature a line of copy that explains what your (or your client's) company offers.

### ACME PRINT
#### LOW COST PRINTERS. HIGH QUALITY PRODUCTION.

Make your contact address details easy to understand.

#### CALL QUEENSTOWN 98 98 98

Leave sufficient 'white space' to distinguish your advertisement from the many others on the page.

As with recruitment advertisements, use borders to add greater emphasis to your advertisement and to help establish a creative advertising style.

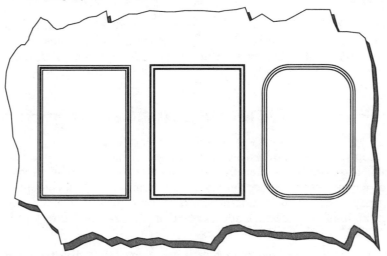

As with off-the-page advertising, consider the use of Freephone telephone numbers to enhance response. If you are advertising in more than one directory, you could also feature a special code to gauge the effectiveness of the local advertisement.

The future for *Yellow Pages* is exciting. By the mid-1990s there was the opportunity in the United Kingdom to advertise on 'Talking Pages', in which telephone operators used the information within the published directory to provide details about local suppliers by phone. In the United States, the telephone is already used to feature special audio information about everything from cinema details to news services, with space at the end of each announcement for a sponsored message. Soon the Information Superhighway will use cable to provide information and advertising direct to people's homes via the computer or television screen.

Another good thing about Yellow Pages is that you can utilise the publisher's own national advertising to enhance your product or service. So you can feature your local ad as part of a greater awareness campaign. On your van, you can sign paint 'Find us in *Yellow Pages*' this adds regional credibility and gives a potential customer the option to go home, open the local *Yellow Pages* and read your advertisement. (Mind you, he or she will also spot everyone else's advertisement, yet as yours is so well written, that shouldn't be a problem!)

Finally, *Yellow Pages* can be used as a source of distribution to include as part of a packaged insert – other material alongside the publication that is delivered with each new edition. See also 'Door-to-door distribution', page 191.

## Other directories

It seems that just about every industry sector has its own specialist trade directory. More often than not, there are several trade directories for each sector. Paper quality ranges from porous to high-quality art paper. Before you decide to advertise, I recommend that you contact an industry's official trade association and ask which directory is best for a specific trade.

If you are offered a free line advertisement space in a directory or if your budget doesn't stretch to a display advertisement, find out how many words you can feature within your limited space. As a guide, in the first line summarise what you offer. In the second line summarise your specialities. In the third line guarantee your offer. In the last line, provide contact details.

### ACME COPYWRITING

[ADDRESS]

AWARD WINNING STRATEGY-LED COPYWRITING AND CREATIVITY.

SPECIALIST IN DIRECT MARKETING, BROCHURES, VIDEOS, RADIO AND SALES PROMOTION.

PROVEN RESULTS, PROVEN VALUE.

CALL QUEENSTOWN 98 98 98 NOW.

If you are writing copy for a very small business or work from home, it is worth considering using a special telephone number exclusively for use in trade directories and other forms of advertising. Firstly, it avoids publicising your private number, and second, you can gauge the level of response without having to feature a code within the advertisement. Incidentally, if you or your client works from home, you also have to decide whether or not to feature your address details. The pros are that people can write to you. The cons are that everyone – including possible weirdos – has your address. Alternatively, you could feature a box number. The pros are that your private details are kept that way. The cons are that it might sound as if your business could be a bit 'shady'. But the choice is *yours*.

## *Directories quick tips*

- Be bold, be brash, be direct.
- Use distinctive borders.
- Always describe your product or service area.
- Include an offer or guarantee (e.g. no fees for initial meeting).
- Make full use of any of the publisher's own national promotions.

# 15
# THE INTERNET

When I think of the broader repercussions of the World Wide Web, part of the INTERNET, I recollect a story told to me by a printer who specialised in advertising. A rich man was often besieged with salespeople trying to sale various items. Each day his butler (who was totally blind) answered the door to would-be suppliers. The blind butler asked for the salesperson's business card. Nine times out of ten, he thanked them and abruptly bid them farewell. However, on a rare occasion after being handed a business card, he smiled and invited the salesperson in. Why? Because that salesperson had his company's details printed through thermography (which raises the image off the card). Hence, the blind person could 'see' that the company he represented was of fine repute.

At one stage, everyone used the thermograph technology. Yet, long term, as a trend, it never really caught on. Nowadays, it seems that just about every company is featuring an additional piece of information on business cards: their e-mail address. Unlike thermography, it looks as though the INTERNET will give rise to a trend that will become an essential part of every copywriter's portfolio.

## Origins

So, what is the INTERNET? The INTERNET is a huge industry in its own right. Its heritage can be traced to the United States. In 1969 the Defence Advanced Research Projects wrote a computer program that enabled researchers based at various locations (four, to be precise) to communicate with each other. Thus, DARPANET was created.

As the years passed so the network of computers able to use the DARPANET system grew. By 1972, 37 computers (or 'nodes') were 'on-line'. Users started to exchange much more than research material. Each had his or her own electronic mailbox. DARPANET had a change of name to reflect a change of agency – it was called ARPANET.

The network grew. The defence agency became concerned that potentially too many people could access sensitive information, so in 1983, a new network was established – MILNET. Technology continued to develop and more US government agencies became interested in the system. NSFNET was created to connect educational locations together. By 1987 so many people used the system that its original purpose (as a means for academic research) was overtaken by a much broader need and network of people worldwide.

Today the INTERNET is a vast interconnecting international 'web' of different computer networks including academic networks, governmental networks and private commercial networks, all of which use a type of language (data communication system) called a protocol such as TCP/IP. Part of the so-called Information Superhighway, the INTERNET, is accessible to everyone.

Each network is like a small community of forums, sites or 'bulletin boards' where ideas and information are exchanged and, from a commercial point of view, products and services are discussed. The INTERNET works on the principle of a very sophisticated bulletin board where, in addition to words, users have access to moving images as well as sounds. As in any community, from a copy viewpoint you have to understand what makes that market community tick. What is acceptable? What is of interest? Who visits the community? Apart from official government or academic networks, you can advertise in many sites.

Advertisers have used the INTERNET from its very early days. Initially, advertisers found it an ideally targeted medium to sell information technology items such as software. Now, with so many different types of users it has become the fastest-growing area for advertisers of all kinds, in the world.

# Marketing on the web

The web has such a broad appeal that it is a tremendously powerful marketing aid (see Figure 15.1).

**Figure 15.1** Estimates (in US$ millions) of commercial size of the INTERNET

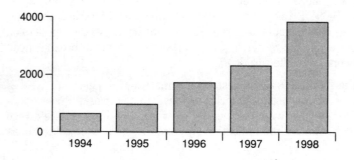

(Includes revenues for expertise, access, software, content and commerce.)

Source: Goldman, Sachs & Co., New York.

**Figure 15.2** Number of people using the INTERNET, Mar–Aug 1995

|  | % of base |
|---|---|
| Intending to buy PC and use the INTERNET | 33 |
| Have a cable TV | 25 |
| INTERNET users living and working in London | 25+ |
| Adults in London hoping to access the INTERNET | 13 |
| Source: NOP Network (Base: 13,000 UK adults) | |

Generally, it is believed that over 25 million people use the INTERNET. By the mid-1990s it was estimated that worldwide, there were around 30 000 sites on the World Wide Web. A site is a platform that allows users – or 'surfers' – to access information through layered data links using a piece of software called a Browser. Popular Browsers include Cello, Netscape and Mosaic. Most Browsers read a special language called HyperText Mark-up Language (HTML). This is used to produce the collection of documents (Web Pages) that may be on computers that are quite literally countries apart but are linked using HyperText to create the World Wide Web.

HyperText, also called Hypermedia, was invented by Ted Nelson in the late 1960s. It is a non-sequential matrix of information, creatively linked by allowing the user (or reader) to click with a mouse on a word or phrase and by doing so, instantly find further details on that word through either further text or even an animated sequence that provides more explanation. Typically, HyperText will link one set of copy to another within a different part of a document.

## The forum of the mind

One way to write an advertisement for the INTERNET is to write an ordinary English (non-HTML) e-mail message for specific forums. Each community or forum bulletin board on the INTERNET consists of people who discuss specialist subjects of interest. This can range from the latest episode of *Coronation Street* to making enquiries about pollution. Instead of using their mouths, individual users use keyboards. This makes the INTERNET a highly personal medium. Users can't see each other in person, instead they literally read each other's minds.

In terms of communications impact, the closest thing to understanding the language of the INTERNET is to consider the telephone. Here, again, you can't actually see the person 'at the other end' but you can use your voice to help illustrate what you are thinking. The INTERNET works on a much deeper level even then this. Instead of giving an instant verbal reaction to what is typed 'at the other end' you have time to construct a written answer using your keyboard. So the two-way communication process is more structured and answers are better considered.

As an advertiser, you have to learn to communicate at this level. Brash graphics or seductive copy is redundant. People want to read facts not sift through sales hype. So keep your copy factual and kick out the superlatives. One technique is to adapt your copy to refer to latest trends and developments. INTERNET surfers love to read about things that are new: fresh ideas, new trends, and so on (called 'cool'.)

Once you have established a knowledge of the community in which you wish to advertise you have to learn about what kind of information is appreciated by that community (forum) and what type is disapproved. The only way to do this is to 'visit' a forum and ask. Information can be provided either by people in the forum, or by eaves-dropping into a forum as a visitor (also known as 'listening'), or by asking via a message to a forum or network representative controller (also known as a System Op).

Once you know what is acceptable, write your e-mail. This, like most advertising copywriting, needs to be to the point. Never write more than three screens full of copy – about 75 lines long. (Remember, you are competing against thousands of e-mails.)

If you can't find a suitable forum to join, consider starting a new one of your own. The advantages are that you run the forum, and providing you get a large enough following, you are able to enhance your credibility as an information as well as service or product provider.

Other forms of INTERNET advertising include: White pages (advertiser database); Pennyshoppers (product-based lists and subscriptions); Billboards (notices in forums or so-called 'newsgroups'); advertising space in INTERNET provider magazines.

## Get yourself on the web

The alternative way to advertise on the web part of the Information Superhighway, is to have a unique 'site' that is similar to a poster on a suburban highway – only, in terms of creative impact and technical possibilities, much more powerful and far more versatile. You can rent a site or own one and become a 'host'.

As you know, posters on suburban highways require short, sharp messages. Sites on the Information Superhighway superficially also feature to the point messages. However, such brevity is skin (or screen) deep. First a reader (or net surfer) has to access your site by typing a unique IP (internet protocol) number – your electronic address or 'domain name' – which you can obtain from one of the network providers. Once a connection to your location or 'node' has been established, your page will appear on the surfer's screen.

Typically, a page is created in layers of information. This is because it takes time to 'download' information via the INTERNET. Most people have modems with connection speeds between 9600 and 14 400 bps. Newer modems are much faster – 28 800 bps. In the United Kingdom it is thought that by 1997 wideband access using a 8Mhz cable channel will speed up connection by 100 per cent.

## HTML in more detail

So your page is transmitted in layered stages. As you know, the computer application that instructs a network program Browser to broadcast and 'read' an advertisement over the net is called HTML. This is a kind of artwork mark-up language that tags documents such as advertisements with data that uses links known as HyperText links to create an interactive cross-platform connection to a broad range of resources on computers around the world (the INTERNET). HTML tells the Browser how a graphic or piece of text should appear on the screen and more importantly where each 'click' of the surfer's mouse should lead via a HyperText link.

An HTML document comprises three parts:

1 A description of the character set to be used and which characters are used to differentiate between text and mark-up tag;
2 A description of the document types and the legally usable mark-up tags for the specific document type;
3 The document, including all the mark-up tags and text.

Depending on the technical sophistication of a Browser program, an INTERNET advertisement using the HTML language, can be 'written' in levels of complexity:

**Level O**
mandatory headings, lists, anchors, and so on
(a text-only Browser is expected to have Level O conformance)

| **Level 1** | **Level 2** |
|---|---|
| images, emphasis | forms, character definitions |

| **Level 3** | **Level 4** |
|---|---|
| tables, figures, etc. | Mathematical equations |
| | (this is still being developed) |

The more complicated your image, the longer it takes to download. When you write an advertisement, you should keep this in mind. If your advertisement is overcomplicated by graphics and text, the surfer may simply switch into a more interesting 'cooler' site. One way to get round this is to feature basic text information and ICONS. When the surfer selects an ICON via a HyperText link, it leads (or 'links') him or her to another layer of information. This could be anything from a picture to a sound or even moving image (which will require specific software to activate).

For example:

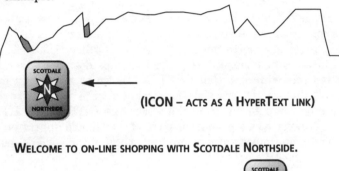

(ICON – ACTS AS A HyperText LINK)

WELCOME TO ON-LINE SHOPPING WITH SCOTDALE NORTHSIDE.

WOULD YOU LIKE TO KNOW
MORE ABOUT OUR HISTORY?
THEN PLEASE POINT AND CLICK HERE.

TO FIND YOUR NEAREST SUPERSTORE
SIMPLY POINT AND CLICK HERE.

WE'RE CELEBRATING **100** YEARS
OF SERVICE AND QUALITY.
POINT AND CLICK HERE
TO JOIN IN THE FESTIVITIES.

WANT TO GO SHOPPING? CLICK HERE.
WE'LL DELIVER YOUR ORDER
'FRESH ON THE DAY' WITHIN **24** HOURS.

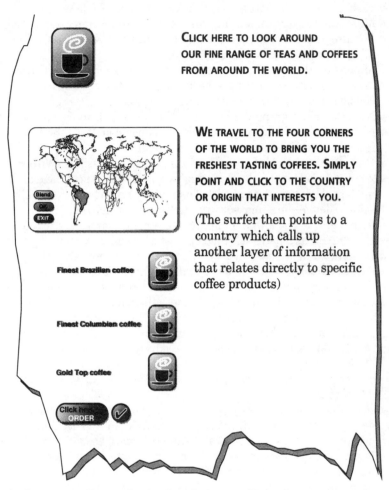

CLICK HERE TO LOOK AROUND OUR FINE RANGE OF TEAS AND COFFEES FROM AROUND THE WORLD.

WE TRAVEL TO THE FOUR CORNERS OF THE WORLD TO BRING YOU THE FRESHEST TASTING COFFEES. SIMPLY POINT AND CLICK TO THE COUNTRY OR ORIGIN THAT INTERESTS YOU.

(The surfer then points to a country which calls up another layer of information that relates directly to specific coffee products)

Finest Brazilian coffee

Finest Columbian coffee

Gold Top coffee

Click here ORDER

And so on, until an order is placed via a credit card account number.

It is important to make your site as interesting as possible. Regularly update it with new information. Why not turn your site into a game panel where, by playing an interactive game, the surfer can learn more about your product or service?

# INTERNET quick tips

- Visit a community forum before asking to advertise in it.
- Make your advertisement information-led rather than creative-led.
- Feature your site web presence and IP address or e-mail address on all company literature and advertising.
- Make sure that all site technical hitches are sorted out in advance.
- Make your site interesting – discuss latest industry issues – consider making your site an interactive game.
- Never overload graphics or colours. Download in layered stages.
- Never send mail bombs (junk mail). In November 1995, the EU issued a directive to ban unsolicited e-mail.
- Ensure that your host computer is as secure as possible. (With over 20 million surfers on the Superhighway, you can expect the odd modern-day equivalent of Dick Turpin may try to hack in to your system demanding your software to 'stand and deliver'.
- Although your potential audience is in its millions, consider the INTERNET as a narrowcast medium which requires careful targeting.
- In addition to any response details within your copy, always suggest that the surfer adds your page site to his or her personal list of interesting pages to visit on the web (hotlist or bookmark).
- Consider forms of asking for payment other than credit card direct via the Net. Perhaps ask people to call a Hotline order number? Hackers may be able to access financial information – many surfers are, therefore, reluctant to provide credit card details. In October 1995 VISA joined forces with software giant Microsoft to release a secure credit card INTERNET package. MasterCard soon followed suit.
- Act responsibly. As the system improves, so legislation is being developed to ensure that information is ethically and sociably acceptable. (In the United States the US Senate has already approved the Communications Decency Act which intends to impose a fine or prison terms for anyone distributing obscene material via a computer network). Even without enforceable rules, those who act responsibly today will probably be those who remain Net leaders tomorrow.

# 16

# PRESS RELEASE COPY

> *News is what someone somewhere doesn't*
> *want you to print: the rest is advertising.*
> William Randulph Hearst

Strictly speaking, public relations (PR) is outside the remit of many copywriters. However, for those writers who are freelance or independent or have to cater for just about any type of publicity writing, PR is another important tool.

PR is not free advertising. Its value far exceeds that. Good PR covers everything from staff communications to product launching to handling bad news to a simple sign by a roadside that apologises for any inconvenience during repair works. According to the Institute of Public Relations: 'Public relations practice is the planned and sustained effort to establish and maintain goodwill and mutual understanding between an organisation and its publics.'

In your capacity as a PR writer you have to act as the special correspondent dealing with your client's interests to every single news media. As such, you have to appreciate the needs of the 'press' and the desires of your client. (Always a delicate balancing act.) As a special correspondent you have to understand how to make an average everyday type of story news worthy. You must be able to present the facts of your story in a form that does away with advertising hype and concentrates on interesting news angles. You have to think like a news hound, ready to track down all the elements of your story as well as the markets who will be interested in printing either your version directly or, more likely, their version as explained through you and your press release. Finally, you have to show a sense of responsibility to your client, the media and the truth. Nobody will ask you for a second story if your first one was eventually discovered to be nothing more than a cover-up or a pack of lies.

As with advertising copywriting, get to know your media. Which kind of publication likes which kind of story, and of the ones which suit your needs, how (in what style) do they like the story explained.

> Ivy Ledbetter lee was the first PR consultant. He opened for business in 1903 and his clients included a circus, bankers and politicians. The first PR company in the United Kingdom, Editorial Services Ltd, opened in 1924. The first PR officer worked for Southern Railway and was appointed in 1925.

## ──── General news release ────

For the purposes of this chapter, let's concentrate on how to write a general news release and accompanying support material. This is the most basic form of PR writing and, as it is written from a broadly neutral stance, offers the greatest attraction to the broadest media sources.

Every news story is divided into three essential components:

1 the headline
2 the lead
3 the body

From a press-release angle, think of the headline as a calling card between you and an editor. It announces in one or two sentences what you have to offer.

BRITAIN'S BEST-LOVED RETAILER CELEBRATES **100** YEARS OF SERVICE.

Notice that the retailer's name was not featured – instead all the words were directed towards the subject features and benefits matter: 'Best loved ... celebrates ... 100 years of service.'

Once you have 'cast your bait' with a headline, you have to 'hook' an editor's interest with a lead paragraph. Within no more than 60 words, your lead has to be sufficiently interesting and relevant for an editor to either read the rest of your press release or get a staff journalist to make further enquiries. Leads are fact- rather than prose-led.

> SCOTDALE NORTHSIDE IS CELEBRATING 100 YEARS OF RETAILING IN THE UNITED KINGDOM. AS PART OF THE FESTIVITIES TO MARK THE EVENT, ON FRIDAY, 8 OCTOBER AT 7 P.M., EACH SUPERSTORE WILL FEATURE A FIREWORKS DISPLAY.

From a practical point of view, it is seldom possible to write a different press release for each publication. However, it is a good idea to target the story to a type of medium. In addition to giving you a theme for your story, you can be more assured that when your lead is read it has a greater chance of working. The Scotdale Northside lead adapted for the popular press would read:

> ON FRIDAY, 8 OCTOBER, THE SKIES ARE GOING TO BE LIT UP FROM JOHN O'GROATS TO LAND'S END. IT'S PART OF YEAR-LONG CELEBRATIONS TO MARK THE 100TH BIRTHDAY OF ONE OF ENGLAND'S BEST-LOVED RETAIL CHAINS, SCOTDALE NORTHSIDE.

The main components of a press release lead are: who is doing what, why and when, and finally, where? Editors often take mere seconds to decide if the story is of interest or not. Avoid sending a press release that discusses something that has already occurred – editors work in the news business not the history library.

Your press release should be 'tagged' as an urgent matter. Consider including a FOR IMMEDIATE RELEASE notice or to add an air of privileged information – NOT FOR EMBARGO UNTIL [DATE]

Never use the word EXCLUSIVE unless the story *really* is exclusive to one publication. If you want to get round this, you can always make your story EXCLUSIVE to one publication and after that SPECIAL for another publication. (Specials may be applicable to local papers who would want a special regional bias given to the story, or to trade publications which wish to discuss a specific business angle.)

Always include **the date** that you sent the press release – if very urgent, **the time**, and of course, your **contact details**.

Next, you move to the body of the release. There are various formulae for writing a coherent and logical product- or service-based press release. One of the best known is SOLAADS:

**S**ubject
**O**rganisation
**L**ocation
**A**dvantages
**A**pplications
**D**etails
**S**ource

We have already dealt with the first three on the list, so now you have to consider the main thrust of your press release. Give further details of what's so different and new about the product or service. Who is likely to want it? What are the benefits to the readers, viewers or listeners? How best can it be used – what kind of problems does it address? How does it shape up? What does it feel like? What does it look like? How does it perform? Who does the editor contact for further information? Where?

## —— Other types of press release ——

Your story may have nothing to do with materials or services. Often the best stories are those with human interest angles. Essentially the format for such a release is similar to those for product- and service-based items.

Always present your copy typed, with double line spacing and ample margin space for editorial comment.

Show where the release comes from:

**More news from**

*For immediate release*

A strong headline, led by the person, features and benefits *not* the company:

RALPH SOAMES SET TO TAKE SCOTDALE NORTHSIDE INTO THE NEW MILLENNIUM.

not

SCOTDALE NORTHSIDE RECRUITS COMPUTER INC'S EX HEAD OF COMMUNICATIONS.

Feature a strong lead-in (non-indented first paragraph):

MARKETING AWARD-WINNING RALPH SOAMES HAS JOINED SCOTDALE NORTHSIDE AS HEAD OF COMMUNICATIONS. "IT WAS THE NATURAL CHOICE," EXPLAINED SOAMES. "THE COMPANY HAS THE RIGHT DISTRIBUTION CHANNELS AS WELL AS SPREAD OF BRANDS TO REALLY OFFER THE CONSUMER SOMETHING TOTALLY DIFFERENT FOR THE NEW MILLENNIUM. I BELIEVE THAT A CONTINUED TARGETED COMMUNICATIONS STRATEGY WILL HELP FURTHER REINFORCE THE COMPANY AS THE UNDISPUTED MARKET LEADER IN ITS FIELD."

Next, include further details about his different approach to marketing and how it will affect the consumer:

(Indented paragraph)

ONE OF SOAMES' MOST FAMOUS MARKETING INITIATIVES WAS THE MOULD-BREAKING ORDER BY NET SCHEME THROUGH WHICH COMPUTER USERS COULD ORDER SOFTWARE DIRECT ON THE INTERNET. "I AM CURRENTLY LOOKING AT FURTHER WAYS THAT THE COMPANY CAN MAKE THE WEEKLY SHOP LESS OF A CHORE TO THE CONSUMER." SOAMES DOESN'T RULE OUT MARKETING ON THE NET. "IT'S EARLY DAYS. ALL I CAN SAY IS THAT ANYTHING THAT HELPS OUR CUSTOMERS WILL BE CLOSELY EXPLORED."

Next – more general information:

THIS YEAR SCOTDALE NORTHSIDE IS CELEBRATING 100 YEARS OF SERVICE TO SHOPPERS. SCOTDALE NORTHSIDE HAS 355 BRANCHES THROUGHOUT THE COUNTRY. SPEAKING ABOUT MR SOAMES' NEW APPOINTMENT, ROGER DALE, CHAIRMAN OF SCOTDALE NORTHSIDE SAID, "WE HAVE FOLLOWED RALPH'S CAREER CLOSELY OVER THE YEARS. WE ARE DELIGHTED TO WELCOME HIM TO THE TEAM. HE WILL HELP TAKE OUR COMMUNICATIONS PROGRAMME FORWARD TO THE 21ST CENTURY."

Conclude with a human-interest angle and closing 'hook':

RALPH SOAMES (AGED 41) IS MARRIED WITH THREE CHILDREN. WHEN ASKED WHERE HIS WIFE MAKES HER WEEKLY SHOP HE ANSWERED, "WELL LET'S JUST SAY IT'S NOT A MILLION MILES AWAY FROM MY NEW OFFICE!"

ENDS

Some companies prefer to mark the end of a press release by typing #######. If the press release continues on to another sheet of paper, write – **more** – and head the following sheet with a suitable *aide-mémoire* line, for example:

SOAMES JOINS SCOTDALE NORTHSIDE PAGE TWO.

Conclude with your contact details:

FOR FURTHER DETAILS
PLEASE CONTACT LESLEY HADCROFT
AT SCOTDALE NORTHSIDE PRESS OFFICE
TELEPHONE 01234 56789
FAX 01234 56789

## Announcement release

You may need to construct an announcement release. This entails brief details about such subjects as a change of address or a new team member. Trade publications often feature short announcements on who's moving to what company. All that is usually required is a few lines of detail: who's moving from where to what position and with what responsibility.

## Background notes release

Another kind of press release is a support piece – the background notes release. This is not usually for publication but provides useful details about technical aspects or historical points related to the main release. Typically, background notes may feature previously published articles, research figures, brochures and company reports. (In the case of Ralph Soames, the background notes could include biographical details.)

## Technical release

The all-out technical release is often longer than the usual one-page, one-side main release. It provides all the additional technical 'homework' an editor or journalist needs to write a complete and accurate account of how a particular product or service developed.

## Television or radio press release

You may be required to write a special press release for television or radio. If this is the case, you have to remember the points discussed previously in the sections relating to the broadcast media – write as people speak. Sentences need to be crisp. Information needs to be distilled to its simple points. Wherever possible, try to include at least one quote that encapsulates the entire message within 10 seconds (approximately 25 words) of 'talk time'. If that quote promises broader repercussions all the better. (This quote is often called a 'sound bite' and is usually an edited highlight from a recording.)

RALPH SOAMES HAS JOINED SCOTDALE NORTHSIDE. "THIS IS ONE OF THE MOST EXCITING DEVELOPMENTS IN OUR ONGOING COMMUNICATIONS PROGRAMME THAT WILL TAKE US INTO THE 21ST CENTURY," SAID SCOTDALE NORTHIDE'S CHAIRMAN ROGER DALE.

RALPH SOAMES IS BEST KNOWN FOR HIS INNOVATIVE MARKETING WORK RELATING TO THE INTERNET. "I AM PROUD TO HAVE BEEN PART OF THE TEAM THAT ESTABLISHED THE INFORMATION SUPERHIGHWAY AS A VALUABLE AREA FOR CUSTOMER TRAFFIC. I AM SURE THAT SCOTDALE NORTHSIDE'S AMAZING BRAND RANGE WILL SOON BE ENJOYED BY THE BIGGEST CUSTOMER BASE EVER SERVICED BY A UK COMPANY."

If you do wish to produce an audio release for the radio, find out what kind of format the recording should be on: reel to reel, DAT or cassette.

Finally, always submit a broadcast release with an accompanying letter explaining what the release is about, how it is relevant to an audience and where to contact you for further information.

# ———— 'Bad news' releases ————

The worst kind of news for a publicist is bad news. For example, a dead cockroach could be discovered in a tin of Scotdale Northside baked beans. A senior member of PenPod's management board could be exposed as a crook. The first thing to accept is that the saying 'All publicity is good publicity' is a fallacy. Too many image-sensitive people have been driven to suicide by bad publicity for the saying to have any real credence.

There are three ways to deal with bad publicity:

1 deny the allegations
2 counter the allegations
3 sue

## Deny the allegations

This is the most obvious course to take. However, there are times when the facts are weighed up too heavily against your client to make any denial plausible. In this case you should resort to countering the allegations.

## Counter the allegations

This is the best option. Journalists want a news story. Give it to them. Only instead of one 'juicy' bit of news, offer another much more tempting morsel. This is a barter method and shows to the journalists that you are on their side to get a *good* story – not a piece of tittle-tattle – and above all, get to the bottom of the *real* truth.

So, if a dead cockroach is found in a tin of Scotdale Northside baked beans, surely the *real* story is not the company's public health checks but who placed it there in the first place? Offer a reward to find the culprits. The public's health is at risk. Scotdale Northside will leave no stone unturned to expose the evil culprits. Go further, announce plans to redesign tins so that they are tamper-proof. Invite journalists to see the production line for themselves. Remember, *your client has nothing to hide*.

If there is simply no way of avoiding adverse publicity, defend your cause by justifying your actions, showing the blatant regrettable victimisation caused by the adverse publicity. (A definite case of kicking a person when he or she is down.)

If you must, face the music and be prepared to admit that a mistake was made. Then 'close' the matter. People will respect you for it. Sometimes, by prolonging a dispute, you can actually make things worse. An early settlement can stop a one-off piece of sensational news becoming a much bigger problem that attracts greater publicity. This is sometimes called the 'David and Goliath' syndrome, when the little guy likes to show up the big corporation.

If applicable to the situation, the big corporation may admit liability early on and then get on with other things, the fight is over. No further battles can escalate. *There is no more news*. The important thing is that a lesson has been learnt. The immediate positive actions taken by the organisation through that experience can only benefit the consumer.

You could take this further, and by doing so gain extra news coverage, by throwing down the gauntlet and asking the public for their opinions. Deviating for a minute from the business world, this technique is often used by movie stars who are caught cheating on their partners – Would you leave your partner if she had an affair? What would you do in his shoes?

Another avoidance technique for movie-star couples who have gone astray is to allow a public debate to have a good 'run' in the press. Then get either the man or woman to make a statement via a television interview. The news of the up-and-coming statement can itself stimulate media interest. During the interview the person who cheated on the partner could apologise for his or her wrong doing. *"It was a one-off mistake. I can only hope that he [or she] will one day find it in his [or her] heart to forgive me.'* Once the interview has been broadcast, the press can again be invited to ask their audience to comment.

The next step is to get the other party to announce that she or he just wants to be left alone to 'figure things out'. About a month later, however, he or she 'comes out of hiding' and announces that love may yet bring them both together again. All this should lead up to a tip-off to a press photographer that the couple are getting away from it all by taking a vacation on an exclusive tropical island. A photograph taken with a long zoom lens, showing the couple walking hand in hand on a beach is then published in the papers.

Soon publicity gets under way to launch one of the couple's latest movie. Or even better, a joint starring-role movie about adultery ... or for guaranteed interest, a movie starring the 'wrong doer' and the 'alleged' one-time, extra-marital partner. Needless to say, it will be a box office success.

Back to the business world and that cockroach in the beans....

From an advertising perspective, avoid producing direct advertising that attacks the parties attacking your client. This is yet another way to highlight a problem and turn it into a longer-term headache. If you have to advertise, produce only advertising that advises on any immediate risks to the consumer and demonstrates a positive response by your client.

## WE'RE RECALLING OUR BEANS BECAUSE WE ARE RESOLUTE IN OUR PROMISE OF QUALITY

HAVE YOU RECENTLY PURCHASED A TIN OF SCOTDALE NORTHSIDE BAKED BEANS (BATCH NUMBER 12345)? IF SO, PLEASE RETURN IT TO YOUR LOCAL SCOTDALE NORTHSIDE. YOU WILL BE GIVEN A VOUCHER WORTH £2.50 THAT CAN BE REDEEMED AGAINST ANY FUTURE OWN-BRAND PURCHASE.

SCOTDALE NORTHSIDE IS OFFERING A REWARD OF £25,000. IF YOU HAVE ANY INFORMATION THAT CAN LEAD TO THE CONVICTION OF CRIMINALS WHO HAVE TAMPERED WITH OUR PRODUCT. PLEASE DIAL 0800 123 123.

WE HOPE THAT THE £2.50 VOUCHER WILL HELP TOWARDS THE INCONVENIENCE CAUSED.

SCOTDALE NORTHSIDE *FOR GOODNESS SAKE YOU KNOW YOU CAN TRUST US.*

## Sue

Whenever possible, avoid legal action. It is costly, drags things out and highlights a problem. Even if you have a good case, libel is difficult to prove. If, on the other hand, you are *100 per cent confident that an injustice has been done*, never be afraid to resort to law. It is, after all, there to *protect your clients interests*.

If all else fails hire a professional publicist. Even a great copywriter like you can only achieve so much!

## *Press release quick tips*

- Try to get all your facts on to one side of a sheet of A4 paper.
- Double line space your text.
- Block copy your lead-in paragraph and indent the rest.
- Show where the news is from.
- Don't use capital letters to write a company name. Scotdale Northside, not SCOTDALE NORTHSIDE.
- Avoid underlining text.
- If there is more than one page of text, use the word MORE at the foot of the page.
- Show the date of embargo or announce on the day – news is now, not history.
- Time embargoes accurately to match a launch or special event.
- Write your story from the top down. Many editors edit from the bottom up.
- Concentrate on facts, not flourishes.
- Show who and where to contact for further information.
- Avoid obvious hidden advertising for products or services.
- Don't try to create a story when there isn't enough news to make it a story worth printing.
- Tailor the emphasis and style of a story to suit a media sector.
- Follow up a press release with a phone call. Does the journalist need any further details?
- Read and write your story as you think an editor would wish it to be received by his or her target audience.
- Double check spelling.
- Only use quotes that are relevant to the story.

# Over to you

1 Write seven press release heading variations which announce that PenPod is launching a new pen.
2 Write a 200-word background biography of your life.
3 Imagine you got caught cheating on your partner. Devise a 12-point plan that would prove your innocence and have you 'coming out smelling of roses'.
4 What does SOLAADS stand for?
5 Construct an advertisement from Scotdale Northside commenting on why a small section of the roof of one of its superstores caved in overnight, narrowly missing a passerby.
6 Write three short sentences that will encourage a news editor to read a press release about an industrial nail manufacturer who wants to announce a new length of nail that is being added to the production line.

\* \* \* \* \*

*I'm a copywriter — still care to join me?*

*Believe in yourself, keep an open mind, read, listen and learn about people, places and events. Practise your craft then people will believe in you and you'll go far.*

*And remember,*

*a simple sentence that can be understood first time is better than a complicated, longer description.*

*Now go out there, write, sell and meet the deadlines!*

# GLOSSARY

**A/B split** 1 the creative testing of two variations of one element in a direct mail package; 2 target testing in a direct marketing or research programme

**above-the-line** originally referred to a form of agency remuneration. Nowadays refers to advertising and marketing budget spent on television, radio or published media. However, this concept has been superseded by 'through-the-line' and 'integrated marketing', which offers a combination of above-the-line and below-the-line advertising

**account** 1 a client of an advertising agency or promotions/public relations agency; 2 a general term given to describe a client's marketing affairs

**account executive** the person, usually at a middle-management or junior-management level who liaises between the agency and client

**account group** agency team that works on an account

**ACORN** A Classification Of Residential Neighbourhoods – a consumer-targeting system which provides a listed selection of residential property information

**advertising** a planned sponsored marketing technique using media to educate and persuade a narrow or broadly targeted audience, thereby building a communications bridge linking a service or product provider, its distributors, users and advocates

**advertising agency** a company that produces advertising and organises advertising campaigns on behalf of its clients

**advertising platform**   the main benefits or facts to be conveyed through a piece of advertising

**advertising rate**   the fee charged for time or advertising space in the media

**Advertising Standards Authority**   the body responsible for overseeing public complaints of printed advertising and cinema (the Independent Television Commission deals with complaints about television)

**advertising wedge**   a product's or service's leading benefit or feature that is highlighted within an advertisement

**advertorial**   a combination of advertising and editorial style of copy to give the appearance of a pure piece of editorial. (Often featuring the words 'advertising feature')

**advocacy advertising**   (see 'issue advertising')

**advid**   an advertising video tape often used by job and US college applicants as an electronic CV

**agency commission**   the fee paid by the media to an agency for placing advertising

**animatic**   a semi-finished animated television commercial often used for research purposes

**answer print**   the final print of a television commercial for approval before broadcast

**art buyer**   a person employed by an advertising agency to commission creative suppliers such as printers and photographers

**art director**   the person responsible for the visual concept design and execution including graphical or photographic management of a creative advertising project. Often advertising agencies team art directors with copywriters, thereby creating macro units of creativity supervised by a creative director. Where such teamwork occurs, generally, creative ideas are jointly conceived

**artwork**   the final creative execution of a piece of advertising material ready for print

**atomistic test**   the research testing of individual parts of a design or advertisement

**author's alteration**   a proofreading correction made by a copywriter

**awareness**   a measurable capacity for people to recall a specific advertisement either when unprompted, 'Can you name a brand of pen?' or prompted 'Have you ever written with a PenPod?'

**back-to-back**   the broadcasting of commercials in a direct sequence

**backgrounders**   public relations support material to aid journalists

**bait and switch advertising**   the now outlawed process of advertising a low-priced item in order to build customer traffic and then switch to selling a higher-priced item

**bang path address**   the original way of writing an INTERNET address

**bangtail**   an envelope designed with an attached perforated 'tail' used as a coupon or order response device

**banker envelope**   an envelope with a flap on the longest edge

**bastard size**   special size of paper, typeface or format

**beauty shot**   a close-up photographic shot used in television or cinema-advertising

**believability**   the scale by which an advertisement is believed

**below-the-line**   advertising and marketing budget spent on advertising, including direct marketing and sales promotions, as well as those areas not dealt with in above-the-line advertising (see also 'above-the-line')

**bill-me-later**   payment charged once the goods have been received

**billstuffer**   (see 'statement stuffer')

**billing**   1   the fee charged to a client by an agency; 2   the net charge made by a media supplier to an agency; the gross charge less the discount given to the agency

**blind ad**   a classified advertisement which does not reveal the identity of a client

**blow-in card**   a loose reply card inserted into a magazine

**blurb**   1   basic product or service descriptive copy; 2   short introduction copy on a book sleeve that highlights, explains and enthuses about the text within the covers

**border**   the perimeter line that distinguishes one advertisement from another on the printed page

**BRAD**   British Rates and Data – a monthly reference source of media and advertising cost and circulation data

**brand**   a name, term, symbol or design (or a combination of them) which is intended to signify the goods or services of one seller or group of sellers and to differentiate them from those of competitors (Source: P Kotler, *Marketing Management*, Prentice Hall, 1991)

**brand association**   the mental link between a specific product or service and its general category

**brand attitude**   a consumer's opinion of a product or service

**brand differentiation**   the degree by which a product or service is perceived to be different from its competitors

**brand image**   the emotive 'gut feelings' conjured up by advertising or marketing, felt by the consumer towards a product or service

**brand loyalty**   the ultimate aim of a brand manager – to secure the continued custom and product or service endorsement from a client

**brand switching**   the act of changing from choosing one brand to another

**BRE**   Business Reply Envelope – a pre-addressed envelope from a mailer to be returned by a recipient

**broadsheet**   large-sized newspaper as opposed to a tabloid

**broadside**   the traditional name given to paper printed on a single side only

**brochure**   a printed, bound pamphlet, derived from the French word meaning to stitch – *brocher*

**bromide**   a photographic print

**buck slip**   a US dollar-sized piece of paper that announces an offer for prompt reply

**business press**   specialist press aimed at the business community often used in business-to-business advertising

**by line**   the name of a journalist responsible for a specific article or report

**campaign**   1   a planned and co-ordinated sequence of advertising, marketing and promotional activities constructed to achieve a calculated result   2   UK advertising publication

**CAP**   Code of Advertising Practice

**caption**   copy that describes a specific illustration or photograph

**Centre Européen des Relations Publiques (CERP)**   European Federation of Public Relations Organisation

**centrefold spread**   centre spread of a publication which can be opened flat to show headlines, pictures and text

**character count**   the overall number of both type and spaces in a piece of copy

**Chartered Institute of Marketing**   Europe's largest professional body for marketing and sales practitioners (founded 1911)

**Cheshire label**   a name and address label used as an alternative to a window address envelope

**circular**   a broadly distributed piece of advertising material

**clean copy**   an error-free piece of copy

**clean proof**   an error-free typeset proof

**clip**   a short edited piece of film

**club line** the unsightly first line of a paragraph at the foot of a page when the rest of the paragraph is printed on the next page or column

**cluster** a group of people sharing a common interest or feature

**cluster analysis** a statistical method for sorting samples of people into clusters

**cognitive dissonance** a consumer's disappointment when there is a vast perceived difference between what is expected from a product and what it actually delivers. Cognitive dissonance can be avoided by stating clear product and service facts within copy and by featuring money-back promises or guarantees if the consumer is not completely satisfied

**cognitive psychology** a general approach to psychology stressing the internal mental processes

**coin rub** (see 'scratch off')

**coined word** a word created for a specific purpose

**cold lists** lists of prospects which have never been previously contacted by an advertiser

**collectable** a one-off or series of objects sold as limited editions using direct marketing techniques

**concertina fold** a paper fold which opens out in the form of the bellows of a concertina

**contact report** a written account of a meeting between a creative supplier or agency and its client

**contest** a sales promotion method that rewards prizes to consumers who perform tasks such as, *'please complete a phrase'*

**continuity writer** a person who writes programme publicity and information copy for commercial broadcasters

**control** the standard by which quality is gauged. Direct mailers feature a control package that has proved the most effective of at least two mailings. All variations of a creative theme are measured against this 'control'. The term is also applied to the most successful creative advertisement within a campaign

**controlled circulation** the free distribution of a publication to targeted addresses

**conversion pack** a direct mail piece that is meant to convert an enquiry to a sale

**copy approach** the main theme or creative thrust in a piece of copy

**copy chief (head)** senior copywriter with management responsibilities

**copy editor**   the journalist who approves and edits journalistic copy produced by reporters

**copy platform**   creative rationale and description based on an agreed advertising strategy

**corporate identity**   material representation based on a corporate goal and philosophy through a logo, corporate colour scheme, uniform or livery of an organisation

**cost-per-thousand**   the cost of an advertisement per 1000 viewers or readers who are not necessarily the ideal prospects (also known as CPM – cost per mille). To calculate, divide the cost of the advertisement by the circulation of the publication. (In the case of television or radio, you have to take into consideration the time at which the commercial is broadcast)

**cost plus**   an advertising execution produced at production cost + agency expenses and fees

**counter card**   a point-of-sale notice highlighting a product name and price

**coverage**   1   the geographic reach of a specific medium; 2   the declared parameters of a market; 3   the percentage of the audience within a market able to see an outdoor advertising poster; 4   the total number of people that buy or receive a publication or see/hear a broadcast

**CPE**   Cost Per Enquiry – the total cost of a mailing divided by the number of enquiries that it produces

**CPO**   Cost Per Order – the total cost of a mailing divided by the number of orders that it produces

**creative director**   employee of an agency who is responsible for the output or creative work and overall supervision and co-ordination of creative staff (or teams)

**creative strategy**   a communications goal based on an intended marketing results

**customer relations**   public relations or advertising programme aimed at consumers using communication devices such as questionnaires, newsletters and after-sales support services

**cut off**   (see 'deadline')

**daily rate**   the fee for advertising space charged for all editions of newspapers published during the normal working week

**database**   a computerised pool of information usually customer details from which selected data can be utilised

**de-dupe** the method of eliminating and identifying duplicate names from mailing lists – once completed, the information is referred to as 'de-duped data' (see also 'merge-purge')

**deadline** the final time a completed advertisement or piece of copy can be accepted

**dealer listing** a list that is included in a piece of copy showing regional dealers who sell a product or service – often replaced by a single dealer telephone number

**dealer relations** PR directed at commercial distributors of products or services

**demarketing** deterring consumers from excessive buying or consuming (e.g. for a summer water conservation campaign – *'By all means splash out on the sun oil, but please, conserve your water.'*)

**demographics** the classification of an audience 'make-up' based on economic and social influences and conditions. Classifications can be segmented by age, sex, income, and working status

**desktop publishing** computer-generated advertising and publications including newsletters, leaflets and press advertisements

**direct mail** the targeted sending of advertising and promotional items direct to likely consumers

**direct marketing** a direct channel of distribution using any form of marketing communication that encourages a response and delivers a quantifiable result

**Direct Marketing Association (DMA)** British professional body for direct marketing practitioners

**dirty copy proof** copy with handwritten comments and amendments

**display face** typeface designed for display-sized advertisements

**DMSB** Direct Mail Sales Bureau – an organisation started by the Post Office to promote the use of direct mail

**donor list** list of people who have donated to a charitable cause

**door-to-door** the direct marketing distribution of material by hand, usually to residential neighbourhoods

**double decker** an outdoor poster stacked in two separate tiers

**double-duty envelope** an envelope designed to be torn yet retain its return envelope features

**dummy** a mock-up sample of a communications piece

**dump bin** a point-of-sale item which carries products in a bin

**edit suites** audio and video post-production facilities for editing purposes

**electronic cottage**   the term given to the residence of a freelance copywriter, designer or person who uses computer technology to link between home and office

**EDMA**   European Direct Marketing Association

**English creep**   the spread of English as an international language – over 345 million people use English as their first language and an extra 400 million as a second

**embargo**   request to withhold press information until a specified date and time

**envelope stuffer**   direct marketing material enclosed in a direct mail piece already containing a business letter, invoice or statement

**exclusive**   a press release or other kind of information written for one media source

**eye camera**   a special camera used to measure the visual response of research volunteers when reading copy

**face**   1   a particular set of typefaces belonging to a 'family' of typefaces; 2   the bare frontage of an outdoor poster; 3   a page which, when opened naturally, faces the reader; 4   the opposite page to a piece of copy

**family life cycle**   1   young single people; 2   young couples with no children; 3   young couples with their youngest child under six; 4   couples with dependant children; 5   older couples with no children at home; 6   older single people

**farm out**   subcontract work

**feedback**   consumer reaction that helps managers assess the overall performance of a campaign

**filler advertisement**   an unbooked advertisement used to fill up blank publishing space

**finger**   a program that shows details of who is accessing your host page on the INTERNET

**flanker**   also known as a line extension brand, referring to a spin-off companion product to a successful brand name (e.g. 'Soft and Gentle Bath Foam' could lead to a flanker, 'Soft and Gentle Shower Gel')

**flat animation**   two-dimensional animation

**flier**   simple, one sheet of advertising material usually found in a mailing piece

**FMCG**   Fast Moving Consumer Goods – products which are meant to have short retail shelf life and high stock requirement based on a fast repurchase demand (e.g. soap, biscuits, butter)

**fount**   alternative word for 'font', meaning a complete set of type of one style and size

**four-colour process**   colour printing featuring primary colours which are separated by a filter

**Frankly I'm puzzled**   traditional style of direct marketing copy which asks why the recipient has not responded to an offer

**free-standing stuffer**   a loose insert 'stuffed' into a publication

**free flier**   an extra insert in a direct-mail piece that offers a special gift for prompt reply

**free keeper**   a low-cost item that the recipient of a mailing piece can keep at no obligation

**free newspapers**   typically weekly local newspapers delivered door to door

**free ride**   cost effective way to save mailing costs by including one specific offer within a different mailing

**free trial**   (see 'sample')

**freelancer**   self-employed person who works independently (e.g. freelance copywriter)

**Freepost**   Royal Mail service whereby the mailer finances the cost of postage

**fuzzy sets**   psychologist term for imprecise language that confuses the reader

**fuzzword**   seemingly defined word that actually confuses a piece of communication, in other words, elegant gobbledegook

**frequency**   the average number of times that a person sees an advertisement during a specified period

**galley proof**   proofed copy text prior to being formatted into pages

**gatefold**   1   leaflet folded so that its two edges meet in the centre; 2   cover of a publication that has to be opened

**generic advertising**   advertising that highlights product or service benefits while omitting the brand name and retailer details

**generic terms**   product descriptions such as cornflakes which describe a product yet are not registered trade names (so one could have *Scotdale Northside Cornflakes*) – opposite 'generic name' e.g. Hoover, Walkman

**ghost writer**   a person contracted to write in the name of someone else

**GIF**   computer INTERNET graphics files (Graphics Interchange Format)

**greek**   also known as Latin – garbled text on a 'rough layout' that represents the size and position where final copy will eventually sit

**guarantee**   an advertiser's promise to a consumer – this can be an extended guarantee

**guardbook**   a portfolio of a client account's creative work

**hack**   a freelance writer who is probably willing to write about anything for any reasonable price

**heart-stopper**   a lottery card sales technique whereby a scratched card reveals all but one number in a sequence required to win a prize. This 'just missed' sequence of numbers usually encourages the purchaser to buy another card

**hidden persuaders**   research for advertising first described by V Packard in the 1950s, sometimes used to describe the role of PR professionals

**Hotline**   a specially-promoted telephone response line which encourages sales, provides information or acts as a form of customer contact service

**house agency**   agency owned and/or managed by an advertiser

**house corrections**   type errors noted on first proof before it is seen by a client

**HTTP**   (Hypertext Transfer Protocol) methodology to broadcast INTERNET web pages

**huckster**   a bygone insolent term for an account executive

**hype**   overstated publicity

**hyphenless justification**   justification of lines of text which avoids breaking up words over two lines

**iconic medium**   medium such as television or video in which images appear as reality

**idea bank**   a pool of creative ideas that are logged and referred to when required

**ideogram**   graphic device that represents an idea or meaning

**illustrated letter**   letter that incorporates some kind of illustration or graphic

**imagery**   figurative language; the illustration and emphasis of an idea by parallels and analogies of different kinds to make it more concrete and objective

**impact**   the tangible effect that advertising has on an audience

**impressions**   1 total number of exposures to a specific

advertisement during a specified period of time   2   the pressure of ink on a printing plate

**in-ad coupon**   featured coupon within a press advertisement

**in-pack premium**   premium item offered free with a product

**in-flight magazine**   magazine published by an airline and placed in the back of seats in an aircraft

**informercial**   television commercial masquerading as a television programme

**in the can**   completed radio, video or filmed commercial

**in-pack coupon**   coupon that can be redeemed at an outlet

**independents**   privately owned and managed media companies or publicity and advertising agencies

**inquiry response mailing**   a mass-targeted mailing meant to generate enquiries rather than orders

**Institute of Direct Marketing**   trade organisation and educational body for direct marketing users, agencies and suppliers

**Institute of Public Relations**   British professional body for PR practitioners

**island position**   advertisement surrounded by editorial

**issue advertising**   (sometimes called advocacy advertising) when an organisation discusses its views on topical issues

**jingle**   musical composition for a commercial

**job sheet**   standard agency administration form describing expenditure and progress of a client project

**joint promotion**   one company endorses another

**junk mail**   unsolicited, poorly targeted mail

**key account**   1   highly valued agency client; 2   important retailer or distributor for a client

**key code**   coding to measure effectiveness of a campaign

**knocking copy**   copy that criticises a competitor

**layout**   sketch or blueprint that shows the intended order of contents and styling of an advertisement mail piece, poster, and so on

**lead**   1   opening section of copy   2   sales enquiry

**lead time**   the time gap between the creative concept and the final result

**LHE**   left-hand edge

**LHS**   left-hand side

**lifetime value**   the entire term value of a consumer to an organisation – typically the costs spent of acquiring a consumer are high; the longer the consumer remains loyal the less the investment costs and so the greater the overall lifetime value

**lift letter**   second letter within a direct mail piece designed to 'lift' response (see 'publisher's letter')

**list ad**   advertisement listing more than one item (for example, a series of records)

**list broker**   agent who sells databases of sales prospects

**list cleaning**   removal of inaccurate data from a database

**list manager**   agent of database lists

**list segment**   section of list chosen against specific criteria such as sex and job title

**literal**   typesetting error by a printer

**live copy**   copy read 'live' on air

**live names**   term that describes active customers contacted through direct mail techniques

**live tag**   'live' message read 'on air' to provide additional local information relating to a pre-recorded national commercial

**livery**   corporate design and styling on all forms of transportation

**logo**   an abbreviation of Logotype – a particular shape, design or trademark that distinguishes an organisation; also known as a signature or sig, or sig cut

**loose insert**   (see 'free-standing stuffer')

**lottery**   sales promotion prize contest based on chance


**Madison Avenue**   generic term referring to the original heart of the US advertising industry

**mail list seed**   'planted' named recipient of a mailing list (also known as 'salting'); seeds are typically used to monitor the effectiveness and accuracy of a direct mail piece

**mail merge**   technique that combines a database with copy for a mailing (see 'merge-purge')

**mailing list test/sample**   random pick of names to test the effectiveness of a mailing list

**mailsort**   term for pre-sorted discounted Royal Mail mailings

**mandatory copy**   legally required copy

**market atomisation**   when each consumer is treated as a unique market segment

**market profile**   term to describe the pyschographic, demographic and geographic characteristics of prospects

**marketing**   the management process responsible for identifying, anticipating and accomplishing customer requirements profitably (Source: Chartered Institute of Marketing)

**marketing department**   organisational department responsible for marketing either for profit or non-profit (in the case of a voluntary organisation); areas of marketing responsibility may include, or be a combination of, direct marketing, sales promotion, advertising, sales, market research, product development and planning and administration

**marketing director**   employee responsible for co-ordination and approval of marketing programmes

**marketing mix**   the combination of promotion, price, product and distribution that creates the foundations of an organisation's marketing agenda

**mass media**   television, INTERNET, press, radio which reaches a large proportion of the public

**media buyer**   advertising agency employee or consultant who co-ordinates and negotiates media schedules

**Media Pack**   sales folder containing information about a specific media publication, programme or resource

**media plan**   proposal that details media budgets and recommended channels for an advertising campaign

**media speak**   journalistic fad corruption of the British language (e.g. 'stalking horse' instead of 'opponent')

**merge-purge**   assimilation of different databases which also removes duplicated or unwanted information (see also 'de-dupe' and 'mail merge')

**mf.**   more follows at the right-hand foot of a press release to indicate a continuation

**MGM**   Member-get-Member or 'recommend-a-friend' or 'word-of-mouth' advertising – when a current customer recommends a product or service to a new prospect

**mini catalogue**   shortened version of a larger catalogue, often featuring special seasonal offers

**mnemonic**   symbol or acronym to aid memory

**mock-up**   near-finished representation of a final creative execution

**modem**   (*Mo*dular/*dem*odulator) device that uses phone lines to link computers

**mood music**   musical track which helps establish a desired atmosphere

**morgue**   written obituaries for VIPs
**multi-mailer**   one mailing containing several loseleaf single promotions
**music bed**   musical background track
**musical logo**   melodic corporate signature

**National Advertising Benevolent Society (NABS)**   highly respected British charitable organisation for professionals working in the media and advertising
**news hole**   the amount of news space in a publication after advertisements have been placed
**newsletter**   organisational journalistic-style publication that contains information of interest to members and associates of the organisation; they provide a sense of belonging as well as a source of planned dissemination of management plans and member or employee developments
**novelty format**   an unusually sized or shaped mailing piece
**nth. name**   direct marketing database technique that divides the total number of names in a list by a required number of 'test' names to produce a sample (e.g. 10 000 'test' names chosen from 100 000 overall total of names would result in every 10th name selected for 'testing')

**offer**   the terms and conditions for a promotion
**on-camera narration**   narration delivered on-screen by a presenter
**on-pack coupon**   coupon attached to the outside of a package
**on-pack premium**   free gift attached to the outside of a package
**one-stage/step**   promotion in which a sales cycle is completed in one step without any need for further following up by letter or telephone (the prospect reads an advertisement and, on its strength, places an order for a product or service)
**open-rate**   the most expensive chargeable media rate
**open end**   1   recorded commercial with allocated space for a tailored ending; 2   programme produced with time for commercials
**opinion research**   research based on opinions rather than facts
**order card/form/coupon**   response device to complete and order by mail
**orphan**   stand-alone line of copy left at the foot of a page

**package insert**   promotional item inserted in a package
**package test**   the evaluation of mailing elements

**page proof**   the printer's proof of a page

**paid circulation**   publication that is distributed to people who have paid a subscription

**pamphlet**   leaflet that contains eight or more pages

**Pantone**   branded colour-matching system

**passive media**   media that requires the viewer or listener to do nothing more than watch or listen

**paste-up**   camera-ready layout

**peak time**   period which attracts the largest television or radio audience figures

**peel-off label**   self-adhesive label that can be attached to an order form

**penetration**   1   another term for 'reach' (see 'reach')   2   a price initially set at a low level

**personalisation**   the inclusion of a recipient's personal address details within a mail piece (research proves that personalisation always increases response)

**piggyback**   secondary offer included within a mail piece

**pitch**   1   new business presentation   2   typeface size

**poco**   brief for 'politically correct', sometimes used by feminists to refer to non-sexist language

**planning**   the activity of predicting future events and using those assumptions to develop strategies that will help achieve the ultimate goal

**portfolio**   case or folder of creative work

**positioning**   strategy that 'positions' a product or idea according to how a consumer perceives that product or service relative to the competitive offerings from providers of similar goods or services

**PPI**   Printed Postage Impression – preprinted Royal Mail licensed mark which typically appears on a direct mail envelope

**premium**   1   free promotional offer to test-trial and eventually purchase a product or service;   2   surcharge for a special advertising position within a publication or as part of a broadcast

**presentation**   formal presentation of creative and strategic concepts and proposals

**press clipping**   published article of interest archived for future reference

**press officer**   PR professional who specialises in press relations

**press pack**   portfolio of information relating to a specific press release or announcement

**price-off**  cut-price strategy to encourage trial or increased usage of a product or service: when intensified between competitors, this can lead to a 'price war'

**production department**  advertising department that co-ordinates and supervises all aspects of technical creative production

**programming schedule**  notification of programme times and dates which aids a media buyer when selecting television or radio commercial time

**promotion**  concentrated marketing method to increase sales of a product or service, usually through using a sales promotion technique

**prospect**  consumer who is likely to become a customer

**psychographics**  classification of prospect according to lifestyle and personality traits

**publication date**  the date a publication becomes available

**publicity still**  photograph used for publicity purposes

**publisher's letter**  'lift letter' from a publisher (see 'lift letter')

**pull**  printer's proof or a measurement of response

**pull quotes**  the enlargement of text of key quotations to give added emphasis

**pull strategy**  method that uses advertising and marketing to stimulate consumer demand and, in turn, encourage intermediaries to handle and promote a product or service

**push strategy**  method to encourage consumer demand and so stimulate intermediaries to stock a product

**Q&A**  abbreviation for 'Question and Answer', usually taking the form of a panel of questions and answers which relate to technical aspects of a product or service. Q&A panels typically appear towards the back of a product or service brochure

**qualitative research**  research designed to measure attitudes and perceptions based on type or circumstance rather than amount or proportion

**quantitative research**  research-based sample quantities based on amount or proportion rather than type or circumstance

**quarterly**  publication published on a three-monthly cycle – as opposed to bi-monthly (every other month) and annual

**questionnaire**  form featuring a sequence of closed or open questions to be completed and returned by a targeted respondent

**rate card**   form detailing specified media advertising costs and support information

**reach**   1   the overall percentage of targeted prospects in a specific area exposed to a specific advertisement during a specified duration (see also 'penetration')   2   percentage of targeted prospects who have made at least one product or service purchase enquiry

**reader ad**   copy-only advertisement that appears to be genuine news or editorial (see also 'advertorial')

**reader profile**   demographic classification of readers

**reader response**   the response of readers to an article or piece of advertising

**readership**   the number of people who read a publication

**rebel advertising**   corporate advertising which aims to appear as 'alternative' for the youth market (aka Generation X advertising)

**repeat mailing**   second mailing follow-up to the same list of names contacted by a first mailing

**repositioning**   planned marketing attempt to reposition a product or service within a market by changing either features, price or distribution – or a combination of all three

**research director**   agency employee responsible for the purchase and analysis of information that influences a marketing strategy

**response**   planned reaction to a planned arousal

**response device**   any piece of communication which accommodates a response`

**response list**   list of individuals who have responded to a direct mail campaign

**retainer**   fee that secures the ongoing negotiated rights to call from time to time upon a person's professional services, such as copywriting

**rhetoric**   the written and spoken language of persuasion – also sometimes refers to pompous style of language

**roll fold**   way of folding paper – usually a leaflet – whereby each printed section is rolled around the next at the paper's edge fold

**rough**   brush stroke layout indicating a general creative concept

**round robin**   traditional name for direct mail letter

**run of book/paper**   advertising space and location determined by a publisher rather than advertiser

**rushes**   rough, unedited print of daily film footage

**sales promotion**   the range of techniques used to attain sales/marketing objectives in a cost-effective manner by adding value to a product or service either to intermediaries or end users, normally but not exclusively within a defined time period (Source: Institute of Sales Promotion)

**sample** 1 individuals typical of a larger percentage of the population; 2 complementary portion, low priced or test quantity of a marketed product (also known as a trial offer); 3 quantity of data picked from a total direct mail database

**scratch-and-sniff** method of incorporating scent on to paper; when scratched, an impregnated scent panel is activated

**scratch off** device (also known as coin rub) whereby a coin is used to scratch a coated paper to reveal a special message

**selective demand advertising** advertising aimed to create awareness and provide information about a particular brand

**self-liquidator** 1 gift or premium which is financed by its offered purchase; 2 sales promotion display provided to a retailer for a fee to the supplier or manufacturer

**sharpening** cognitive process in which the information retained becomes more vivid and important than the event itself

**shelf life** 1 the amount of time that a product can remain on a retail shelf; 2 the longevity of a product or service, based on its popularity and demand

**shelf strip** a point of sale printed strip attached to the facing edge of a shelf (see 'talking shelf strip')

**shirt-board advertising** advertising printed on the cardboard used to support laundered shirts – popular in the United States

**sleeper** unpublished 'seed' name (see 'mail list seed')

**sponsored programme** 1 television or radio programme that is part-financed by a named advertiser; 2 any event that may be financially subsidised for marketing or advertising purposes

**statement stuffer** printed advertisement inserted in an envelope containing a bill (see also 'bill stuffer')

**stock** 1 music, art, graphics or photographs available from specialist libraries 2 recommended reproduction material

**style book** manual of approved corporate styling ad design

**suit** generic term referring to a non-creative employee of an advertising agency

**suspects** consumer who may or may not become a customer

**sustaining advertising** advertising that maintains rather than increases demand

**sweeps** the months of November, February and May set by a US television rating service to establish the ranking of television network shows: this sets the level of advertising rates for local stations

**sweepstakes** a below-the-line technique in which prizes are offered according to the rules to participants on a random chance, no-skills basis to win. An assumption is made that the technique will eventually encourage the consumer to buy a product (no immediate purchase required).

**take one** 1 leaflets or pamphlets freely distributed via a sales promotional desktop or mounted dispenser; 2 in the United States, a 'take one' is an attachment to a transit advertising vehicle card. The 'take one' is a coupon or information request sheet. It often incorporates an envelope or is part of a pad

**talk** an INTERNET discussion or 'newsgroup' which debates a wide range of issues: ideal for subtle advertising

**talking heads** television production featuring extreme head and shoulder close-ups of subjects discussing a specific item or area of interest

**talking shelf strip** point of sale printed strip or item attached to or near the facing edge of a shelf, which contains a movement-sensitive electronic device. As the consumer passes, the device triggers a prerecorded soundtrack which discusses the product. (Belgian advertisers claim that such devices could increase sales by 500 per cent. In 1995 a dog food manufacturer became one of the first advertisers in the UK to use such a device)

**target audience** the ideal prospective audience which would be interested in a specific product or service

**tear sheet** page torn from a publication sent to an advertiser as proof of publication

**teaser campaign** series of brief announcement advertisements which stimulate curiosity

**telemarketing** measurable market prospecting, selling, servicing and informing via the telephone

**television director/producer** person employed to manage and co-ordinate the production of television commercials

**test marketing** (see 'zone plan')

**thank you letter** direct mail copy technique in which a customer is thanked for making a purchase or enquiry

**threshold effect** the stage at which the effectiveness of an advertising campaign can be seen to be working

**thumbnail**   miniature, rough layout

**tie-in promotion**   promotion which markets more than one product or brand

**time-sheet**   a standard form to record the amount of time spent working on a client project

**tip-on**   coupon reply card or sample glued to a printed piece of advertising

**tip in**   loosely placed publication insert (see 'free-standing stuffer')

**tombstone**   originally a US Wall Street financial advertisement used, among other things, to announce new stock issues; so called because the copy provides only the bare-bones facts

**tone of voice**   general attitude, expression or approach given to a message

**traffic building**   an advertising piece of communications that can include sales promotion or direct marketing, designed to encourage retail store traffic

**traffic department**   the department within an advertising agency which co-ordinates the work flow of projects between departments

**treatment**   an overall styling or approach to a piece of advertising

**trial close**   copy technique whereby the reader is asked for an order at an early stage of a direct mail letter. The copy then directs the reader to the coupon. This technique can be repeated several times during one direct mail letter

**trial offer**   sales promotion marketing technique to encourage future consumer purchase, made within a particular period of time (see also 'sample')

**TV shopping**   also known as 'Shop-at-Home'. Television programmes or channels that are likened to shopping catalogues. (This area is also embraced by the INTERNET)

**two-stage/step**   promotion in which a sales cycle is completed in two steps with a further follow-up by letter or telephone. The prospect reads an advertisement and, on its strength, applies for further details of a product or service. (Opposite = One-stage/step)

**ultra**   short for an 'ultra-consumer' who insists on purchasing the very best – regardless of personal income

**usage pull**   the power of advertising to encourage individuals to purchase an advertised service or product

**USP**   Unique Sells or Selling Proposition – the outstanding benefit or family of features which distinguish a product or service from its competition

**voice**   breadth of media coverage
**Voice Over**   the voice of a narrator or presenter
**voucher copy**   copy of an entire publication sent to an advertiser as proof of publication and advertising position as agreed

**white mail**   letters sent to mail-order firms which result in more paper work (e.g. complaints and enquiries)
**white space**   unprinted space which gives greater emphasis to remaining printed advertising space
**window envelope**   an opening or 'window' die-cut into a direct mail envelope which shows part of the contents of the mailing inside. The cut is usually covered by glassine which is a type of transparent paper
**wraparound**   cover/holder which carries a mail-order catalogue and supporting material such as sales letters and order forms

**X-factor**   the undefinable aspect within a person or a company that can't be copied but equals success

**Yes/No envelope**   response-direct mail envelope which encourages readers to reply to an offer, irrespective of whether or not they intend to make a purchase
**Yes/No stamp**   similar to the Yes/No envelope response-enhancement device; instead either a YES, NO or MAYBE stamp is attached to a response device. This encourages customer involvement and gives a sense that the mailing is an 'active' item

**Z fold**   method of folding paper such as a sales letter into three equal parts. The centre forms a diagonal column, as in the letter Z
**zip envelope**   direct mail envelope which is opened by pulling a tab
**zone plan**   strategy to test a new product or service using advertising in a highly-targeted small geographic area (see also 'test marketing')

# APPENDIX A

## Typical all-embracing creative brief form

### JOB START

| CLIENT | | JOB NUMBER | |
|---|---|---|---|
| PRODUCT | | TRAFFIC CONTROLLER | |
| DATE | | ACCOUNT HANDLER | |
| DESIGN BUDGET (INCLUDING PRODUCTION) | £ | ADVERTISING BUDGET (INCLUDING PRODUCTION) | £ |
| PROPOSED BRIEF ISSUE DATE | CREATIVE REVIEW DATE | INTERNAL REVIEW DATE | CLIENT PRESENTATION DATE |
| DESIGNER | | CREATIVE TEAM | |

REQUIREMENT:

| ESTIMATE REQUIRED? (PLEASE TICK) | | TOTAL FIGURE ONLY? | | SIMPLIFIED BREAK DOWN? |
|---|---|---|---|---|
| PRINT: | WHO WILL PRINT? TMG | | DELIVERY DATE | |
| | CLIENT | | | |
| MEDIA: | PUBLICATION | DATE | SIZE | COPY DATE |
| INVOICE DETAILS: | COMPANY | | | |
| | ADDRESS | | | |
| ATTENTION OF: | | | | |

# BACKGROUND DESIGN/CREATIVE BRIEF PART 1 (OUT OF 3)

| CLIENT | |
|---|---|
| PRODUCT | DATE |

1. WHAT DOES THE CLIENT DO?

2. IN THIS INSTANCE. WHAT IS THE CLIENT'S PRODUCT?

3. HOW WILL THE PRODUCT BE SOLD? (PLEASE TICK)   VIA BROKERS    DIRECT RESPONSE    RETAIL OUTLETS

# SUMMARY DESIGN/CREATIVE BRIEF PART 2

| CLIENT | |
|---|---|
| PRODUCT | DATE |

---

1. IN ONE PARAGRAPH, WHAT IS THE CLIENT'S REQUIREMENT/PROBLEM?

---

2. WHO IS THE CLIENT TALKING TO?

---

3. WHAT TONE OF VOICE SHOULD WE CONSIDER?

---

4. WHAT IS THE KEY THING WE WANT PEOPLE TO UNDERSTAND?

---

5. WHAT ELSE IS RELEVANT TO THE PROBLEM?

---

**APPROVAL OF BRIEF**

| ACCOUNT DIRECTOR | CREATIVE DIRECTOR | TECHNICAL CONSULTANT (IF INVOLVED) | CLIENT |
|---|---|---|---|
| SIGNATURE | | | |
| DATE | | | |

# CREATIVE BRIEF PART 2 (FILL IN AS MUCH AS REQUIRED)

| CLIENT | |
|---|---|
| PRODUCT | DATE |

**IF DESIGN**

| |
|---|
| 1. QUANTITY? |
| 2. HOW DOES THE CUSTOMER RECEIVE IT? |
| 3. ANY RELEVANT RESEARCH? |
| 4. IS IT A NEW CONCEPT, OR MUST DESIGN FIT WITHIN AN EXISTING STYLE? |
| 5. IF NEW, ANY CORPORATE GUIDELINES? |
| 6. IF NEW, CAN WE COMMISSION PHOTOGRAPHY/ILLUSTRATION? |
| 7. IS SIZE FIXED? |
| 8. NUMBER OF COLOURS AGREED? |
| 9. IS COPY SUPPLIED? AND IF SO, IS IT FINAL OR OUTLINE? |
| 10. WHAT DO WE NEED? (PLEASE TICK)  FINISHED VISUALS   ROUGHS |

**IF ADVERTISING**

| MEDIA | PUBLICATION | DATE | SIZE | COPY DATE |
|---|---|---|---|---|
| | | | | |
| | | | | |
| | | | | |
| | | | | |
| | | | | |
| | | | | |
| | | | | |
| | | | | |
| | | | | |

**IF DIRECT MAIL**

| (PLEASE TICK) OUTER ENVELOPE | BRE/BRC | LEAFLET | FLYER | LETTER | OTHER (SPECIFY) |
|---|---|---|---|---|---|
| 1. QUANTITY? | | | | | |
| 2. WILL THE PROMOTION TIE IN WITH ADVERTISING? | | | | YES | NO |
| 3. WILL THE PACK BE PERSONALISED? | | | | YES | NO |
| 4. STANDARD OF FINISH?  FULL COPY/FINISHED VISUALS | | | OUTLINE COPY/ROUGH VISUALS | | |

**APPROVAL OF BRIEF**

| ACCOUNT DIRECTOR | CREATIVE DIRECTOR | TECHNICAL CONSULTANT (IF INVOLVED) | CLIENT |
|---|---|---|---|
| SIGNATURE | | | |
| DATE | | | |

# APPENDIX B

## Sample production time plans

(All times may vary according to computer-generated design and production techniques.)

### <u>MONO AD TIME PLAN</u>

| | |
|---|---|
| CLIENT | DATE |
| PROJECT | JOB NUMBER |

| | <u>Dates</u> |
|---|---|
| Client's brief received by account group start job raised | day 1 |
| Creative brief formulated and full agreement obtained | day 3 |
| Start creative work | day 4 |
| Creative review/internal review | day 5 |
| Client presentation | day 6 |
| Client approval | day 9 |

---

| | |
|---|---|
| Research out | |
| Research in | } If required allow 3 weeks |
| Research debrief | |

---

| | |
|---|---|
| Copy brief in | day 10 |
| Pre production meeting | day 10 |
| Photography briefed | day 11 |
| Prints, agency & client approval | day 13 |
| Retouching out | day 14 |
| Copy final approval | day 14 |
| Mechanical in hand | day 16 |
| Mechanical final approval | day 17 |
| Retouching final approval | day 18 |
| Artwork in hand | day 19 |
| Press deadline | day 20 |

# 32-PAGE FOUR-COLOUR BROCHURE TIME PLAN

32 pages, location photography, A4, 4-colour throughout, 15 photographs, tint laying on pie charts, 40 000 run, delivery to Midlands.

| | |
|---|---|
| CLIENT | DATE |
| PROJECT | JOB NUMBER |
| | <u>Dates</u> |
| Client's brief received by account group job start raised | day 1 |
| Creative brief formulated and full agreement obtained | day 3 |
| Start creative work | day 4 |
| Creative review/internal review | day 7 |
| Client presentation | day 8 |
| Client approval | day 12 |
| Copy brief in | day 13 |
| Pre production meeting | day 13 |
| Photography briefed | day 14 |
| Prints, agency & client approval | day 21 |
| Retouching out | day 23 |
| Copy final approval | day 23 |
| Mechanical in hand | day 24 |
| Mechanical final approval | day 25 |
| Transparency final approval | day 26 |
| Mechanicals to print | day 27 |
| Proofs, agency approval | day 31 |
| Proofs, client approval | day 32 |
| Print by | day 45 |
| Delivery | day 46 |

# TV TIME PLAN (USING LIVE ACTION)

| | |
|---|---|
| CLIENT | DATE |
| PROJECT | JOB NUMBER |
| | <u>Dates</u> |

| | |
|---|---|
| Client's brief received by account group job start raised | Start of week 1 |
| Creative brief formulated and full agreement obtained | weeks 2/3 |
| Start creative work | week 4 |
| Creative review/internal review | week 6 |
| Production company estimate | week 6 |
| Client presentation | week 7 |
| Client approval | week 8 |

| | |
|---|---|
| Research out | |
| Research in | } If required allow 3 weeks |
| Research debrief | |

| | |
|---|---|
| Final script approval. Client & Broadcasting Advertising Clearance Centre | week 9 |
| Budget presentation and approval | week 9 |
| Special effects/model work in hand | week 9 |
| Casting | week 9 |
| Pre-production meeting with client | week 10 |
| Set build and shoot | week 11 |
| Rough cut | week 12 |
| Fine cut/opticals | week 13 |
| Record music | week 13 |
| Rough dubb | week 14 |
| Optical double head client approval | week 16 |
| Answer print | week 17 |
| Transfer and final clearance | week 18 |
| Playout/GS Pools | week 18 |
| On air | week 19 |

# USEFUL ADDRESSES

## United Kingdom

The Advertising Association
Abford House
15 Wilton Road
London
SWIV 1NJ
Tel: 0171 828 2771

Advertising Standards Authority
Brook House
2-16 Torrington Place
London
WC1E 7HW
Tel: 0171 580 5555
(Independent body responsible
for ensuring that the British
Codes of Advertising and Sales
Promotion works in the public
interest.)

Broadcast Advertising Clearance
Centre
200 Grays Inn Road
London
WC1X 8HF
Tel: 0171 843 8000
(Approves national TV
advertising copy)

Broadcasters' Audience Research
Board
Glenthorne House
Hammersmith Grove
London
W6 0ND
Tel: 0181 741 9110

Broadcasting Standards Council
5/8 The Sanctuary
London
SW1P 3JS
Tel: 0171 233 0544

British Institute of Management
Management House
Cottingham Road
Corby
Northants
NN17 1TT
Tel: 01536 204222

Chartered Institute of Marketing
Moor Hall
Cookham
Maidenhead
Berkshire
SL6 9QH
Tel: 016285 24922

Chartered Society of Designers
29 Bedford Square
London
WC1B 3EG
Tel: 0171 631 1510

Committee of Advertising
Practice
2 Torrington Place
London
WC1E 7HW
Tel: 0171 580 5555
Copy rules advice on
advertising and promotions –
tel: 0171 580 4100.

CAM Foundation
Abford House
15 Wilton Road
London
SW1V 1NJ
Tel: 0171 828 7506

Datamonitor
106 Baker Street
London
W1M 1LA
Tel: 0171 316 0001

Data Protection Register
Wycliffe House
Water Lane
Wilmslow
Cheshire
SK9 5AY
Tel: 01625 535777

Direct Mail Information Service
5 Carlisle Street
London W1V 6JX
Tel: 0171 494 0483

Direct Marketing Association
(UK) Ltd
Haymarket House
1 Oxendon Street
London
SW1Y 4EE
Tel: 0171 321 2525

Direct Mail Services Standards
Board (DMSS)
26 Eccleston Street
London
SW1W 9PY
Tel: 0171 824 8651

Henley Centre
9 Bridewell Place
Blackfriars
London
EC4V 6AY
Tel: 0171 353 9961

ICSTIS (The Independent
Committee for the Supervision of
Standards of Telephone
Information Services)
3rd Floor
Alton House
177 High Holborn
London
WC1V 7AA
Tel: 0171 240 5511
(Offers a free checking service
for copy written for use over
premium rate telephone lines.)
Internet address
http:/www.icstis.org.uk/

Incorporated Society of British
Advertisers
44 Hertford Street
London
W1Y 8AE
Tel: 0171 499 7502

Independent Television
Commission
33 Foley Street
London
W1P 7LP
Tel: 0171 255 3000

Institute of Directors
116 Pall Mall
London
SW1Y 5ED
Tel: 0171 839 1233

Institute of Direct Marketing
No. 1 Park Road
Teddington
Middlesex
TW11 0AR
Tel: 0181 977 5705

The Institute of Packaging
Sysonby Lodge
Nottingham Road
Melton Mowbray
Leics.
LE13 6NU
Tel: 016645 00055

Institute of Practitioners in
Advertising (IPA)
44 Belgrave Square
London
SW1X 8QS
Tel: 0171 235 7020

Institute of Public Relations
The Old Trading House
15 Northburgh Street
London
EC1V 0PR
Tel: 0171 253 5151

Institute of Sales Promotion
Arena House
66–68 Pentonville Road
London
N1 9HS
Tel: 0171 837 5340

Mailing Preference Service
No. 5 Reef House
Plantation Wharf
London
SW11 3UF
Tel: 0171 738 1625

Market Research Society (MRS)
15 Northburgh Street
London
EC1V 0AH
Tel: 0171 490 4911

The Marketing Society
St George's House
2–5 Pepys Road
London
SW20 8NJ
Tel: 0181 879 3464

NABS
199–205 Old Marylebone Road
London
NW1 5QP
Tel: 0171 723 8028

The Newspaper Society
Bloomsbury House
74/77 Great Russell Street
London
WC1B 3DA
Tel: 0171 636 7014

NOP Research Group
Tower House
Southampton Street
London
WC2E 7HN
Tel: 0171 612 0100
e-mail: PatrickD@Nopres.co.uk

Public Relations Consultants
Association
Willow House
Willow Place
Victoria
London
SW1P 1JH
Tel: 0171 233 6026

Radio Advertising Bureau
74 Newman Street
London
W1P 3LA
Tel: 0171 636 5858

Sales Promotion Consultants
Association (SPCA)
2nd Floor
47 Margaret Street
London
W1N 7FD
Tel: 0171 580 8223

## Australia

PRIA (New South Wales)
PO Box 1728
North Sydney
NSW 2060
Tel: 2 369 2029

PRIA (South Australia)
PO Box 194
Marden
South Australia 5070
Tel: 8 362 1559

PRIA (Queensland)
PO Box 1492
Milson
Queensland 4064
Tel: 7 368 3662

PRIA (Tasmania)
PO Box 163
Hobart
Tasmania 7001
Tel: 0 233 4439

PRIA (Western Australia)
190 Hay Street
East Perth
Western Australia 6004
Tel: 9 421 7555

Australian Marketing Institute
Level 2/464
St Kilda Road
Melbourne
Victoria 3004
Tel: 3 820 8788

The Advertising Institute of
Australia
79 Macleren Street
Adelaide
SA 5000
Fax: 8 21 21 238

Australian Direct Marketing
Association Ltd
7th Floor
22–30 Bridge Street
Sydney
NSW 2000
Tel: 2 247 7744

## Canada

Canadian Public Relations
Society Inc (CPRS)
Suite 720
220 Laurier Avenue W.
Ottawa
Ontario
K1P 5Z9
Tel: 613 232 122

Canadian Direct Marketing
Association
1 Concord Gate, Suite 607
Donmills
Ontario
M36 3N6
Tel: 416 391 2362

Institute of Canadian
Advertising
30 Scrudan Avenue
2nd Floor
Toronto
Ontario
M45 1U6
Tel: 416 482 1396

## USA

Advertising Council Inc.
261 Madison Avenue
11th Floor
New York
NY 10016
Tel: 212 922 1500

American Advertising
Federation
1101 Vermont Avenue
NW Suite 500
Washington DC 20005
Tel: 202 898 0089

American Marketing Association
250 S Wacker Drive
Suite 200
Chicago
IL 60606
Tel: 312 648 0536

American Association of
Advertising Agencies
666 3rd Avenue
13th Floor
New York
NY 10017
Tel: 212 682 2500

Direct Marketing Association
1120 Avenue of the Americas
New York
NY 10036-6700
Tel: 212 768 7277

International Advertising
Association
342 Madison Avenue
Suite 2000
New York
NY 10173
Tel: 212 557 1133

Marketing Research Association
2189 Silas Dean Highway
Rocky Hill
Suite 5
CT 06067
Connecticut
Tel: 203 257 4008

Point-of-Purchase Advertising
Institute
66 N Van Brunt Street
Englewood
NJ 07631
Tel: 201 894 8899

Public Relations Society of
America (PRSA)
33 Irving Place
Union Square
New York
NY 10003
Tel: 212 995 2230

## Hong Kong

Public Relations Association of
Hong Kong Limited (PRAHK)
GPO Box 1264
Hong Kong

## Recommended education courses

Buckinghamshire College
Queen Alexandra Road
High Wycombe
Buckinghamshire
HP11 2JZ
Tel: 01494 522141
**Course** Graphic Design
and Advertising

Institute of Sales Promotion
Arena House
66–68 Pentonville Road
Islington
London
N1 9HS
Tel: 0171 837 5340
**Course** ISP Diploma;
ISP Certificate

The Institute of Direct
Marketing
No. 1 Park Road
Teddington
Middlesex
TW11 8BR
Tel: 0181 977 5705
**Course** Diploma in
Direct Marketing
Certificate in Direct Marketing

CAM Foundation
Abford House
15 Wilton Road
London
SW1V 1NJ
Tel: 0171 828 7506

The Communications
Advertising and Marketing
Education Foundation at Part 1
(Certificate) Level and
Part II (Diploma) Level

West Thames College
London Road
Isleworth
Middlesex
TW7 4HS
Tel: 0181 568 0244
**Course** Higher National
Diploma in Graphic Design
and Advertising

West Herts College
(Watford Campus)
Hempstead Road
Watford
Herts
WD1 3EZ
Tel: 01923 257500
**Course** Advertising
Copywriting/Art Direction

# INDEX

above-the-line 114
acronyms 58
action 999 approach 210
AIDA 10, 23, 47, 70
AIDCA 24
*aide-mémoire* brief 49, 52
all-embracing brief 49
alliteration 68, 106
animatic 234
anticipation headlines 83
art director 70
Audit Bureau of Circulations 123

BARB 123
below-the-line 114
blindfold test 80
bodycopy 61, 92
brainstorming 28
braintyping 26
brand core values 40
brand loyalty 40
brands 40
brief 48
budget 51
bulletin boards 271
business-to-business 131

call to action 12, 94
caption 72, 100, 156, 178, 203
catalogue 203
CAVIAR 124
challenge headlines 80
charity 206
charity mailings 197, 206
circulation 116, 118, 123
clichés 56, 62
coin rub 183
colloquialisms 64, 109
comparison headlines 79

copy dates 117
copy fitting 109
copy platform 54
copy style 97
copy tracking 95, 100
corporate advertising 140
coupons 132, 151, 156, 193
cross selling 159, 169

DAGMAR 25, 47
Dale–Chall Index 107
declining sales 138
demonstration headlines 87
Descartes, René 19
direct mail 101, 132, 166
direct marketing 151, 152, 166
display advertisement 125, 128
door-to-door 124, 191
dream copy 201

ellipses 67
Elvis factor 38, 85
e-mail 197
emphatic full stop 67
eye-tracking 175

facilitator 29
family brands 41
Fax Back 163, 197
Flesch Formula 107
FMCG 4
Fog Index 107
foreign words 99
formulae 23
forums 271, 274

'G' spot 39, 85
gadgets 182
GIGO 23

grammar 61
greetings card device 84
Grim Reaper approach 180
guarantee 142, 181, 204, 268
Gunning, R 107

Haas, C R 107
headline themes 74
Hotlines 161, 204
HTML 275
humour 25, 57, 99, 136

idioms 62
impulse purchase 92
incentives 154
in-store posters 259
Institute of Practitioners in Advertising 58
INTERNET 31, 70, 197, 213, 242, 254, 270
invitation headlines 81
involvement, reward and fun 3

jargon 135, 151
JICNARS 58, 123
JICPAR 124
jingle 69, 232
journalism 61
jump-to-it headlines 78, 165

Latin 69
layout 70
lead-in sentence 94, 102
leading...teaser headline 84
left brain 26
lifestyle copy 98
lifestyles 58, 220
line-ads 126
list broker 166, 170
location headlines 85
logo 71, 174

mail bombs 198
'Man in the Hathaway shirt' 86
marketing objectives 50
Maslow, Abraham 26
media 113
Media Pack 46
media planning 114, 116
media spend 114
Media Register 121
member-get-member 192

MOPS 152
multi-media 130, 242

needle-drop music 254
newsmaking headlines 87
niggling-itch effect 84
ninepoint cross examination 36
nostalgia 17

off-the-page 151, 267
OSCAR 124
OTS 121
own-label brands 40, 139, 142

PETA 124
Plato 19
Platonic ideas 19
poetry 99
positive or negative attitudes 55
postcard decks 190
posters 119
press release 78, 280
product life cycle 42
product line brands 41
promise headlines 82
proverbs 65
psychographic targeting 58
public domain music 254
public relations 280
punctuation 66
puns 90

question and answer panels 188
question headlines 74
quotations 75

radio 119, 244
rate-surfers 42
ratings 240
read 'n' ring recruitment advertisement 127
Reading Ease Score 108
recruitment advertising 125
Register–MEAL 2, 124
repetition 65, 69, 106
representation headlines 85
research 37, 135, 138, 150
response device 151, 152, 182, 189, 191, 238
right brain 26
role playing 11

sales promotion 4(

sex 29, 222

slice of life 220

slogan 62, 103

socio-economic groups 50,

SOLAADS 282

spinners 42

SRBRA 23

story board 223

strapline 63, 103

strategy 38, 44

SWOT analysis 46

synectics sessions 34

taboo 51

talking heads 224

targeting 15, 55

taste of the things to come, approach 84

telephone response 52, 127, 132, 151, 157,
160, 238

testimonial 74, 99, 209, 223

tests 169, 257

TGI 123

three Ws 179

trade publications 116, 131

television 119, 212

typeface 62, 71, 129, 175

umbrella brand 41, 98, 139, 141

Unique Sales Proposition 35, 39, 50, 54,
71, 94, 95, 138

Values and Lifestyles (VALS) 58

VFD 124

word pictures 65, 88

writer's block 21

*Yellow Pages* 266